ELUSIVE INNOCENCE:
SURVIVAL GUIDE
FOR THE
FALSELY ACCUSED

by Dean Tong

HUNTINGTON HOUSE PUBLISHERS

Huntington House Publishers
P.O. Box 53788
Lafayette, Louisiana 70505

Some individuals names throughout this book have been
changed to protect their identities.

Library of Congress Card Catalog Number 2001092717
ISBN 1-56384-190-8

Contents

Acknowledgments

Words cannot express my appreciation for the steadfast support and guidance of Lily, my wife.

To my children, who at the time this book will be published will both be adults . . . I love you always!

To my parents, Kenneth and Claire Tong, for their emotional, psychological, and financial support during my own trials and tribulations.

To my grandfather, Cyrus Gardner, who, although deceased, taught me early on to stand up and fight for what is right.

To my grandmother, Emma Gardner. Thank you, Gram.

To Kathy Rapp, free-lance writer, for putting up with me.

To Charles Jamieson, Esq., for his contribution. Thank you, Counselor.

To Dr. Ron Leymaster for his contribution.

To Dr. Bob Fay for his contribution.

To Dr. Bruce Ewart for his contribution.

To Huntington House Publishing, specifically Kathy Doyle and Mark Anthony, for believing in my work and making this project a reality.

To all investigators of alleged abuse cases . . . may this book be your beacon in the night.

To all attorneys and judges in all courts . . . may this book be by your side for quick reference.

To all legislators . . . may this book be your *reason* to make child protection safer for everyone.

To all those wrongly accused . . . may this book be your inspiration.

And, finally, to all child victims of true and false abuse accusations . . . YOU are the reason I stay in the fight!

We will not win the war against child abuse
until we first win the battle against
false accusations.

Introduction

The cycle of child abuse and domestic violence is twofold. Since Dr. C. Henry Kempe's presentation of the Battered Child Syndrome in 1961-62, to the legislative enactment of the Mondale Act (Child Abuse Prevention and Treatment Act) of 1973, society has become less resistant to keeping child abuse "the yucky secret." There were only 160,000 cases of suspected child abuse and neglect reported in 1963. That statistic mushroomed to 1.7 million alleged child abuse and neglect reports in 1985, and 3.5 million alleged child abuse and neglect reports in 1998. According to the National Center for Child Abuse and Neglect, there were 1 million confirmed reports in 1998. Of these, approximately 71 percent were unfounded and false.

Child protection agencies, nationally, are charged to guard our most vulnerable and precious resource, our children. Children who suffer disorganized attachments, who are molested by situational and fixated pedophile caregivers, do refrain from telling on their perpetrators. They're afraid of the separation anxiety and loss of their abusers. We must prosecute to the fullest extent allowed by law those who violate our children, and women who are responsible for continuing this vicious cycle of abuse.

Elusive Innocence is my attempt to help parents, attorneys, and other professionals who fall victim to, champion, and don't understand the aforesaid 71 percent unfounded and false cases of alleged child abuse and neglect. This is what I call the reverse cycle of child abuse. According to most published reports, false allegations of child abuse occur only about 10 percent of the time. That means that only about one in ten allegations are fostered in malice. About 2/3 to 3/4 of all good-faith, but unfounded, reports of alleged child abuse and neglect are the result of improper interview techniques, confirmatory bias, source misattributions, and delusional accusers. This book takes you, the reader, through heart-rending actual case studies, to the accused, the accusers, the agencies, and the courts. It will stimulate your gray matter regarding the suggestibility of young children's disclosures of abuse, usage of anatomically exaggerated dolls, and inherent problems facing our social work, mental health, and legal professions.

Wielding children as pawns in protracted divorces, visitation disputes, and custody battles is not in the children's best interests. Motive-laden abuse excuse tactics in alleged child abuse or domestic violence cases is not in the children's best interests. We are reminded of the Elian

Gonzalez case and the psychological torment that boy was put through. Psychologists Hickman and Reynolds from Texas A&M University, in their publication, "The Effects of False Accusations Upon Children and Families," remind us that it is no longer safe for judges to err on the side of caution, on the side of the children. Theses cases are not gray. They are black and white. If abuse did not happen, we must not allow emotions, politics, and hysteria to get the best of us. We must not treat non-abused children as real abuse victims. We must recognize the emotional and psychological damage to child victims of both false accusations of child abuse and domestic violence. The results are neither benign nor innocuous.

Elusive Innocence aids those unjustly accused, defense attorneys, social workers, therapists, guardians-ad-litem, police officers, teachers, prosecutors, judges, legislators, et al., navigate the labyrinth of false accusations. From fighting false allegations of child abuse and domestic violence to borderline personality disorder, problems and solutions, dos and don'ts, to ten appendices, including how to choose your attorney, a look at science in the courtroom, a critical view of alleged medical findings, interrogatories of false accusers, and investigative flow chart, wrongly accused victims and their attorneys are armed with state-of-the-art defense tactics for litigation.

As a litigation consultant and soon-to-be-expert testifying in live court cases, I see too many wounded innocents fall prey to Alford, *nolo contendre*, or guilty plea bargains. If innocent and pleading *nolo*, one waives his or her right to appeal. In a criminal sexual child abuse proceeding, pleading *nolo* forces one to register under Meagan's Law with the police. In a domestic violence proceeding, pleading *nolo* means you will not attain normal visitation rights or acquire custody in family court under Violence Against Women's Act (VAWA). Thus, it is incumbent upon the falsely accused and his or her attorney to assert his or her rights. This book provides you with a vehicle for doing so, for reversing the mindset of guilty until proven innocent. I implore those who have been accused to complete my two-prong test; prove your innocence via testing and impeach the credibility of your accusers. To do so requires willpower, stamina, resources, and experts.

We have created a system that encourages child abuse, child neglect, and domestic violence reports, and is vehement in prosecuting these. If falsely accused, your defense team must also be vehement in exonerating you, and clearing your name. In my caseload, I see too many parents expend tens of thousands of dollars, needlessly, because it took them five attorneys and three psychologists to affect justice. Be forewarned! Be forearmed! If unjustly accused, do not let innocence settle on the horizon. Do not let your case vacillate and meet its demise because innocence is elusive. It does not have to be. Reclaim your good name, your children, and your rights. Read *Elusive Innocence*!

1.

Massachusetts 1980—Florida 1994

She was a sociable, young woman, small to the point of petite. Her shoulder-length, dark hair fell in natural waves, serving as a frame for her sparkling eyes and the flashing smile that she shared with most of us at the Medical Center. That smile brightened the day for employees in the lab where I worked, and in the veteran benefits section of the center where she was a volunteer helper. It was July of 1980. I was 24-years-old, and Carla was twenty-two.

We initially met through my work as a lab technician in the outpatient laboratory. Carla had been diagnosed with epilepsy, which was controlled by medication. Once a week, I ran the tests that monitored her drug levels to assure her continued health. During those weekly visits, I learned that Carla had been honorably discharged and retired from the Army as a result of the epilepsy. I also learned she was going through a divorce from her first husband and was naturally upset and depressed by the domestic situation.

Our laboratory friendship quickly progressed to courtship. Gradually we began sharing more and more of our previous experiences, current hopes, and future dreams. As I began falling deeply in love, I envisioned our life together: sharing all the good times and bad times, building a family, growing old in the glow of the love we felt for each other. I recognized the serious nature of Carla's illness and was concerned with the frequency of her seizures, but Carla never let it get her down. She often viewed the seizures as a joke, and when people commented sympathetically on her condition, she made it clear that she didn't feel sorry for herself and neither should they.

Unfortunately, during the late summer and early fall of 1980, Carla's seizures began coming more frequently and were of longer duration. After talking with her doctors in Boston, we made the decision to relocate to Fort Pierce, Florida, in the hope that the warm Florida climate would decrease the seizure activity.

In fact, her convulsions and their frequency worsened, often requiring that she be rushed by ambulance to the local hospital. An increasingly bad temperament was directly proportional to the prevalence of her seizures; both worsened as time passed. This was a result not only of the natural progression of the disease, but, more important, because Carla was often careless about taking her medication, often neglecting it totally.

We had our up days and our down days, as any new couple. They sometimes seemed more extreme because of the added stress of dealing with Carla's illness and her intense mood swings. I blamed her periodic withdrawals and days of shrewish behavior on the illness, the drugs, anything I could use as an excuse for her behavior. There was no way I could accept the fact that the woman I had fallen in love with had been a temporary personality, now replaced by the "real" person behind the mask.

In January of 1981, Carla announced we were to become parents. This placed our relationship in an entirely new light. Up to this point, Carla and I hadn't worried about the legalities of living with and loving each other; it hadn't seemed important. Now, however, we agreed that we wanted a family; we wanted our children to have a mother and father who were legally bound in the eyes of God and the state. We flew back to Massachusetts on Memorial Day weekend and were married in a private ceremony attended only by my family and close friends.

Carla's pregnancy was a difficult time for her, although the frequency of her seizures was reduced. Initially, during the first few months, she was not only lethargic but, like many pregnant women, felt miserable. For a period, I felt I was running in circles, changing hats from lover to nurse to orderly, then playing house husband and breadwinner. The first few months, Carla required being waited on hand and foot.

To my dismay, we grew further apart during the course of the pregnancy and our relationship became one of not only disharmony but distrust. When she began feeling better, Carla returned to her job as a cocktail waitress at Franky & Johnny's Lounge, and I would periodically slip into the bar to watch her. Her actions did nothing to alleviate my concerns about her feelings for me, the future of our new marriage, and the prospects for a happy family. It was not unusual to watch her use her skimpy uniform to gain the notice and attention of the male customers. I tried to justify her actions by telling myself she was trying to make me jealous, afraid that as she gained weight with her pregnancy I would no longer find her attractive. Her actions over time progressed from flirtatious to promiscuous.

Our daughter, Diane, was born on 3 November 1981, almost exactly a year after we had relocated to Florida to start our new life. I had hoped the birth of our daughter would mark the beginning of a resurgence of love and togetherness in our marriage, the beginning of the happily-ever-after I envisioned when I first asked Carla to come to Florida with me.

Our marriage, however, continued to be a series of ups and downs. We had delightful days at the beach watching Diane daring the tide to touch her toes, pleasant evenings out to dinner or the movies, shopping expeditions to the mall and fishing trips in our boat on the Indian River. Interspersed with the good times was Carla's ever-present jealousy, which included my success in my career, any contact I might have with other women professionally, and my close relationship to Diane. Added to the jealousy were anger and the ever-present seizures. Nonetheless, we both worked hard to develop a good marriage. Carla wanted another child, a son. She saw Diane as "Daddy's girl" and commented on the close father/daughter relationship, saying she wanted to enjoy the same natural mother/son closeness. Carla had hoped that Diane would be a boy; we decided to have another child, and this time Carla got her wish.

With the realities of two children, rapid inflation and the reduction of opportunities in the lab technician field, I decided to attend medical school at the University of St. Lucia, even though it meant a temporary separation from my wife and children. Of primary consideration was the fact that St. Lucia did not require taking the Medical Collegiate Aptitude Test, thus the qualifying time was greatly reduced, and I was able to gain quick acceptance into their medical school, an important fact given our family and financial requirements. In addition, the acceptance criteria was easier to meet, and they taught all courses in English, even though they were located in the West Indies. The decision, when made, seemed a resolution to the many problems we were facing as a result of an increasing family and decreasing cash flow and an answer to my yearning to help others.

Robert was born in July, just before I was to leave for school. Carla was elated with the new baby, but distraught over my departure for school. We had moved to Boston so Carla and the children could live with my parents while I was away. This arrangement assured the grandparents of the opportunity of knowing their grandchildren, and more importantly, assured Carla that she would have assistance in caring for two babies, and someone would always be available should she have any medical problems.

Carla continued to waver in her attitudes and emotions; in November I was called home because of her persistent irrational behavior and pseudo-seizures. While I was at school, she sent a continual stream of depressing correspondence, noting her increased seizure activity, how much she and the children missed me, and how unhappy they all were. In addition, she and my mother were constantly bickering, until they finally reached the point of fisticuffs. When Carla was admitted to the Medical Center the first of November, it marked the end of my medical studies.

We returned to Florida, this time settling in St. Augustine, where I could work as a medical technician and Carla still had the advantage of warmer weather throughout the year. My return to the States seemed to have no positive effect on Carla's personality, our marriage, or her irrational mood swings. Her behavior became more and more negative. She persistently ignored medical advice, often, in fact, going against the advice of her physicians. Her care for the children became erratic. It wasn't unusual for me to arrive home and find Diane in soiled diapers, left lying on urine-soaked sheets. When I changed the sheets and diapers, an argument over the necessity of such actions and my trying to "take her place" would inevitably ensue. The marriage was rapidly deteriorating and Carla was not subtle about seeking solace elsewhere. In September of 1984, she moved in with a male friend from one of the local bars, and I learned what being "Mr. Mom" was all about.

Two months later, Carla returned to the house and attempted a reconciliation. Within days, things were back to normal, with Carla unhappy and unpleasant, me unhappy, confused, and frustrated, and the children confused and frightened by the frequent shouting. Feeling it was unfair to expose them to our continuous fighting and wanting to subject them to as little change as possible, I moved out of the house and found an apartment near my job, in a town about fifty miles away. Little did I realize that this error would have long-reaching consequences. Unbeknownst to me, Carla moved her boyfriend into our home almost as soon as I moved out, a fact of which I was unaware for over two weeks.

My wife now had full control of the children, their environment, their well-being, and their emotions. In the state of Florida, it is the public policy to assure that each minor child has frequent and continuing contact with both parents after the parents separate or the marriage is dissolved. Both parents are encouraged to share the rights and responsibilities of child rearing, and theoretically, the father is given the same consideration as the mother in determining the primary residence of a child, irrespective of the age of the child.

Carla sued for divorce and temporary custody in mid-December. With her boyfriend living at the house, my wife's irrational and inconsistent behavior over the past few years, and potential future medical problems, I felt it appropriate for me to counter-sue, requesting full custody of the children. I sought the legal assistance of a local attorney, being unaware at the time that, in cases of custody disputes, one is best served by locating and retaining an individual with extensive knowledge and experience in divorce courts, public agencies, and ex-wives. Had I initially retained such an individual, there is the possibility that he would have forewarned me of the potential for not only a long up-hill fight, but the real possibility that not all fighting would be clean and straightforward. Unfortunately, I knew none of this at the time.

At this point in the process, I made a major mistake in reacting to my concern for my children. After an evening visit in the children's home, Carla and I had one of our frequent verbal disagreements just prior to my leaving. A short distance from the house I realized I had left my jacket. Returning to the house, I found the front door ajar, the master bedroom door closed, and the children left unsupervised in their respective bedrooms. Taking advantage of what I thought to be the perfect opportunity to remove the children from a negative environment, I hid in my son's bedroom.

At 3:00 A.M., I packed up the children and drove north to my parents' home. Arriving in Massachusetts, I immediately contacted an attorney to try and get custody of the children. His efforts were a waste of his time and my money; a superior court judge ruled that Florida had jurisdiction over the children.

The following day we returned to St. Augustine. Within twenty-four hours of our return, I was not only served with divorce papers, but advised that my wife had motioned for a restraining order. Under the Shared Parental Responsibility Act, Carla had moved the court for temporary custody. At the end of that month, I counter-petitioned for full custody under the Uniform Child Custody Jurisdiction Act of 1977. Because of innuendos Carla had included in her motion, intimating that I had done such things as physically abusing her, had kicked the front door ajar and had threatened to wreck her car, for example, I filed a motion for contempt. Because of my response to her innuendos, she motioned for contempt. The actions, first by my wife and then by myself, began a game of back-and-forth accusations and innuendoes that built a mountain of evidence that could be used to the detriment of either party.

A hearing was set for 27 February 1985 in St. Augustine. During the two months prior to that time, Carla's behavior continued to fluctuate. Early in February, she brought the children to my laboratory office, despite repeated orders from her doctors that she was not to drive. Her visit resulted in a heated argument, witnessed by my co-workers who expressed concern about her irrational and belligerent behavior. While her erratic behavior could, in a minor way perhaps, be attributed to organic or seizure related causes, the behavior was primarily inorganic in origin. Carla's actions were the result of personality factors that would be identified in later psychological tests.

A few days later, Carla apologized, and we conversed on a mature adult level. Prior to the court hearing, Carla allowed me to visit the children, creating no problems and initiating no arguments. The children appeared well cared for; Carla's attitude seemed stable, and I began to feel the game of tug-of-war was not in the best interest of the children. I still loved my wife and felt guilty in the extreme for the situation the children were in.

The hearing, held at the end of February, proved to be non-adversarial. Carla and I appeared with our respective attorneys, and I reluctantly gave Carla temporary custody of the children, toddler's, ages three and one. This error in judgment on my part would complicate future problems tremendously. Carla was to receive three hundred dollars a month in child support, and I was granted reasonable rights of visitation.

The judge did not grant dissolution of the marriage that day. He instead ordered the Department of Health and Rehabilitative Services (HRS) to conduct a home study, witnessing the interaction each of us had with the children. The findings of that study would be instrumental in the final decree of custody. Although such studies are not routine during a divorce proceeding, they are typically ordered if there is disagreement between parents regarding custody rights. Such a study supposedly allows HRS to recommend to the judge which of the individuals is the most fit, most mature, and best all-around parent for the children.

Under the visitation order granted at the February hearing, I saw my children twice a month. During this period of time, I began to suspect physical abuse was occurring in their home; bruises on Diane's legs and on Robert's arms raised my concern about their well-being. I took photographs of the children, showing the bruises and documenting my concerns. Additionally, the general overall health and appearance of the children deteriorated, and I began regretting my decision to afford Carla temporary custody.

In early April, I made another of many mistakes that would have long-term and negative ramifications. Concerned about the children and unable to discuss the situation rationally with Carla, I called the local hot line number and reported questionable physical child abuse and potential neglect, naming Carla as the perpetrator of the abuse. The call incited an investigation of the report by the Department of Health and Rehabilitative Services (HRS) which was handled by an unmarried male in the local office. The result of the investigation was that neither physical nor emotional abuse could be substantiated and nothing more was done by HRS concerning the matter. At the time, I questioned the agency's handling of the report and ensuing investigation, but was unfamiliar with standard procedures and policies.

I know now that there was a much better way to handle my concerns. Given that I already had the pictures, my best course of action would have been to take the children to a doctor for a physical examination and then contact my attorney, requesting he motion for an immediate court appearance. My experience has proven that the one constant, when involved in a divorce and custody battle, is to avoid the HRS at all times.

Unfortunately, my allegations set the stage for Carla's revenge. Unknowingly, I had taken a number of steps that would place me in the classic setting for a Sexual Allegations In Divorce (SAID) case.

I was at work at the lab, running routine tests and making plans for the weekend visit with Diane and Robert. It was 18 April 1985, and the divorce was not yet final, nor was the question of custody resolved. Responding to a paged message, I cradled the telephone receiver against my shoulder as I examined the specimen in my hand. It was my attorney.

"Dean, it's Ron. I've just been advised that you've been accused of sexually molesting Diane."

Dropping the serum specimen, I stared at the shattered pieces of glass on the floor as I stated, "Ridiculous hogwash, Ron. She's only three-and-a-half, and I'm her father!" There was silence on the line.

"Is Diane okay? Why would Carla do this, Ron? It was Carla, wasn't it?"

Ron confirmed that Carla had made the accusation. Supposedly, Diane had complained to her mother that "she hurt down there," after returning home from the last weekend visit with me. Ron advised me that a court hearing had been set for determination of probable cause on 21 April 1985.

At the onset of the hearing I was, of course, nervous, but felt I had no reason to be intimidated, as I had done nothing wrong. The judge informed both parties of the proffered medical evidence "vaginal lacerations." I began to wonder why my attorney didn't question this evidence. Where was the M.D. who reported the findings? How could we cross-examine a report, hearsay evidence?

The judge ruled the accusation was unfounded or unsubstantiated, based on the fact that Diane would not talk. In other words, there was a lack of evidence. I had mixed emotions. I felt relieved that the court sought justice, and I was not going to be charged. However, how could they rule "lack of evidence?" There was no evidence at all! Suddenly I had more questions than anyone had answers for. Why had DHRS gone through such steps to try and have me charged? Why was my young and innocent daughter brought into this courtroom? Why didn't Carla testify? What was I doing here?

I had several concerns, in addition to protecting myself from Carla's actions. The major concern, of course, was the evidence of vaginal lacerations. Since I hadn't seen or talked with the doctor issuing the report, I had no idea exactly what he meant by the statement nor how he determined the existence of such. If there were lacerations, how had they really happened? Could Carla be extreme enough, in her search for vengeance, to hurt Diane in order to get at me?

Was it possible that her current live-in boyfriend was responsible for the lacerations? I had learned that in two-thirds of the cases of child abuse in a divorce setting, the abuse occurs at the hands of the live-in boyfriend or stepfather.

Was there a chance that Diane had hurt herself while masturbating? She was going through a rough time, adjusting to her father being gone and a new man in her house, her mother's care and attention being given sporadically. It is not unusual for young children to masturbate when under emotional stress of some kind, and Diane's fingernails were unkempt most of the time.

I wondered about the possibility of Diane's soiled underwear causing irritation and discomfort, the lacerations occurring when she rubbed or scratched herself in response to the itchiness.

Finally, of course, there was the possibility that Diane had fantasized the entire ordeal, and Carla had taken advantage of it. Although I continued to probe and prod at these questions and possibilities, there were no conclusions.

Carla motioned the court twice, attempting to suspend my visitation rights, based on the first allegation of child sexual abuse. Her efforts were unsuccessful. Our divorce was finalized on 6 May 1985. The HRS home study recommendations called for Carla to be awarded primary residential custody with me having liberal visitation.

On 24 September 1985, I was in Orlando, Florida at a sales demonstration meeting. It was my third week as an employee of Professional Medical Sales, a distributor of clinical laboratory products, and I was optimistic about my new position, if nothing else in my life at that time. During the meeting, I received a message to call Ron at 9:15 A.M. Knowing Ron would only call me at this meeting if there was something important happening, I obeyed the summons. My attorney advised me tersely that I had, for a second time, been accused of sexually molesting Diane. I dropped the phone, left the meeting and drove home to Baldwin, pondering this second allegation and reviewing every detail of my last visit with the children.

As soon as I arrived home, I was on the phone with Ron, a conversation that lasted an hour and a half. We went through the events of the most recent visit with the children the previous weekend, and I assured him it had been without incident, as always. "Did you have anyone with you and the children? Could anyone attest to the activities of the weekend state that no abuse occurred?" With a deep sigh, I responded, "No." It simply hadn't occurred to me that it would be necessary to have someone always at my side, to testify as to my behavior with my own kids. The attorney asked what I wanted him to do; I didn't know.

Two days later, a juvenile detention hearing to determine probable cause commenced at the county courthouse. DHRS had filed a petition for dependency against me to get the hearing. Ron and I were totally unprepared for the hearing, let alone its outcome.

Entering the courtroom, I saw several faces there I had never seen before. Although my attorney urged me to remain calm, I was nervous, and I was beginning to get angry, feeling the victim of a conspiracy, an ambush. Carla was flanked by her new attorney, a DHRS intake counselor, and an assistant attorney general representing the DHRS. In spite of my innocence, or because of it, I was beginning to feel a strong sense of paranoia building.

My fate was sealed by hearsay evidence presented by the intake worker. The "evidence" that led to losing my children consisted of a social worker repeating a statement she claimed Diane made, a social worker repeating the statement of an unnamed doctor who stated there were vaginal abrasions present, and a social worker stating that Diane had acted out the sexual actions with dolls while a video tape was made.

It is interesting to note that the first hospital physician to examine Diane found no evidence of abuse. However, two hours later, at another hospital, a Child Protection Team physician found positive evidence of trauma. I had not seen my daughter in the two-hour period between the two examinations. The second physician's report was accepted as evidence of abuse.

My next shock was at the amount of authority and judicial latitude assumed by the presiding family court judge, the same judge who had presided over the hearing when the initial allegation had been made. Based on the hearsay testimony of the intake worker, he found probable cause that I had sexually abused my daughter and terminated my visitation rights with both children pending further investigation by the DHRS.

My mind went blank, and my body was numb as I walked out of the courtroom. I was devastated from the experience of a living nightmare. I couldn't even express my feelings and the pain I felt. I didn't want to talk to anybody, especially my attorney. I thought I might still see the children for a last weekend visit. That, of course, did not happen. I didn't know when, or if, I would ever see my children again.

The first weekend after the hearing was tearful and depressing. I stared at the toys laying motionless in my living room while my home seemed to cry out for the children's presence. I became easily agitated, not wanting to associate with anybody. Nothing held any interest for me—the television, radio, working on my car. I couldn't sleep, my mind constantly racing with thoughts that circled to no conclusion. I was finding it difficult to function as a person. Throughout this entire ordeal, my parents were, fortunately, a very positive support for me. During that first weekend, I talked with them several times on the phone. They encouraged me to persist in my efforts, to fight for what I knew was right. I agreed, but thought they were seeing things too simply, not understanding the complexity of all I was facing. Nonetheless, throughout, they prodded and encouraged me to be strong for myself and for the children; they reminded me to remember this wasn't Diane's fault.

On Monday, 30 September, I received yet another call at the office from Ron. "There's a warrant out for your arrest, Dean, criminal charges of sexual battery. You need to turn yourself in. I'll meet you at the Jacksonville Sex Crimes Unit at nine o'clock Wednesday morning."

I hung up the phone, nauseous, and shaky. After a trip to the men's room to splash my face with cold water and try to get a grip on my nerves, I went to see my supervisor. Putting into words the fact that I had been accused of such a horrible action toward my daughter made it no more real, but a great deal more painful. We talked briefly, and I tried to explain the sequence of events, my beliefs as to what might be behind the accusation; I assured him of my innocence. He accepted my verbal resignation.

My reaction to the criminal accusation was predictable: a mixture of chills, sweat, and tears. I arrived at the sex crimes office as scheduled and found my attorney waiting for me there. We were greeted by a detective, who informed me that I was under arrest for probable cause of committing sexual battery, handcuffed me, and sent me off to jail. I had no time to confer with my attorney.

Following instructions, I emptied all my belongings onto a counter as another officer read my arrest report. He looked at me in total disgust and yelled, "That's sick, man! That's sick!" While I had not seen the report, I knew the charge and could only agree to how sickening the entire fiasco was, as I stared at the ground, listening to his abuse. My short stay in the booking room convinced me that until I could prove my innocence, I was guilty in everyone's eyes, or so it appeared. I used my one phone call to contact my mother, calling collect to bring her up to date on my current ordeal.

When I entered my cell, the eyes and odors of twenty other inmates greeted me. My intuition told me that they knew what I was in for. I hadn't even made it to my bunk when a black man growled in my face, "Baby Raper." As the sweat poured down my brow and between my shoulder blades, I reminded myself that I had to maintain control of my thoughts, emotions, and actions.

With lightning speed, the bond hearing the following morning came and went. Although my attorney was dependable and likable, he was not experienced in the area of criminal law and, as a result, the judge denied bail. Back in my cell, I tried to remain calm, despite my spinning head and shaking hands. It seemed that the state must feel they had a solid case against me if bail had been denied, and I realized their goal was to send me to prison. The fact that the majority of my cell mates were hardened, repeat offenders, familiar with various prisons throughout Florida, did nothing for my morale or feeling of well-being.

The first week in jail slowly passed. There were constant questions chasing each other through my mind. Why did it take so long to get another bond hearing? What will this do to my reputation? Could I get another job? Should I, could I, sue for false arrest? Was this really America, where the arrested are suddenly guilty until proven innocent? The more questions I asked, the more depressed I became.

Eventually I was permitted bail. My parents managed to raise the twenty-five thousand dollars in bail money, but fighting the false allegations was time-consuming and costly. In December of 1985, HRS closed the arrest case as "indicated," and I was placed on the Child Abuse Registry for seven years. An "indicated" case is one in which the HRS feels some type of abuse did occur, but leaves the perpetrator unnamed. Ron was replaced by two attorneys experienced in criminal law. First, there was the psychosexual testing. Then my attorneys viewed the videotape of Diane with the dolls, a tape taken by the Child Protection Team, which is a branch of Child Protective Services affiliated with the HRS, and obtained Carla's deposition. I knew the two attorneys and psychologist fees had to be expensive. I knew I couldn't afford it. How could my parents pay for such expenses? I was referred to Dr. David More of Jacksonville at Frank's request. I had no idea what to expect or what he expected. Did he think he was meeting and evaluating a sexual deviant? Was that what he was supposed to look for and verify? I spent an entire day with Dr. More, was exposed to a battery of psychological tests. Unfortunately, the results were cloaked in secrecy, and it was months before I had any indication of what those tests had revealed.

We received no notification of anything that was happening or had happened, and I had to obtain all my files personally. This further accentuated the stigma of being an accused abuser of children. So far, there had been no criminal charges formally filed, for which I was thankful. Frank said the state's case against me was growing weaker every day. However, the assistant state attorney, who was prosecuting the case, wanted me to see a "psychologist for the state." He wasn't satisfied with Dr. More's conclusions, which I still had not seen. I wasn't looking forward to another session with another psychologist, but it appeared I had little choice. I didn't want to face a future arraignment and criminal indictment.

The first part of 1986, I met the "psychologist for the state" in Orange Park, Florida. It was clear this was not going to be an objective relationship and things were tense from the beginning. The doctor's direction was clear. He was to interview me and administer a variety of tests, then recommend whether or not the state should prosecute. His analysis and conclusions as to whether or not I was a pedophile would be persuasive, directly affecting the actions of the state attorney's office.

The results and conclusions reached by the state's psychologist were contradictory in a number of areas and only increased my frustration, confusion, and growing anger at a system that more and more appeared not to have the best interests of my daughter or justice as a priority.

Initially, his statements were encouraging: "Mr. Tong's Minnesota Multiphasic Personality Index (MMPI) is one which necessarily raises doubts about his capability for responding to therapeutic intervention." With this statement, I was in total agreement. Since I had not compromised my daughter, why would I want to respond to "therapeutic intervention?"

"His responses to the group of psychosexual disorder questionnaires fall within normal limits, i.e., there are no findings from these self-reported instruments that this father endorses aberrant or deviant values or beliefs about any form of engagement in sexual behavior and, in particular, there is no reflection of overt pedophilic tendencies." I thought that made things pretty clear. However, the report continued. "In this psychologist's consultations with professionals who interviewed Diane, it was their strong belief that the child's reports of having been molested by her father were credible. My review of the videotape of Diane, taken by the Child Protection Team, also points to the same conclusion." Suddenly, I couldn't believe what I was reading.

The psychologist's final conclusions were damning as far as I was concerned. "This clinician would be reluctant to render any conclusive and unequivocal opinion regarding the actuality of the allegation that Mr. Tong has molested his child." Well, that meant he wasn't recommending prosecution, at least. "However, there does appear to be a strong likelihood that Mr. Tong has engaged in some form of inappropriate, erotic behavior with his young child. Accordingly, it is my recommendation that Mr. Tong be referred for therapeutic participation in an outpatient sex offender program to further explore his responsibility for misdirected effectual behavior with his young child. While the charge that Mr. Tong has molested his daughter is certainly a serious one, I do not see a compelling cause to prosecute this individual, provided he shows a willingness to cooperate in correcting his psychological and sexual deficiencies. This psychologist would support the present exclusion of parental and other visitation rights of Mr. Tong."

I was devastated. First the man states that I am "normal" in the areas of sexual behavior and have none of the characteristics of a pedophile. He further stated his doubts that I would respond to therapeutic intervention, based on the results of the MMPI. He then turned around and recommended that I continue to be denied access to my children and, while he wouldn't recommend prosecution, that recommendation is qualified by the requirement to attend therapy for an action he indicates I don't appear to have committed. At this point, I was convinced I was the victim of a conspiracy by the state agencies and my ex-wife. Not only was the report of the state psychologist contradictory, he and his findings never were presented in court, nor was the doctor ever cross-examined.

As seemed to be the case throughout the long ordeal, a doctor or agency seemed to know all about me, while I knew nothing about them.

Frank's job was to keep me out of jail, and he was delighted that I wasn't recommended for prosecution. I was happy to stay out of jail, but I wanted more than that. I wanted my innocence proven, and I wanted to see my children. I went to a session of outpatient therapy, at Frank's advice. There I sat, in a room filled with twelve "guilty" sexual deviants, individuals who blatantly stated they committed inappropriate sexual acts. When my turn came to speak, I said nothing. I knew I shouldn't be there in the first place. I wasn't guilty, as they proclaimed me to be. My personal story was none of their business.

I called Frank the next day, told him of my actions and reactions at the therapy session and said I wasn't going back. Frank informed me that if I didn't complete the ninety-day program, my case would linger in the state attorney's office. I was willing to let that happen, perhaps forcing the state to either prove my guilt or admit my innocence.

In November 1986, I moved the court for supervised visitation with my children. The family court granted my motion, after learning that the state was going to drop the felony charge. In December 1986 the sexual battery charge was dropped. I was never indicted, and this was not a case that was *nolle prosequi*. That term is the state's way of saying that, even though you've been formally charged, they decline to prosecute at that time. In my case, I was not formally charged, only arrested and detained for probable cause.

It had taken fourteen months and thirteen days for the capital felony charge of sexual battery to be finally dropped by the state attorney's office. During this time, I had been under a court order not to see or contact my children. I had no visitation rights at all, even though I had been arrested for probable cause only. Although formal charges were never filed against me, I still had to prove my innocence to the juvenile and family courts and the world. I had to prove that it was safe for the children to be with me.

In October 1986, I moved to Georgia, hoping the change of residence would aid my emotional state. I began seeing Dr. David Fox for assistance in dealing with my depression, isolation, and other negative emotions. He attempted to work with the Florida Department of Health and Rehabilitative Services, but wasn't even afforded the courtesy of responses to his letters, let alone any increase in my visitation with my children. That spring I went through another series of tests with a psychologist in North Carolina, and these tests and interviews again stated that I was not pedophilic. In June, I hired Hoffman and Associates, known as the "A Team" for their extensive knowledge of and work with false allegations of child sexual abuse. Mr. Hoffman filed the appropriate motions for visitation. A month later I went to Athens, Georgia where

I underwent a series of psychosexual tests, including the penile plethysmography test, which indicates an individual's natural and involuntary reactions to a variety of audio and visual sexual stimulations. As in earlier cases, my test results clearly indicated that I was not an individual with any pedophilic characteristics. This information was added to the results of my polygraph, which proved that I was not lying when I denied any inappropriate behavior with my daughter.

In April 1988 there was a hearing at the St. John's County Courthouse that included expert testimony from the Georgia doctors, David Fox and Henry Adams, all supportive of my case. In June 1988 there was another hearing at St. John's County Courthouse following our motion for normal visitation and/or a change in custody, a restraining order against Carla, a requirement for her to have a psychological examination, a finding of contempt or removal of the children to a foster home. The following day we received an order giving us one full day at a final hearing to be held the end of September.

In July, my attorneys lodged a vigorous objection to the admissibility of using the videotape of Diane with the anatomically correct dolls as evidence in court, stating that the tape was unduly prejudicial and contrary to due process, and that we would need to question the Child Protection Team (CPT) personnel who were involved with it. Carla had a psychological examination on 13 September, ten days before the final hearing, which really wasn't final at all.

On 21 October, Carla's recommendations were submitted to the court. A week later, on 27 October, we submitted our final arguments. In spite of the results of the psychological evaluations and testimony submitted to the court, in spite of the fact that Carla was proved an unfit mother, in spite of the fact that Carla had threatened a day care center with an accusation of child sexual abuse to avoid payment of her bills, on 5 December 1988 the court awarded Carla full custody of Diane and Robert and allowed me only supervised visitation with my children. We filed an additional memo, but were denied a motion for a rehearing.

On 5 January 1989, I filed my first Notice of Appeal against health and rehabilitative services. On the 27th of the month, we filed a rebuttal memorandum and an amended motion for rehearing. As a result of this action, the judge set aside the order of 5 December. However, five days later, when he issued his second order, there was little difference from the first. Carla retained custody, and I still had only supervised visitation. However, this order did contain the stipulation that HRS was to investigate Carla as a result of some question about her being an abusive parent. This investigation was never performed.

On 8 March 1989, I filed my second Notice of Appeal, this time against Carla. On the 17th of the month, the Fifth District Court of Appeals in Daytona Beach granted my Notice of Voluntary Dismissal, and the HRS appeal was dismissed. Three months later, in June, the HRS case was dismissed in full. In August, I submitted my initial brief to the Fifth District Court of Appeals. At the end of August my supervisor for visitation was changed again-for the fifth time-and my visitation increased to provide for nine hours on alternate Sundays, four hours the other Sundays.

In November 1989, I filed a Motion for Oral Argument and to expedite appeal. On 7 December my motion to expedite the appeal was denied. We never did receive a ruling on the Motion for Oral Argument. In early March 1990, I lost my appeal, as the Fifth District Court deemed the case *Per Curiam Affirmed* (PCA), not even rendering an opinion. This meant the Appellate court reaffirmed the lower court's decision. On the 20th, we filed motions for rehearing or clarification and also attempted to go to the state supreme court and request the entire Fifth District Court of Appeals to review my case. On the 22nd, the PCA became a mandate because of untimely filing of these motions by my attorney.

On 3 April we filed motions to recall the mandate and to reconsider my motions. On the 20th, all motions were denied and ruled as "moot." In July 1990, I had a one-hour hearing before the trial judge to modify visitation. For the first time in five years I was allowed unsupervised visitation with both children, four hours on one Sunday, nine hours the following Sunday, progress indeed.

During the five years following these allegations, I spent over eighty thousand dollars, hired six attorneys, saw five psychologists, took a polygraph test, a penile plethysmography test, and was subjected to countless other psychosexual tests. Although I proved a prima facie case of my innocence and my ex-wife was declared an unfit mother in court, she retains custody of the children. It wasn't until late summer 1990 that I was allowed to see my children without the supervision of an appointed chaperon, thanks to the A-Team! Regardless of my innocence, I was still considered guilty by the system that regulated my relationship with my children.

In fall 1990, I decided to file a lawsuit against all parties responsible for the deprivation of my civil and constitutional rights in federal court. To do so was not an easy task. I learned that because of the legal arguments of the abstention doctrine, *collateral estoppel* and *res judicata*, I could not seek equitable relief in the form of increased visitation rights or custody in federal court. But, according to the advice of a few civil rights litigators, I could, under 42 USC 1983, file a complaint for the violation of my constitutional rights and negligence incurred *ultra vires* (beyond one's reasonable authority), associated with same under the color of state law. I learned that federal court would be a more impartial forum to hear my complaint and that there was no limit on monetary damages sought. I was intent on making someone pay, literally, for the total destruction I incurred as a direct and proximate result of the false abuse accusations. Moreover, if I won in federal court, I knew I would be opening the floodgates for scores more lawsuits to be filed against the governments arbitrary and capricious manner in investigating and interviewing alleged child victims of sexual abuse. I learned that according to the federal rules of civil procedure I had four years to file such a complaint, from the time I knew, or should have known through due diligence that I was injured. After retaining an attorney to file the lawsuit we decided the statute of limitations didn't start running until at least 5 December 1988, the date the family court judge ruled in Carla's favor.

I learned that the filing of the lawsuit would be a long, arduous paper-trail battle. I learned that I would have to prevail not only on the statute of limitations issue, but also on the issues of absolute governmental immunity under the eleventh amendment, stating a clear cause of action upon which relief could be granted, and jurisdiction. I soon learned that I would be battling one of the top assistant attorney generals in the state of Florida.

We filed suit in federal court in the Middle District Court in Jacksonville, Florida in November of 1990 against my estranged spouse, the state of Florida-DHRS, and various other governmental officials responsible for my plight. We sued for intentional (now called negligent infliction of emotional distress) infliction of emotional distress, invasion of privacy, defamation of character, interference with familial relations (formerly called alienation of affection), and the violation of my due process rights under the Fourteenth Amendment. Total monetary damages sought surpassed two million dollars. The suit was covered by the local media. According to my attorney, the police had probable cause to arrest me. That said, we couldn't name the authorities as co-defendants in the lawsuit, or sue for false arrest or malicious prosecution. The basis of our lawsuit was a negligent videotape made by the child protection team in cooperation with the DHRS of my then 3½-year-old daughter, a tape that was allegedly electronically altered and doctored. In essence, we alleged fraud perpetrated upon the family court in St. Augustine, Florida, by the government, since the judge viewed the video and rendered an opinion and order from the same.

We alleged that the videotape was edited, that it was spliced by the government, to create an *impression* that I allegedly molested my daughter. It took my attorneys a lot of time to get the video in their hands. And, when they finally did so, they didn't know if they had the original tape! Fortunately, we had the video scientifically analyzed by the Institute for Psychological Therapies (IPT) in Minnesota, which stated the video was not original, and that the one shown to the court was comprised of 66 percent leading and suggestive questions and reinforced behavior. In other words, the state, via the anatomically exaggerated dolls (see chapter

10) and other play therapy techniques, goaded my daughter to confabulate false accounts.

All co-defendants filed timely (within twenty days) motions to dismiss my lawsuit. We countered the same via motions to strike, but I became unglued when I learned that my attorney had no legal foundation to sue the state of Florida, or one of its agencies. The legal case law proved the state was correct. According to *Gamble v. Florida* DHRS, 779 F. 2d 1509 (11th Cir. 1986), the state of Florida was/is immune from suit in federal court brought under 42 USC 1983. My attorney failed to inform me about the Gamble decision, or, in the alternative, wasn't aware of it. Yet, the Gamble court did expound upon Florida's intentional tort statute, 768.28, to state:

> No provision of this section, or of any other section of the Florida Statutes, whether read separately or in conjunction with any other provision, shall be construed to waive the immunity of the state or any of its agencies from suit in federal court, as such immunity is guaranteed by the Eleventh Amendment to the Constitution of the United States, unless such waiver is explicitly and definitely stated to be a waiver of the immunity of the state and its agencies from suit in federal court. This subsection shall not be construed to mean that the state has at any time previously waived, by implication, its immunity, or that of any of its agencies, from suit in federal court through any statute in existence prior to June 24, 1984. (emphasis added)

I was shocked! Surely, my lawsuit would be dismissed, with prejudice, or, at best, I'd be required to amend it.

In fact, over the next four years of very tedious litigation, we amended our lawsuit several times. My attorney agreed that we needed to delete the State of Florida-DHRS, as a named co-defendant. Even after we did so, it seemed the well was poisoned as far as the magistrate and judge were concerned. I did not file a politically correct lawsuit, and, because I (State House of Representatives candidate in 1994) and the lawsuit accumulated a lot of press attention, I paid the price, literally! In 1994, the federal court dismissed my lawsuit with prejudice. I lost. It was not an appealable decision. And, to pour gasoline onto an already incendiary situation, the court sanctioned my attorney and I, requiring us to pay the state's attorney fees for litigating the lawsuit over four years.

After ten years of litigation in six different courts, eight attorneys, six psychologists, and over $120,000.00 in costs to defend myself, I enjoyed unsupervised visits with my children for eight hours every Sunday. In other words, I was prevented from having my children sleep overnight with me at my house until they reached the age of majority.

During the interim of the litigation, my estranged spouse married twice, and once thereafter, for a total of five marriages to date. I married a beautiful and very supportive Vietnamese woman by the name of Lily in 1998. We've had no children together thus far.

2.

England 1977—Ohio 1991

William Smith was an unhappily married man. His wife of seventeen years had gone back to college in the early seventies. The children were almost grown, and she wanted her own career, her own life. William was in the process of starting his own business in an effort to raise their standard of living. The return of his wife to college, and her constant exposure to the new men of the seventies and the new attitudes, created a number of situations with which William was uncomfortable, but which neither of them chose to face nor discuss. William quietly decided to wait until the two children left home and obtain a divorce.

Into this set of circumstances walked Patti, twenty years younger, entrancing, vivacious, and beautiful, with a mind that was active and bright. William tried to ignore Patti, knowing she was provocative in the extreme to him, knowing he was not yet a free man, and his master plan said he would get a divorce and then take his time finding a woman with whom to begin anew. Love doesn't necessarily follow one's management plans for life.

Patti began her studies in music at college, and William vowed to put her out of his life and out of his mind. For a few months, he honored that vow, until he got a call that Patti wanted to meet him. Events moved rapidly, their love being the stuff that romances are made of. William left his wife, and he and Patti lived together. William had met Patti's father, to explain his intentions, and was happy to find that her father wished them well. However, he had cautioned William that Patti often had emotional and personality swings, but both men considered these would be resolved as she gained maturity. Following the finalization of William's divorce, they were married on 27 August 1977.

Life with Patti was an emotional roller coaster. She'd run for days in high spirits and then crash down into the blues. Much of this appeared to be the result of her relationships with her family. Her mother seemed to have, an unusual effect on and control over Patti. One day her mother approved of the couple; the next she withdrew that approval. One day Patti loved her mother; the next minute she hated her.

In 1978, Patti was pregnant with their first child. Her relationship with her mother worsened during this period. They were happy, however, finalizing plans to move to the United States from England, so William could help start a business there. Patti looked forward to putting some distance between her and her mother and regaining full control of her life. All was going well and planning took much of their time.

One morning, after leaving home with the usual happy farewell, Patti waving good-bye from the front door, a movement in the rearview mirror caught William's eye as he started down the quiet main road, a parked car pulled out from the side of the road and turned down their lane. He slowed and swung the car around, back to the village. As he circled the one-way street, William saw the car parked outside the cottage and a man entering the front door, greeted by his very pregnant wife. Caught in the system of one-way streets, he was unable to get to the house before the man, warned by Patti, had returned to his car and left. She claimed the man was someone from her past, and it was all unexpected, that he had called to see her on impulse. William had strong suspicions this was not true, particularly as the man had appeared to be purposefully waiting for his morning departure, but, loving Patti and considering her condition, he didn't feel he should pursue the matter.

That fall, the Smiths moved to the United States, visiting the East Coast sights before settling in Ohio. They had a lovely home, and he worked out of the house, developing new ideas for machinery and supporting a new license for his original technology. Janice had been born the winter of 1978, and Johnny was born in 1980. In spite of his love and the children, Patti still seemed to be haunted by her personality problems, the problems her father had tried to explain to him before he and Patti had married.

In 1981, a young man had moved in with the neighboring couple, whether a friend or relative was never clear. Much of the time he'd appeared to be out of work and would be in the house with Patti when William came back from daily business excursions. William was curious and concerned, but gave his wife the benefit of the doubt. Years later, he learned from the neighbors that they had sometimes seen the two hand in hand. During one of William's overnight trips, they had seen the young man returning to the house early in the morning, barefooted and with no shirt. Eventually, the young man had gone off to Oregon with another male neighbor. There were other dubious situations. It seemed almost as if Patti had two personalities, in total contrast to each other. William tried to put the concern out of his mind.

In 1982, through a combination of "innovative financing" and money from his late father's estate, William moved the family to a beautiful house with woodland acreage and a small lake in a suburb of Cleveland. Life with Patti and the two children seemed close to perfection. In 1983,

William went to England for a week on business. Shortly after his return, Patti mentioned inviting a man to tea. William tried to find out just what that meant, but with no success. It was two years later that he was advised that the man had stayed at the house for several days during his absence.

By 1984, he was getting on his feet, although they were not nearly as wealthy as they appeared to be. The future looked good, his technology was being accepted well, and his company was set to receive growing royalties for years to come. William's oldest son from his first marriage graduated from London University and, at Patti's invitation, came to live with the family the first of the year. As was true with the various members of her own family, Patti seemed to have a love/hate relationship with Brandon after he arrived. He got a job and moved into his own apartment in May. Patti's mother came out to visit that summer. Although Patti said she dreaded the visit, when her mother arrived, she acted as though she'd been reunited with her best friend. They had lengthy conversations, which stopped when William came near, and he began to feel uncomfortable and upset. It seemed that her mother's pub in England was failing, and Patti asked if her mother could come live with them. He said definitely not, knowing what her mother's constant presence would do to Patti as well as to him.

William found that he needed to take a long overdue business trip to Japan and Australia that fall, if his business was to continue to prosper. He would have preferred to stay home, fearing that Patti might go to pieces again while he was gone, but felt forced to schedule the trip for October. Usually, Patti was not keen on his leaving, but this time William was surprised to find that she actually supported his going. On the day of his departure, Patti was angry and jealous about his older daughter's graduation from London University. Patti dropped him at the departure area for the two-week trip and drove off. During that two-week trip, he talked to Patti every day, with the exception of one weekend when he couldn't reach her at the house. William arrived home on 10 November, exhausted and looking forward to time with his family. Patti met him at the airport, alone, and advised him that something terrible had happened to the children. Fearing an accident or serious illness, William was stunned when Patti handed him three documents, one from a social worker, one from a psychologist, and one from a physician, all stating that the children had been sexually abused. With little expression, she informed him that Brandon was in jail, a rape charge had been filed, and William's choice was between Brandon or her and the children. He got the distinct impression that his wife was enjoying herself.

Arriving home, William discovered that Patti's mother had come over from England and was staying with them. Suffering from the shock of the accusation and the jet lag that accompanies a trip such as that he had just completed, William kept quiet and simply listened. Later that evening he went down to the police station. His son's first words were, "Dad, I'm sorry about Patti." Not knowing what Brandon meant, William simply nodded his head and assured himself that Brandon was okay.

Over the next few days, he began to pick up facts and pieces of information that started to confirm a rather ugly picture. With an air of arrogance, Patti informed him, that she had slept with Brandon earlier that year. Now, Brandon's comment made to William in the jail cell made sense. A second visit to the police revealed that Patti had told them she had slept with Brandon while he was residing in her home and had done so to stop him from abusing the children. This made no sense at all to William, as he knew she had asked Brandon to baby sit over the several months following her having slept with him. Therefore, she was either knowingly leaving the children with a child abuser, or she was lying. The police officer told William that he had considered the abuse allegations a setup after the first interview with Patti, and he had another officer confirm that he'd stated so at the time. However, the police said they were bound to proceed because the Human Services were proceeding. William felt that they were playing a political game and was thoroughly disillusioned. He was now totally on his own.

Later, while putting his passport away in the file, he found that Patti's passport and those of the children were missing. Although he shouldn't have been surprised, he was.

Within a week, Patti began developing scenarios aimed at getting William out of the house. On one occasion, he was tickling the children's feet, as requested by Janice and Johnny, and she walked into the room, stating he was abusing the children. Walking up behind him, she struck him on the head with heel of her high-heeled shoe, as her mother watched. Instead of retaliating as she had hoped, William called the police and showed them the cut. He has since learned that actions such as these are commonly employed by the wife, who hopes the husband will retaliate, and she can then have him removed from the house on the basis of domestic violence.

William insisted upon attending what appeared to be a routine follow-up interview with the children by the psychologist who had stated, in writing, that the children had been sexually abused. He perceived the report as unscientific and therefore dangerously unprofessional, since it stated that abuse had definitely taken place. He got a shock when, in front of him, the psychologist gave Janice a "good touch-bad touch" book and proceeded to ask her if the bad touches were ever given to her by her father. At this point, it appeared that the case could take on an additional angle.

Patti's mother returned to England, but the following weeks were difficult at best. Patti continued her attempts to bait William into some type of negative action, while acting the distraught mother who hoped to see Brandon rot in jail. Throughout this period, he met several social workers of one sort and another, not one of whom impressed him, but rather convinced him that they were running the investigation on some agenda other than that of truth. On 17 December, Brandon was indicted for eight counts of rape and four counts of gross sexual imposition. Four days later, William took care of the children while Patti went to the Witness/Victim Center to sign a release. He asked her to bring him a copy, but her only response was anger. The task that was supposed to take an hour stretched into six hours, but Patti refused to discuss where she had been or what she had been doing, although she was visibly upset when she returned. The next day she attacked William with a kitchen knife, in full view of the children. When her attempts at forcing William out of the house failed, Patti left the house with the children, coming back with the police for some of her possessions and moving to a women's shelter in Cleveland. She then filed for divorce. The divorce request included domestic violence and the fact that Brandon, his son, had been indicted for sexual abuse of the two children. Unknown to William and unauthorized to do so, she had withdrawn all of the money in the company account, totaling eight thousand dollars, and had run up a bill for fifteen hundred dollars worth of clothes on a credit account.

The events that followed were an ongoing nightmare. Christmas Eve was a perfect picture as snow began failing over the landscape. The children's presents were grouped at the foot of the Christmas tree, and William's faithful german shepherd remained at his side. Somehow, William retained his sanity.

The weeks that followed blur in retrospect. William could see that Patti had become deadly, not caring about anyone, not even the children, in her attempts to crush them all. He would wake in the night, thinking it was all an impossible bad dream.

In early January, William received a letter from the Department of Health and Social Services (HSS) requesting he meet with them. During a telephone conversation regarding that request, he learned that Patti had alleged that he had also sexually abused the children; HSS never pursued those allegations. During this time, Patti advised the police that Brandon had a criminal record of child abuse in England; they found this to be untrue when they attempted verification.

William began the process of obtaining legal representation for the divorce. Since Patti had stolen the money from the company, he had to find money to cover the operating bills. Meantime, Brandon's grandparents sold their home in England to come up with the twenty-five thousand dollars down payment for a criminal defense lawyer for him. There were two cases, Brandon's criminal case and William's divorce case, and he had to be prepared to fight a potential criminal case against himself as well.

On 24 January, with no warning of any kind, Patti fled to England with Janice and Johnny, leaving via Canada. She filed and had the children made "Wards of Court" in England. Patti's affidavit made unbelievable claims, including statements that both Brandon and William had been found to be sexual abusers against Janice and Johnny. She further claimed that the family burned coal in their home, and that it was damp and cold. The documents arrived within hours of a hearing in which William would have lost all his rights as a parent. Although this appeared to have been Patti's intent and purpose, he managed to get a British attorney immediately. More debts were accumulated.

Finally, in February, William was allowed to see Johnny and Janice under the supervision of a policeman. Although it seemed to him that both children were depressed, they had always had a close relationship and were almost immediately as close as they had been before Patti's flight to England. For the next several months, he was allowed to see them one hour on Friday and one hour on Monday every fifth week, in England, under the supervision of a social worker. The agreement was that if all went well after several months of supervised visits, there would be support for his contention that the children should return to their home in the United States. After several months, he was told the children obviously loved him, but it would be traumatic for them to leave England. William felt that both he and the children had been tricked by the change in the terms, and he told the social worker/supervisor. He managed to ask the kids what they wanted, out of hearing of the supervisor. They said they had no regard for their mother, because of all that had happened and because she had told them they didn't have a father anymore. They hated living with her family and complained about their treatment. Fortunately, their mother had been unable to destroy the close relationship William had with the children. Even at such an early age, Janice and Johnny were able to see themselves as part of a team and to exercise patience, knowing they were working together to be together.

Finally, in June 1985, William had his ammunition. The rape case had been dismissed as *"Nolle Prosequi"* in April. The Ohio police had written to Patti in March about leaving unlawfully with the children and about her availability for the local case against Brandon. Also, in March, the guardian *ad Litem* issued an affidavit for the return of Janice and Johnny to Ohio. The fact that there had been two full months of nonprotective guardianship of the children later raised some question as to her competence. Armed with new passports for Janice and Johnny, William flew to England, not knowing when or if he would be returning to the states. It seemed so bizarre to him. He was then still a British subject, about to put himself in jeopardy with the British authorities in order to get two American citizens back to their own country. None of this should have been necessary in the first place. (There is now a Hague convention in place between Great Britain, the United States, and other countries, to ensure the return of children to "their place of habitual residence.")

William had to consider more than the next few hours or days. He questioned Patti's mental condition and what she might do to the children in the short and long term. What she had done thus far had been grossly abusive to all of them in different ways. She had obviously intended to put Brandon in prison for the rest of his days and then follow up with the same fate for William. In doing so, it appeared she was willing to destroy the children's family and their lives. As on his other visits, William stayed with Patti's father, Fred, and his second wife, Annie. They could see what was going on and shared his concern for Janice and Johnny. When he announced that, somehow or other, he was going to get Janice and Johnny back home to the States, Fred jumped right in and announced his help. This meant risking his livelihood as a dental surgeon and his friendship with local members of the royal family. Nonetheless, he was with William 100 percent.

William had several outlined plans for the escape, intending to settle on the best option by midweek. There were several major obstacles to be gotten over: how to get the children away from under the nose of the supervisor and out of the building; how to travel several hours to an airport or seaport, get past police, past security and immigration checks. It was inevitable that there would be a national security system alert within minutes of their leaving the building, and he was well aware of the efficiency of that system. Once and for all, he had to make sure the children knew exactly what they were doing, and had no doubts about their actions or leaving their mother.

On Friday, the children secretly reaffirmed their wish to go back to the States, fully aware that their mother might not follow them home. In fact, their enthusiasm to get going and their lack of interest in Patti's plans was somewhat overwhelming to both Fred and William, a subject that they often discussed afterward. By nine o'clock that evening, William, Janice, and Johnny were in France, ready to fly to Cleveland. The next day they were back in the United States.

William had complete responsibility for the children for nine months. They had a grand time together, and the children gradually opened up about what had occurred when Patti started the rape allegations two years earlier. According to their matching stories, they had been taken to a motel about a mile from the house over the weekend while William was in Japan. This was not a total surprise, as he had found the receipt for the stay at the motel.

Janice told him that she and Johnny were told, over and over again, what to say about Brandon having sexually abused them. Patti had even drawn pictures of what had happened. They had no toys, and Janice remembered playing with tissues and having to sleep on the floor. Johnny remembered Patti calling the police to come talk to them at the motel, but the police didn't come. Both children covered other details, such as when they were finally interviewed by the police, and Patti sat behind Johnny, pinching and flicking him with her fingers. It appeared that the pressure may have caused both children to lie as instructed, although Johnny remembered saying "No, no, no" to a social worker. Having listened to the tape made by the HSS agency, it had been apparent to William that the children were pushed by the social worker over and over again until she received the right answer. However, the real crux was that both children denied ever being touched wrongly or abused in any way by Brandon, or anyone else for that matter. It was apparent they were thoroughly disgusted with the whole subject.

During the time William had the children, they were in counseling, which confirmed the above reports they had given him and identified their negative attitude toward their mother for having put them through the trauma of the sexual abuse allegations, their removal from their home, their father, their country, and their loss of Brandon, whom they considered a great friend. Brandon had moved out of the area, away from the family, and was attempting to build a new life of his own. Patti had returned about three months after William returned the children to the United States. Throughout this time, she failed to comply with any of the court-ordered, twice-weekly visitations with the children, although she was living nearby in Cleveland. Nonetheless, she continued to make her presence felt through various legal motions, and William was ordered to pay her support money. He started to do so, but stopped due to a lack of money and the fact that he was close to going under financially.

In January 1986, Patti filed an affidavit, accusing William of violence toward the children. In what William considered to be a move to stop her father from being a witness against her in the pending divorce and custody case, Patti accused her own father of having sexually abused her as a child. Through her mother, pressure was brought to bear on the English court to bring about two allegations of child abduction, citing the children's return to the Untied States. William won against both charges. Shortly after Patti's return to the States, both parties were to complete a Minnesota Multiphasic Personality Index (MMPI) test. Upon completion, the results of Williams's testing was available but, mysteriously, Patti's results never came to light. Patti changed attorneys and her new attorney and the guardian *ad Litem* for the children quickly requested that new tests be done for both parties, but by another psychologist. Amazingly, both MMPI tests were allowed to be taken at home and without supervision. A report was later submitted to the court, based on the interpretations of these latest MMPIs and interviews with the family.

William had questioned the psychologist as to the validity of the MMPI's, since under the testing circumstances, they could have been completed by anyone and could well have been done by an outside party. His concern was ignored. For reasons best known to himself, the psychologist had Patti take yet another test some months later. That in itself was not scientific, because William was not asked to repeat the test. The question was (and is) why? That and more became the subject of a lawsuit.

In March 1986, a hearing was scheduled regarding the children's current and future custody. After waiting for hours, the judge said she had made up her mind, the children were to be returned to Patti. This decision was made without benefit of hearing William's witnesses or reading the psychological reports from the children's counselor. His attorney was astounded and attempted to have a full hearing scheduled. At five-thirty that afternoon, they were advised that the hearing would be held that evening and that it must be completed within an hour and a half. At that point, their witnesses were long gone, but Patti's attorney had two on standby. One of these was the psychologist and the other a social worker who testified that, among other things, William had a face like a martian's sex organs. From this, you may imagine the quality of the hearing. The end result was that William had to instruct Johnny and Janice to gather their belongings and go to their mother. They didn't cry; they screamed.

Dr. Hill, the children's counselor, immediately protested to the Ohio court authorities that the hearing had been improperly held and that significant information had not been available regarding the children and actions in their best interest. There was no response from the courts or the guardian *ad Litem* and custody was established as twelve days with Patti, two days with William. Those involved with the children were stunned. Throughout the preceding months, the children had constantly and consistently repeated that they had been made to lie about the sexual abuse and had evinced a great deal of anger toward their mother for making them lie and for taking them to England and away from their father.

Next began years of pain, frustration, and expense, as William set out to prove not only that the allegations of sexual abuse were false but that it was in the best interest of the children for him to have at least, joint, if not full custody. On the advice of his attorney at the time, William took the children to Dr. Carl at the University of Arizona, in the event there might be further allegations of child abuse made against him. Dr. Carl stated that, in her opinion, the children had not been molested by their father and that she considered him a good candidate for custodial parent. In November 1986, Janice described a clash with her mother, regarding her being made to lie in the original allegations against her stepbrother. According to Janice's report, Patti had tried to smother Janice by putting one hand over her mouth and holding the girl's hands and knees with the other. She said the act was interrupted by an inquiring neighbor.

After hearing this, William took both Janice and Johnny out of state for an in-depth evaluation at Loyola University. The evaluation was recorded on video and was the subject of a comprehensive report, which was later blocked from use as evidence on a technicality raised by the guardian. William's concerns about Patti's emotional state increased as it became clear that the children were being subjected to physical, verbal, and emotional abuse. This fact was confirmed by psychologists considered experts in the field of child psychology.

There were what seemed to be continuous motions, appeals, and counter appeals to the legal system and the state HSS agencies. Each time there was a chance for a change in custody, the children became hopeful. Each time custody remained with Patti, the children resisted that custody, more than once having to be forcibly taken to their mother's home. No one, it seemed, thought it necessary or advisable to listen to the children. William had filed a police report due to his concern for the safety of the children if Patti became desperate about the discovery of her perjury and brainwashing of the children. In November, Janice wrote a letter to the police, asking that it be given to the judge in charge of their case so they could return to their father.

In January 1987, prior to the divorce and custody hearing which had finally been set for May 1987, William learned from the children that they had been taken for drug tests at the local general hospital and that they had been questioned about his giving them drugs. William received the bill for the tests.

He couldn't afford an attorney by the time of the divorce hearing and represented himself. The case ran for most of a month, and although the outcome was predictable from the start, William was determined to bring out evidence and put it on record for future use. Of the thirteen witnesses he'd brought in, perhaps the most interesting was the teacher who testified to being approached by Patti and asked to lie, to say that she, the teacher, had started the abuse accusation. William had always suspected that Patti would do her best to cover her tracks.

For three years, William continued to battle for custody. For three years, HSS and the courts refused to listen to the pleas of the children or to consider the reports from the University of Arizona, from Loyola Medical School, and from Ross Counseling, where the children had been under consistent therapy at the order of HSS. During the course of 1989 and 1990, Janice and Johnny suffered further physical and emotional abuse from their mother. On one occasion, they called the police to their mother's home. On another occasion, they ran away from their mother outside the juvenile court and defied six police cars in the local garage.

Johnny, at the age of ten, fought two sheriff's deputies so as not to be returned to his mother, who was watching the struggle. Although, at one point, a judge declared there was "clear and convincing evidence of abuse," the case was dismissed without a hearing several days later. HHS told William to keep the children and then denied doing so to a judge who subsequently stopped William's visitation. Never once were the children allowed to testify, to act as witnesses.

In June 1990, Janice, then twelve years old, filed an affidavit with the court, documenting the events of the past six years. In that affidavit, she pointed out that filing the affidavit was especially important; she and her brother had never had the chance to speak or to be heard in a court.

Janice first stated that while her dad was away, their mother took them to a motel and kept them there for two days, telling them that their stepbrother had done bad things to them and drawing pictures for them to look at. She told of being taken to England by her mother, who told them they didn't have a dad anymore, and then of returning to Ohio with their father. She stated that they were very happy living with their dad and that they didn't want to see their mother, but were taken away from William and forced to go live with her.

Janice documented the fact that her mother had physically abused both her and her brother and that she was afraid of her mother. After a particularly frightening display of abuse, Janice had confided in her father during their weekend with him. She said William made some calls and they were allowed to stay with their father until they could go to court and tell the judge everything. However, when they arrived at the courthouse, they were not allowed to see the judge and were sent home with their mother.

One of the saddest parts of this particular case study was this affidavit and the statements made by Janice regarding the dilemma of the children:

> I told a social worker about that (physical abuse) when she came to visit us. Mrs. M. said she was my friend and that I need not tell anyone because my mother and father were going to get together again. I asked my dad and he said it wasn't true. I told a teacher at our school, Mrs. K., and she said she would help us. I also told Mrs. R. They didn't. This year my mother began to punch Johnny and I tried to stop it. I climbed out a window to get help. The police came and they said they would help us. The police did not help us. I talked to a man on the phone and he told me that Johnny and I could stay (with William) until they came to see us. They never did come to see us.

I tried to see the judge, but they wouldn't let me. It was the worst day of our lives and Johnny and I tried to run away but the police caught us and made us get in the car with our mother. A lady called Cheri talked with us and said she would help us speak to a judge the next day, but it never happened. It is another summer and the court has stopped my father from seeing us. It is so difficult living with our mother because we never know what she is going to do. We have asked our dad to never give up fighting for us.

As of this writing, William continues to be denied any visitation with his children. He continues to pay child support and lives abroad much of the time. Each month the children are growing stronger and closer to freedom from oppression. Like the Berlin Wall, William believes it is inevitable that time will tell, and the barrier of lies separating him from his children will crumble.

3.

Colorado 1984-1991

Marsha and Rick were married in 1977 and had three children: Andrew John, born in 1979, Cecil Wayne in 1980, and Sheila Marsha in 1982. Like most couples, they had their fights, but Rick loved Marsha dearly and thought she loved him. He was concerned about the fact that she was a screamer, instructing and disciplining the children in a strident voice that made Rick as nervous as it did the children. During the course of their marriage, Rick was often concerned about the many times Marsha stayed out late with girlfriends, later learning that she had been lying to him about where she was and with whom.

The couple separated for three months in 1979. In July 1984, they again separated. Marsha filed for divorce in November 1984, but stopped the proceedings based on the belief she and Rick could work out their difficulties. She returned to him in April 1985, and they made a second attempt at a working marriage. Rick had purchased a large cabin for the family and was doing finishing work on their new home, while Marsha and the children lived in a trailer in town. Marsha had termed the cabin unlivable, and Rick was trying to bring it up to her standards. She left him again in June 1985, and they lived separately thereafter. Rick had continued working on the cabin, ever hopeful that once all the comforts had been installed and the finishing touches completed, Marsha and the children would move back there to live. He and Marsha had been seeing a marriage counselor, and although Marsha felt they could not reconcile their differences, Rick continued to hope.

Throughout the spring and summer, Rick continued to see his three children, although not as often as he would have liked. Marsha contended that his attempts to see her and the children constituted harassment. On one occasion, when Rick came in to see the children while she was visiting her mother, Marsha had him arrested for causing a major disturbance, threatening to take the children and damaging her car. A few weeks later, Marsha had called the sheriff's office, contending that he was harassing her at work.

Unknown to Rick, Marsha had contacted a therapist in June and taken the children to see her. When he learned of the therapy and asked

Marsha what was going on in the sessions, she told him she couldn't say exactly. In August, Rick advised Marsha that, because of her behavior in seeing other men and her inability to support the children, he was going to sue for custody. On a sunny day in September, Rick heard the crunch of gravel and looked up to see Marsha's car coming down the drive. Since she rarely came to the cabin, he started toward her car, hoping she was coming to see how work was progressing. It was then he saw the second car. The officer in the squad car had come to arrest Rick for sexually molesting his 3-year-old daughter.

From the cabin, Rick was taken directly to jail and denied any contact with friends or relatives, told the phone was out of order, and generally ignored. The next day he was taken to court for formal charges and returned to jail. Three days later, he was taken to a second court for filing of criminal charges. Fortunately for Rick, the criminal court judge was so agitated about the manner of arrest and confinement, he ordered Rick released on his own recognizance. It was only during the court appearance that Rick found out the charges had been made by a policeman. Later investigation revealed the charges had been made based on Marsha's allegations. The policeman was Marsha's boyfriend, who had frequently been seen at the trailer by neighbors.

Marsha had filed a handwritten affidavit in which she had made the allegations of child sexual abuse, stating it had occurred when the children had one of their rare overnight visits with Rick. The visit had originally been scheduled to take place at his parent's home. Following an argument with him, Marsha decreed that the children would, instead, spend the night with her mother, and Rick was so advised. He went to his mother-in-law's house, picked up the kids, and returned to his parents' home, as had been originally planned.

Marsha's allegation stated that Rick had taken the children for visitation 26 August, spending the weekend at his parent's home. When the children returned, Marsha learned that the boys had slept upstairs and Sheila had slept downstairs with Rick. When Sheila went to the bathroom, she said "my pee-pee hurts." Checking her daughter, Marsha noticed the entire vaginal area was red. She asked her daughter what happened and Sheila replied, "Daddy kissed my booby and pee-pee." Then Sheila said "no, her daddy didn't do this, her grandfather did." Then Sheila said "no, her grandfather didn't do it, it was because she had slept on the carpet." Marsha contacted social services the next morning.

As is common in cases such as this, Rick had no idea of the steps Marsha had taken that resulted in his arrest. Marsha was a good friend of a therapist at Department of Social Services (DSS), and with her assistance had set up an entire scenario to establish charges of child sexual abuse. As a result, the county DSS, juvenile division had filed a petition stating that Sheila had been sexually abused, and both boys had been physically abused. The dependency petition, dated 26 September 1985, stated that the boys said their father had hit them with his belt and left bruises. It further stated that due to Sheila's age (she was three at the time), she could not talk about the abuse and referred the child to an agency therapist (ironically, the same close friend of Marsha's) for purposes of obtaining more information on the sexual abuse to substantiate the allegation. The agency therapist's letter to the DSS stated that she had received a call on 30 August 1985, from Sheila's mother stating she had reported further information supporting the allegation to social worker Jane Storey. In a letter to the social worker, the agency therapist said that in her sessions with Sheila, the child had remained consistent about her father having lay on top of her with his clothes on and that he goes "potty" on her.

In the meantime, a report had been filed by a district attorney investigator, following an interview with Marsha. During the course of that interview, Marsha made clear allegations of sexual abuse. She began by discussing the fact that from the time Sheila was 3-weeks-old, she had noticed a thick white discharge with a strong offensive odor coming from the child's vaginal area and contended that during the periods when she was separated from her husband, the discharge and odor seemed to be reduced. Marsha also stated that Rick walked around their home often with no clothes on and expected to engage in intercourse when the children were in the bedroom. She specifically discussed an incident when Rick was in a chair with no clothes on and, Sheila, crawling into his lap, grabbed his penis and said "Daddy, you got a big peter." Marsha said Rick laughed about the incident.

According to Marsha's report, when she left Rick the second time in June of 1985, she made an appointment with the agency therapist at the county mental health for therapy for the children. She also took Sheila to see a doctor, who said it would be hard to determine sexual abuse unless Marsha brought Sheila in immediately upon noticing anything out of the ordinary.

When he was released from jail, Marsha and Rick met at the marriage counselor's house. She had gone to him earlier to try to undo what she had done that week. She showed Rick a list of the written charges she had made against him and a list of the recantations, telling him she had not meant for him to be arrested, but things had gotten out of hand. He was absolutely shocked at what she had done and the charges she had made, and immediately asked for a divorce. In the short period of time that elapsed, a week that had seemed like a month to Rick, the district attorney had gotten involved, as well as, social services. The recantations meant nothing to them; they contended Rick had threatened Marsha into making them. In addition, there was a charge of physical abuse, based on an incident when he had lifted Sheila over a porch railing. In the process, she hurt her elbow, and they had taken her to a doctor to have it checked. There had been no report of abuse by the doctor, as it had been a simple accident. Social services viewed it as another weapon in their arsenal and used it against Rick in future hearings and considerations.

Suddenly Rick had only very limited access to his three children as supervised visits were required. More often than not, these were either scheduled when he was working, or Marsha canceled them arbitrarily. Because he refused to confirm the charges and maintained his innocence, he eventually lost all rights to visit the children.

On 26 September 1985, based on a letter from the social worker stating it was her opinion that sexual abuse had occurred, a decision was issued by the Department of Social Services stating that Rick would not visit with the children unless supervised by the county DSS or an assigned agency; that the sheriffs department and DSS would be notified of when Rick would be visiting with the children (time, place, and date); and that, should the agreement be broken, visitations by Rick would immediately cease and the children might be removed from their home.

The formal statement from the social worker asserted, "Based on information Sheila and her mother provided me, it is my opinion sexual contact has occurred between Sheila Doe and her father, Rick." Rick's access to his children was based primarily on statements made by his ex-wife and Marsha's interpretation of Sheila's statements, which she repeated to the social worker. No one seemed to be listening to anything he had to say. All actions were based on what Marsha said or what the social services workers said.

The following weeks were an ongoing nightmare. Rick saw his children only under supervised conditions, the supervisor being the Department of Social Services or an assigned agency. Because of agency policy, most visits continued to be scheduled during Rick's work hours, and Marsha continued to cancel the visits arbitrarily, usually at the last minute. Meanwhile, the children, his two sons and daughter, were in ongoing therapy under the direction of DSS, who treated all three children as if they had, in fact, been abused and issued consistently damaging reports and summaries regarding Rick's actions with the children and their feelings about their father.

On 12 May 1986, the agency therapist sent a letter to the county DSS, stating her concern about the visitations of Rick with his children. Criminal and juvenile petitions were still pending, alleging physical and sexual abuse of the children, and Rick was to meet the conditions set out in the September edict. The agency therapist contended that Rick was not following the rules, that he had frequently been in the presence of the children and had been emotionally abusive to them, telling them he didn't love them, and he didn't want them. She further stated that the children reported being frightened of their father and of his following them and Marsha around. The therapist recommended that visitation be disallowed until the disposition of the criminal and juvenile matters. She based her recommendation on her analysis of the children's reports, Rick's hostility toward the DSS, and her feeling that his attitude was disrupting their therapy progress.

On 16 May, the therapist sent a letter to DSS stating that Rick's son Cecil had shown her, with anatomically correct dolls, "bad touches." He indicated that Rick had touched his penis, fondling him when he was in bed, and also showed her how his father had fondled Sheila's vagina. A comprehensive report was submitted by the agency therapist on 1 July 1986, to DSS. This report indicated that both Marsha and Rick had previously been married, and that Rick had two daughters who lived with his ex-wife. Marsha said the ex-wife had told her that Rick had been physically abusive to her during their marriage, and Marsha contended he had continued that pattern during his marriage to her. Over the ten years of their marriage, Marsha and Rick had separated several times.

The agency therapist contended that all three children demonstrated behavior characteristics of physical, emotional, and sexual abuse victims. According to the therapist, Andrew exhibited an extremely low self-esteem and had difficulty expressing any positive item about himself, frequently stating he was "unlovable." He perceived the world as an unsafe environment, showed antisocial behavior, and acknowledged little personal responsibility. Both Cecil and Sheila were said to demonstrate a mistrust of adults. Cecil demonstrated difficulty in concentrating and a basic "don't care" attitude. Sheila exhibited angry, defiant, oppositional behavior to any monitoring or restructuring of her activities. In summarizing the benefits of the therapy the children had been undergoing, the agency therapist stated that Cecil's increased feeling of being protected allowed him to discuss the incestuous behavior of his father. She further stated that Sheila's progress included improved identification of her feelings concerning the sexual abuse and improved expression of feelings concerning family roles, boundaries, and relationships. (I find this to be an impressive accomplishment for a 3-year-old, as did Sheila's father.) In conclusion, she recommended that legal custody of the children be returned to Marsha and, due to the fact that criminal and juvenile court petitions were still pending, a strong case management system be implemented.

At the end of July, the court gave legal and physical custody of the children to Marsha Doe with DSS retaining protective supervision, requiring that the children and Marsha remain in therapy, and stating that Rick was to have no visitation and no contact with the children unless he agreed to enter therapy, at which time the restrictions would be reviewed.

On 1 August 1986, the courts issued the divorce decree, recognizing the orders in effect from the juvenile court, denying Rick any contact with his children, and stating that Rick was not to visit Marsha unless a time had been previously arranged and a third person of Marsha's choosing was present. On 27 August, a motion was filed requiring that the victim (Sheila) be made available for a psychiatric examination prior to Rick's trial on child sexual abuse.

While Rick's attorney was successful in getting the criminal charges of sexual abuse dropped, due to lack of any substantial evidence, he was not helpful in his suggestion that Rick plead *nolo contendere* to the charges of physical abuse. Following his attorney's advice, in an effort to simply end the nightmare, Rick made a fatal mistake in this pleading, a mistake that resulted in the possibility of the juvenile court using that plea to prevent Rick from ever seeing his children again.

Unknown to Rick, a videotaped interview of his daughter was ordered by the deputy district attorney, based on the therapist's opinion that it would be emotionally traumatic for Sheila to testify in court. The tape was made, but Rick was not present, never saw the tape, and when he learned of it and asked to view it, his request was denied. Unfortunately, this is not unusual in cases of this nature. It is interesting to note the list of questions asked during the interview was provided by the deputy DA. In any analysis of interviews, the types of questions often dictate the types of answers received, and it is quite possible to lead the witness through the proper questions. Included in this listing were a number of closed and leading questions which placed the interviewer in a much more active role than the child. Questions such as:

- Has Rick Doe ever touched her where she didn't want to be touched?

- Where did he touch her?

- With what did he touch her?

- Did he touch her more than once?

- Did the touching hurt?

- Has Rick Doe ever lay on top of her?

- Has she ever lay on top of him?

- Did they have their clothes off?

- Has Rick ever made her touch him?

- Where?

- Did Rick ever tell her not to tell anybody?

Although sexual abuse charges were dropped by the criminal prosecutor due to a lack of substantial evidence, social services held to the sexual abuse, as well as the physical abuse charges. The public defender, who represented Rick, advised him to plead *nolo contendere* to the physical abuse; after all, the incident in which it was alleged his daughter's arm had been hurt did happen. So there he was, charged with child abuse, sentenced to four years of probation and denied any access to his three children. Rick found himself in the typical position of one who has been falsely accused of sexual abuse. The agencies and courts were determined to treat a condition that didn't exist and solve a problem that wasn't there. Meanwhile, his children were deprived of any contact with their father.

In final court orders, Rick's ex-wife received full custody of the three children, Rick was put on probation for four years, ordered to pay four hundred and twenty dollars a month in child support, as well as full restitution to the court, and was advised by the court that he would never see his children again. Any attempts to visit or contact the children would result in his arrest. It was a no-win situation. He couldn't admit to sexual child abuse that had never occurred; he couldn't see his children, and he couldn't find anyone to help.

On 8 October 1986, the agency therapist drafted a clinical summary update in which she recommended that the county social services discontinue their involvement with Marsha and the children. She indicated that all three children were afraid of their father. She stated that the agency continued to work with Cecil and Sheila as incest victims and that Marsha had joined a weekly adult incest survivors group. On 11 November 1986, a memo from Rick's probation officer stated that he had a letter from their family counselor, stating that Marsha had told him she had trumped up the charges against Rick because she believed she had been caught by him in an incriminating relationship with another man. Marsha had initialed the report from the counselor. The memo further included statements from Dr. R., indicating that he did not believe Rick suffered from mental illness, was not an alcoholic, and did not appear to him to be a child abuser. The probation officer recommended that Rick participate in mental health counseling.

The court-ordered evaluation done by Dr. R. was, for all practical intents and purposes, ignored by the court. Overall, the evaluation pointed out that Rick was a candid, straightforward man, one incapable of perpetrating child sexual abuse. It is interesting to note that Dr. R. questioned the use of the anatomically correct dolls, pointing out that an inappropriate setting and the use of leading questions can provoke desired responses, rather than accurate or true responses. He indicated that the public defender felt Rick was the victim of a legal sequence of events derived from what he felt was incorrect procedure, poorly carried out, in Aspen by the mental health worker. In closing, Dr. R. cited the fact that Marsha had admitted to the marriage counselor that she had made false allegations of both physical and sexual abuse in an effort to protect her custody of the children in the face of her extramarital relationships. He then stated: "Accordingly, then, the whole issue of counseling may be moot, since there is, in my opinion, no significant issue to be dealt with."

Two months later, January 1987, in spite of the above positive report, DSS issued a six-month treatment plan for Rick that required the following: therapy with a professional whose background experience was in working with perpetrators who have sexually abused, a psychological evaluation, no visitation or telephone contact with his children unless specifically recommended by Rick's therapist and agreed to by the agency therapist, entry into a perpetrator's group, preferably with a mental health center recommended by DSS. The stated goal of the treatment was "to have Mr. Doe in therapy so that he is able to resolve past issues that led him to abuse his children."

Rick was referred to a female therapist. She insisted he admit to sexual abuse prior to any therapy. Because he was innocent of those charges, he refused. DSS then referred him to a second therapist, the agency therapist who was convinced he was an abuser, who had filed allegations based on her work with his ex-wife and three children, and who continued to counsel the children as sexual and child-abuse victims. As a result of maintaining his innocence and refusing to enter a perpetrator's group and admit to being an abuser, the court, based on recommendations of DSS in August 1987, dismissed the juvenile case with the following orders: Legal and physical custody of the children would be with Marsha; Rick would have no custody and no visitation or contact, direct or indirect, with his children; Rick would enter therapy and be evaluated; Rick should be in individual therapy for one year to work on issues related to sexual abuse of children. If Rick progressed through this therapy, he would then have to attend parenting classes for a minimum of eight weeks and, following that, enter counseling with Marsha to allow them to establish a dialogue in which the two could work toward the children visiting their father. Meantime, Marsha remarried, providing a substitute father figure for the children who were denied their own father by the system.

In December, the agency therapist left the mental health center and was replaced by a second therapist. Unknown to Rick, the second therapist provided the district court with a clinical summary update on 6 April 1987. Many of her statements and recommendations were in marked contrast to those of the original therapist, i.e. "recognizing and working through personal concerns such as ambivalent feelings toward their father and mother, age-appropriate issues around trust and abandonment which may be exacerbated by their family problems." The new therapist further stated that she thought it important to the children's emotional well-being for them to reestablish a healthy relationship with their father. Toward this end, she recommended Rick consistently attend a minimum of twelve consecutive weeks of therapy in individual or group format and attend eight weeks of parenting classes, following which he should be allowed supervised weekly or biweekly visits with his children. She also recommended that Rick and Marsha attend joint therapy for purposes of helping them function together in the children's best interests.

At the same time this occurred, the social services agency in their county was under fire from a number of families who had been treated much as Rick had been and whose rights had been badly abused. There was a great deal of media attention, resulting in a state investigation that culminated with resignation of the director and a general shake-up in the employees.

During this time, Rick continued to look for a good lawyer. Most didn't want the case, as they felt they could be of little help due to his pleading guilty to the child abuse. Others didn't want to fight the Department of Social Services. Finally, he located an attorney who said he could approach it from the standpoint of restoring Rick's visitation rights. At least, he might get to see his children again after three and a half years.

In April 1989, Rick went back to court for reinstatement of visitation rights, represented by a new attorney. It had now been more than three years since he had seen his children. One of the items pointed out by the attorney was that Rick found himself in a lose-lose situation. The psychological report indicated no basis for the charge of sexual abuse and no issue for which to seek resolution through therapy. His ex-wife admitted she had concocted the charges. The criminal courts had dropped the charges. Yet, as a condition of seeing his children, he was required to admit he had perpetrated sexual abuse and enter one year of sex abuse therapy. Rick's attorney sought supervised visitation, supervision to be supplied by a clinical psychologist who agreed with Dr. R.'s findings regarding Rick and who had offered his services to assist in establishing contact between father and children.

On 17 October, an order was issued regarding visitation. Initial visitation was scheduled in the DSS office, with the agency therapist supervising. It was ordered that, prior to Christmas, reports would be filed by the therapist and the guardian *ad Litem* describing the course of the visitations and addressing the issue of holiday visitation. Marsha's response to this request was to file a motion asking that visitation reinstatement not be considered until after a guardian *ad Litem* was appointed for the children and said guardian had the opportunity to review the case and make some judgment regarding the merit of reinstating visitation. The motion requested that the guardian *ad Litem*, who had been appointed for the juvenile case be reinstated.

A guardian *ad Litem* was appointed, and in December she entered a report to the court in which she recommended that visitation continue, but that there be no unsupervised visitation allowed at that time. She requested that she be allowed to determine when unsupervised visitation became appropriate. Attached to the guardian *ad Litem's* report was a report from the therapist, indicating that the visitation was occurring on a weekly basis with both Rick and Marsha attending the visits. She stated that the children exhibited increasing comfort in Rick's presence and some lessening of prior levels of fear, although they continued to express strong reluctance to be alone with their father. It was recommended that the children spend an extended Christmas Eve visit with Mr. Doe at his parents' home, with his parents supervising. She further recommended that visitation times be increased and be supervised by a non-related person, gradually moving into an unsupervised visit in a public place, then at Rick's home.

Rick's girlfriend encouraged him to continue to fight for his innocence, but the attorney told them this would cost a lot of money. If they wanted to put his kids through college, he didn't mind, but he was very discouraged regarding the cost. At that time, the end of January, they felt they had their hands full just dealing with the visitation issue. The guardian was prejudiced against Rick from the court records she had read and her interviews with Marsha and the therapist during the supervised visits. The only thing keeping the couple going was their visits with the kids. The children remembered Rick, in spite of the years of separation; the father and children began getting acquainted again and their hope was that time would resolve the problem.

Eventually, the guardian and Rick began communicating; her attitude seemed less one-sided. She was bothered by some things she'd heard from his ex-wife, some things that didn't click. Over the course of several visits, Rick gained ground with the guardian. His girlfriend sent the guardian a copy of an article she had seen in an issue of the *Florida Bar-Commentary* and suddenly, the visits were extended and unsupervised. When the guardian *ad Litem* advised Rick of her approval of unsupervised visits, she cautioned him that his girlfriend should always be present. It seemed that his ex-wife would cooperate under those circumstances. Rick now got to see the kids for two hours one day a week and every other Saturday from 9:00 A.M. to 7:00 P.M.

In April 1990, Rick and Marsha were asked to draw up a visitation agreement with the guardian *ad Litem* for purposes of establishing visitation. Both Rick and Marsha were dissatisfied with the supervision and therapy of the second therapist and asked for her dismissal. Rick signed the agreement drawn up by Marsha, unaware that both agreements were to have been reviewed by the guardian *ad Litem*. As always, his major concern was avoiding delays in spending time with the children. Rick's agreement had requested unsupervised visits of eight hours in length, beginning in April, every other Saturday. He had then requested overnight visitations beginning in June and including either Friday or Saturday night stays every other weekend, increasing in July to visits every other weekend starting on Friday evening and ending on Sunday evening. Provision was made that if visits were missed because of their mother's plans, those visits would be made up.

Marsha's agreement, which he signed, provided for visits every Tuesday night for two hours and every other Saturday from nine in the morning to five in the evening, such visits to be unsupervised if the children were comfortable. Dr. T. recommended such arrangements, and the judge approved. She requested freedom to change the visits if unforeseen plans occurred.

In spring 1990, Rick again filed for joint custody of the children and liberal visitation. In May, Marsha produced two letters, one from Cecil's teacher and one from Andrew's teacher. The letter from Cecil's teacher was particularly upsetting to Rick, as she stated that his visits with Rick were having very negative effects on the child. She also said that she was familiar with children who had suffered from physical and sexual abuse, clearly indicating that she felt Cecil's problems were directly related to his being abused and forced to visit with his father. No one seemed to consider that the issue here might not be visiting with Rick, but the fact that the time with Rick was restricted. Perhaps, if they had been allowed more time with their father, these problems would have gone away.

During 1990, psychological evaluations were ordered on all three children, partially as a result of the above letters. Andrew's evaluation was done first, consisting of testing and interviewing, then interviewing both Marsha and Rick. The evaluations were done by a psychologist requested by Rick's ex-wife (not an independent Ph.D.), who appeared to accept the allegations of abuse as fact and whose findings on all three children indicated behavior "consistent with abuse."

Her summary of emotional considerations included statements that Andrew had a distorted image of an aggressive father figure that he wished a less powerful figure in that role. During the Children's Apperception Test, she stated that after producing a plot, Andrew could not resolve the hostile conflicts between parents and children unless the father figure was killed or left. The Sentence Completion Test, in conjunction with an interview, suggested to the psychologist a cry for help in improving his relationship with his stepfather and resolving his ambivalent feelings of wish/fear toward his father. In addition, she stated that he seemed to have great difficulty relating to the mother figure during the Rorschach testing and that he was angry and unfulfilled by parent figures. Scattered throughout the evaluation were comments such as, "The physical and emotional abuse has clearly had a significant deleterious effect upon him," and, "He suffers significant emotional problems consistent with a physically and sexually abused child."

Included in Andrew's evaluation were recommendations for family therapy and focus points. She felt it was important that Andrew work through his aggression and his fear of Rick in order to redevelop a more positive relationship and, at the same time, work to develop a stronger attachment with his stepfather and stronger bond between him and his mother.

The evaluation report on Sheila, now eight years old, was submitted in July. In the summary of emotional considerations, the psychologist stated that Sheila described the family environment as a hostile, dangerous place in which the father was angry at the child and physically attacked the mother. In her stories, she and her siblings routinely rescued and protected the mother from the powerful father. The psychologist then stated that Sheila believed that her natural father had sexually molested her, which resulted in Sheila's significant anxiety and ambivalent feelings toward him. The constant thread throughout the evaluation and recommendations was recognition of the fact that Sheila often felt sad, lonely, and insecure and that she needed a much closer, more trusting relationship with both parents and her stepfather, but particularly her mother.

Cecil's evaluation also was done in June 1990. He was ten. The summary of emotional considerations indicated that Cecil was seeking adult help in solving, among other things, the continued strife between his parents. The psychologist stated that Cecil seemed angry at both parents and at court officials for not hearing or understanding what he was saying. Emotionally, Cecil appeared very attached to his mother. The psychologist stated that because of his fear and unsafe feeling with his father, Cecil said he could not ask his father to stop the bitterness between the two families. She felt Cecil had a strong attachment to his stepfather, but felt confused and tense when Rick did not support Cecil's affiliation with his stepfather. One of the key issues of this evaluation was the negative impact being caused by the bitterness between Cecil's parents and his desire for everyone to be happy. It appeared that Cecil was sensitive to the anger and tensions between his mother and father and sought to solve the conflict by severing contact with Rick. During his interview, Cecil indicated that he wanted to get along with his family and that meant he didn't want to see Rick. At one point, he reported to the psychologist that when he was two or three he sat on Rick's lap, and Cecil thought Rick had touched him. This conflicted with the original report of abuse filed by DSS years earlier.

In a letter to the psychologist, Rick's attorney raised several points. Among these was the fear that some of the allegations made against him were a result of the separation and divorce and had nothing to with abuse, that the child-abuse charge to which he pleaded no contest had been an excuse for those allegations. After reviewing the psychological evaluations, the attorney sent another letter to the psychologist. In this letter, he raised a number of questions. First, the parties involved in the upcoming August hearing had agreed to the necessity of not bringing up old rumors and allegations concerning child abuse, yet the reports from the psychologist seemed to dwell on the past to a large degree. Secondly, he questioned the assumption that the aggressive father figure was Rick, not the stepfather. Andrew had referred to the aggressive and abusive figure as "dad." The attorney pointed out that the children were not allowed to call Rick "father" or "dad," but were to refer to him by his given name, while instructed to refer to their stepfather as "dad." He went on to question the fact that in Sheila's evaluation and Andrew's evaluation the exact same opening to a statement was made: "I would do anything to forget the time that I had bad bruises from Rick," and "I would do anything to forget the time that I was hurt by Rick, his bad touches." He pointed out the fact that the same wording was used is a potential indication they were told what to say.

A hearing was scheduled for July 1990, to address Rick's requests. Marsha asked for a continuance of that hearing and again requested that the court appoint a guardian *ad Litem* to represent the best interests of the children. An order was issued granting her requests.

Court hearings were canceled three times. The therapist was out of town and the guardian *ad Litem* was tied up with a different case, and Marsha's lawyer requested a continuance. Finally, a November hearing was scheduled. Rick's girlfriend called the attorney weekly, ascertaining there would be no more changes, no more delays. Waiting for the hearing was a long, difficult exercise. Always, the situation was on their minds; always they faced the possibility that Marsha would come up with new and different schemes, more attempts to alienate the children.

It was hoped that by forcing the issue of therapy/mediation between Rick and Marsha prior to the court date, some truth might be revealed which would counteract the negative effects of Marsha's manipulation. However, the guardian denied their request for Dr. S. to serve as the therapist. Rick was already behind on his debts to lawyers and therapists, as well as his support payments, and it was contended he didn't need additional debt. In addition, Marsha wouldn't agree to the therapy.

When they finally had their day in court, it all seemed very strange. The two opposing attorneys chatted amicably, and it was agreed that Rick should have the normal visitation he had requested. Effective immediately, he would see his children one day every week and every other weekend, as well as having them for a week during Christmas break and two weeks during the summer. Nothing was mentioned about the alleged abuse.

The judge stated that she remembered the case from years ago and was impressed that the parents now seemed to be cooperating on behalf of the children. A therapy session for Rick and Marsha was instated, both of them seeing Marsha's therapist, whose involvement was left to her discretion. Although nothing was resolved as far as Rick's innocence, there was satisfaction in knowing his visits with the children had been successfully negotiated and court-ordered.

Currently, Rick has what appears to be normal visitation and the ability to return to a somewhat normal life. But the fear and uncertainty are always there. Will his ex-wife continue to cooperate or will she do something to disrupt the visits yet again? Will the children, who are still in therapy, be treated for what is really wrong or will the focus of the therapy continue to be abuse that never occurred? For how long must Rick and his girlfriend walk a tight rope, before they can really relax and be natural and open around the children? And finally, will Rick's name ever be cleared? Will he be removed from the Central Abuse Registry? And what of the emotional trauma and financial ramifications resulting from the false allegations? Will life ever return to what most people perceive as normal?

4.

Texas 1986-1991

The Mark Doe case made headlines in Texas and throughout the nation. As a result of the many negative ramifications caused by false allegations of child sexual abuse filed against him, Mark filed a multimillion dollar lawsuit against his ex-wife, her attorneys, Texas Child Protection Services (DPRS), and mental health institutions and professionals who were involved in the case, alleging malicious prosecution and conspiracy, citing the violation of his constitutional rights and extortion and racketeering attempts used by his ex-wife and her attorney to gain divorce and custody settlements. Among other charges he states that the individuals involved knowingly provided false information to the county district attorney, false information that led to his indictment on child sexual abuse charges. Mr. Doe has also engaged the Racketeer Influenced and Corrupt Organizations Act (RICO Act). Although the charges against him were dismissed in August 1988, as of late fall 1990, Mr. Doe still had severely restricted visitation rights with his children, and it remains to be seen what effect or feelings of alienation may result from the events of the last four years. Currently, Mark Doe fought for a twofold purpose-to gain normal, unsupervised visitation with his children, or better yet, custody, and to set a national precedent as the hallmark case in false child sexual abuse charges.

Mark and Judy Doe were married in 1978. A year later their son, Norman, was born. In 1984, they had a second son, Bill, and in March 1986 became the proud parents of a daughter, Paula. Mark owned two successful businesses, a cafeteria and a medical equipment supply firm. Unfortunately, their marriage was not building as successfully as their family and businesses, as Judy had been seeing other men. The couple separated in September 1986; in October, Mark filed for divorce and custody of the three children, on grounds of adultery and abandonment. He had been both mother and father to the children for some time prior to the separation. The court awarded Mark temporary custody of the three children. Mark consented to joint custody, pending the arbitration property settlement proceedings, hoping that Judy would want to become a parent for the children's benefit.

In January 1987, Judy's attorney, Mr. L., filed an application for a family study to be conducted by the DPRS. This request is highly unusual as, by law, the CPS is not involved unless there is suspicion, or allegations of child abuse, as occurred in my own case. At that point, there had been no indication of abuse of any sort. Mark's counsel was not advised of the request. It was later learned that the order for the home study was never signed, nor entered by the family court. The motion, as filed, was in violation of the court's orders for noninterference by attorneys during the arbitration process. As is often the case in custody disputes, the Does were instructed to undergo psychological evaluations to determine the best interests of the children. The evaluations were done by a professional recommended by Judy's attorney.

By the time the psychologist saw Mark Doe, she had already seen Judy and Bill several times, and had concluded that Mark had sexually and physically abused his son. She stated this opinion to the authorities. With her conclusion already made, she reviewed Mark's tests as pathologically as possible, concluding he had "obsessive-compulsive tendencies, high defensiveness, and an intense need to control," that "his rigidly defensive posture does not adequately bind the underlying anxiety and trepidation of doing poorly." Later review by forensic psychological experts indicated that nowhere was this conclusion supported by empirical data, nowhere did the psychologist indicate that not all tests were performed under supervision, and nowhere did she give any allowance for the acrimonious situation in which Mark currently found himself.

The psychologist's interpretations of the Rorschach, stating she saw "an undercurrent of anxiety, unrequited love, and cloaked sexuality . . . difficulty with relating appropriately to others . . . polymorphous perverse orientation to the environment . . . fantasies (that may include) homosexual, bisexual, and exhibitionist feelings . . . hostility toward women," were termed by the forensic experts later reviewing the case to be arbitrary, personal, subjective, and idiosyncratic interpretations.

Citing serious omissions in her educational requirements, the experts reviewing the case raised questions as to the psychologist's competency and training for providing the type of services she did for the Doe family and questioned her competency in representing herself as an expert and making the far reaching recommendations regarding the entire family. Throughout the evaluation process, the psychologist had numerous contacts with Judy's attorneys, a highly irregular occurrence. As an objective arm of the family law court, her mission should have been to form an impartial evaluation of the family members, based on contacts with those family members, not on contact and information supplied by the wife's attorney. Throughout this period, there was no contact with Mark or with his attorney.

Arbitration broke down on 28 April 1987, with no agreement on property settlements or custody arrangements. On 29 April 1987, Judy began seeing a therapist and taking Bill, their 3-year-old son, with her. The therapist agreed to prepare a statement that she suspected Bill was the victim of physical or sexual abuse. Although she stated in notes, documenting her meetings with Judy and Bill, that she suspected abuse, Ms T. did not report the suspected abuse to CPS, as she is required to do, in writing, by law. As a matter of fact, although Ms T. saw both Judy and Bill numerous times and concluded there had been child abuse, there were no case notes available to be surrendered to the criminal court regarding any of these therapy sessions. However, such information was made available to the court and counsel when she was personally sued by Mark Doe. In this instance, the therapist had perjured herself in criminal court by denying the existence of notes and records.

In June 1987, CPS received a call from Bill's daycare center. The school had been requested by Mark's ex-wife to report that they suspected sexual abuse because of his behavior. The suspicion was ruled unfounded on 2 July, after CPS initiated an investigation. Bill denied having been abused by anyone when he was questioned by the CPS caseworker. In spite of these findings, Judy and her attorney persisted in making the allegation an issue in family court proceedings, attempting to force Mark to settle the divorce and custody issues on their terms.

On 9 July, less than a week before the family court hearing, Judy called CPS from the psychologist's office to report Bill's declaration that he had been abused by his father. This allegation made no sense, as Judy stated that Bill had told her about the abuse on 6 July and again on the 7 July. Yet, Judy had allowed Bill and his older brother to stay overnight with their father on 7 and 9 July, after Bill had allegedly told her about the abuse. The report to CPS wasn't made until the 9 July. That report alleged that Bill had told his mother that Mark had tied his legs with a chain and played with his penis. Based on Judy's allegation, CPS reopened the investigation into allegations of child sexual abuse involving Mark and Bill.

On 10 July, unknown to Mark or his attorney, Judy took Bill to the CPS offices, bringing with her a blue bicycle chain. Bill was interrogated by CPS and later interviewed on videotape. During the videotaped interview, Bill repeatedly denied having been touched in his private area. Finally, the caseworker led Bill to mumble, "Daddy touched me there." Terminating the interview, the caseworker asked Bill if he was telling the truth or a lie. Bill responded, "It's a lie." The same question, eliciting the same response, was repeated three times.

As too often happens, the interview was conducted using a number of repetitious and leading questions and employed the use of anatomically correct dolls, which are highly suggestive by their very design. A review of the tape clearly showed that this was not Bill's first introduction to the dolls or to the questions being asked of him. In the video, he identified the dolls as the ones he had seen at his mother's house, and it appeared that he had been coached by his mother in using the dolls and in responding to questions and comments. Nonetheless, his answers were confusing and not credible. Throughout the interview, the caseworker routinely touched or pointed to the "private parts" of the doll when asking where daddy had touched Bill. In addition, Bill was not yet toilet-trained at the age of three and, naturally, his father would have touched what the caseworker referred to as "private parts" when cleaning him after an accident or when bathing the child in preparation for bed.

However, where Judy and her attorney were concerned, the only important part of the tape was that Bill said, "Daddy touched me there." In spite of the fact that CPS knew the Does were involved in a bitter divorce and custody battle, generally the type of situation that fosters the possibility of false allegations, no further investigation was done. As too often happens, the social worker made an immediate initial decision that Bill exhibited the behaviors and attitudes of an abused child, based on the assertions of the child's mother. The therapist's subsequent opinions, conclusions, and recommendations were derived solely from information and opinions provided her by Judy Doe. Ms T. became Judy's support person and, due to her prejudice, was unable to act in the best interest of her supposed client, Mark's youngest son.

On 13 July, at five in the afternoon, Judy and her attorney filed allegations of child sexual abuse, and the next morning the psychologist submitted her report to the family court, stating she suspected Bill had been physically and sexually abused by his father. A review of the evaluations done on Norman and Bill showed that, while the psychologist recognized that the stress of the acrimonious divorce was causing problems for Judy and Norman, she concluded that Bill's problems were due to his having been physically and sexually abused, "most likely by his father."

Mark wasn't advised of the allegations against him until immediately prior to the family court hearing. Judy's attorney and the trial court judge expelled Mark Doe from the courtroom during the proceedings. Why? The psychologist and the therapist had prepared highly biased and inaccurate reports, in which they represented themselves as experts and concluded Bill was probably the victim of sexual abuse and the abuse was most likely from his father. She recommended that Judy be given sole custody of the children and that Mark be allowed only very limited and closely supervised visitation. She further recommended that Bill be hospitalized for further evaluation and psychiatric treatment, based on her statement that Bill exhibited the demeanor of an abused child.

Mark's visitation rights were immediately terminated. On 17 July, during the courtroom negotiations finalizing the divorce between Mr. L. and Mark's attorney, the psychologist issued her threat, telling Mark's attorney that unless Mark agreed to Mr. L.'s property settlement, the custody arrangements, placing Bill in a hospital for psychiatric evaluation and treatment, and submitting himself to therapy, she would use her efforts to have all three children removed to foster homes. Consumed with fear and concern for the three children, Mark, on his attorney's recommendation, agreed to the terms, having been told he had no real choice. He certainly didn't view foster care as being in the best interest of the children.

On 20 July, the divorce papers were signed by the court. Mark paid one hundred thousand dollars to Judy's attorney, as "agreed" under the terms of the settlement he had been forced into accepting. Mr. L again reminded Mark that if he didn't go along with the terms and the system, he would never see his children again. Mark took the threat very seriously.

Bill was hospitalized at Duchein Children's Center on 21 July, based on the psychologist's recommendation and with CPS approval. While the medical staff at Duchein was aware there was no evidence of abuse, they provided treatment as if such abuse had occurred. In addition, the psychologist diagnosed the 3-year-old as anuretic and encopretic when, in fact, the child was simply not yet toilet-trained, and neither diagnosis is valid at such a young age. Nevertheless, Duchein treated these conditions as well. Mark was refused permission to see his son for forty-five days. A week later, the CPS caseworker was instructed to follow up on criminal charges against Mark.

It became apparent to Mark that CPS was not going to conduct any further investigation of the alleged abuse, and it was equally clear that the staff at Duchein had decided there had been abuse and that Mark was the abuser. He contacted CPS, the psychologist, and the doctor at Duchein, informing them that he intended to find out if Bill had actually been abused and, if so, by whom. Mark took a polygraph test and submitted the results to the Duchein staff and all professionals involved. The lie detector test indicated he had not abused his son. In addition, he obtained affidavits relating to his ex-wife's live-in boyfriend and the sexual molestation of the boyfriend's three daughters. Judy subsequently married the boyfriend, a convicted child sexual abuser. The information was submitted to everyone involved: the trial court, attorneys, professionals, and hospital staff. As Mark continued his battle, he obtained evaluations by forensic psychologists. After a great deal of thought, Mark decided to go back to domestic court and attempt to regain custody of his children. He trusted that the psychologist would be reluctant to force his children into foster homes, with the evidence he had gathered showing the falsification of the allegations, and he hoped that Judy wouldn't allow such a thing to happen out of vindictiveness toward Mark.

On 4 September, Mark went to CPS to inquire about child visitation rights and rulings. He found that all records of the investigation were missing. When Mark spoke with a CPS supervisor and explained the situation, the supervisor's reaction was, "Oh, no; not again!" When Mark questioned the man's reaction, he explained that there were other cases he was aware of, in which Mr. L., Mark's ex-wife's attorney, had injected charges of child abuse or child sexual abuse in custody battles. Further investigation into Mr. L.'s records has already revealed there are at least five other parents and their children who have suffered as a result of this attorney's tactics.

Mark was becoming more and more concerned about his children, particularly since he had learned that Judy's live-in boyfriend had a documented history of being a child sexual abuser. He was equally concerned about the psychological and emotional effects that staying in Duchein might have on his youngest son, particularly given the fact that the staff continued to treat him as a victim of child sexual abuse. Bill was the youngest child there. Duchein had been designed to treat disturbed adolescent or prepubescent children, and there were no programs available for Bill, who was only three years old. The therapies used by the staff were too advanced for Bill. The staff had decided that Bill had been abused by his father. The observations, interpretations, and diagnoses were made with the goal of supporting those allegations, rather than investigating the possibility of abuse.

One incident particularly bothered Mark. It occurred the first time he was allowed to see Bill within the supervised confines of the hospital. Bill had greeted him with a hug, and they had played a variety of games. When Bill was hit on the nose with a nerf ball, he ran to Mark, who kissed it to make it better. Bill, hearing noises, appeared frightened and said someone was coming to get him, that a lady would take him back to the unit, and instead he wanted to go to his daddy's house. The observer's interpretation of this was that Bill was frightened by his father's close physical reaction. She stated she felt the physical closeness triggered a reaction in Bill.

On 27 October 1987, Mark was indicted by the county grand jury for allegedly having sexually molested his son Bill, in spite of psychological evaluations clearly stating that there was nothing in his background, nothing in the interview, and nothing in the evaluation results to suggest any reasonable concern. It was further stated that he did not exhibit the personality characteristics, behaviors, background, or attitudes typically associated with individuals who do admit to such inappropriate acts. The evaluating psychologist pointed out that the level of involvement he has with his child is unusual for the typical sex offender. Mark persisted in denying the allegations and began the long, frustrating, and expensive process of seeking to prove his innocence. Evidence introduced against him was all hearsay-the allegations of his ex-wife and statements from biased therapists who persisted in treating Bill as an abused child. On 15 July 1988, the criminal trial court judge ruled that Bill was not a competent witness and therefore could not provide credible testimony . . . once again, an incompetent witness, whose statements are only given credibility when repeated by an adult.

Throughout this period, Mark went through the emotions and turmoil typical to one who has been falsely accused. He was unable to focus attention on anything but the false accusations and their ramifications. He suffered the frustration of not being able to see his children and experienced deep concern about Bill and the potential effects of his experiences at Duchein. Mark was humiliated, frightened, and lived in self-imposed isolation. He experienced a constant state of severe depression. He still cries out in his sleep at night. In addition, investigations that included examinations by a forensic document examiner revealed that records at CPS and the mental health clinic had been altered in order to bolster the case against Mark. Ultimately, the assistant district attorney became convinced that the state wouldn't be able to prove its case, and the indictment was dismissed on 1 August 1988.

Mark Doe lost his media-riddled suit in federal court. It is unclear to this writer if Mr. Doe ever attained joint or sole managing conservatorship of his children. As a result of conditions contained in the divorce settlement, Mark religiously attended the parenting therapy required by Dr. G., seeing the director of the Fairmont College of Medicine Sex Abuse Clinic. During the first three months of therapy, the discussions related primarily to Bill. During the following four months discussions centered on the situation of false allegations. It was Mark's belief that following this action would lead to discovery of the truth and restoration of his children. In February 1988, Mark was released by his therapist when the therapist found that Mark had hired one of the foremost defense attorneys in Texas (a federal court specialist) to represent him, an attorney with a reputation for "catching liars." The state's district attorney, apparently fearful, avoided Mark's attorney, and neglected to show up in court for scheduled hearings until so ordered by the trial court judge. The institution where Bill was sent was sued by the State of Texas for Medicaid fraud and, in a plea bargain settlement, paid back the money identified as defrauded from Medicaid.

In spite of the fact of his innocence, Mark will live the remainder of his life under the dark cloud of a serious social stigma, the result of false allegations brought by a malicious attorney and his ex-wife. He will never be able to be a boy or girl scout leader, an activity he had hoped to share with his children. He will never be able to work with and teach blind children, something he had done in the past. And, to this date, there are many people who will never forget the accusation and indictment reported in the local papers for all his friends and customers to see.

5.

A Summary of the Case Studies

Unfortunately, these four cases are not isolated or unique situations. False allegations of child sexual abuse occur daily across this country and the globe against teachers, daycare providers, coaches, volunteer program directors, psychologists, etc. However, the most frequently accused perpetrator is the ex-husband or divorcing husband who is involved in a visitation dispute and/or custody battle where young children are involved. The similarities in these case studies and other cases reviewed should sound a warning to individuals, professionals, and agencies.

First, all cases studied involved divorcing parents. Second, all cases studied involved a current or potential custody suit. Third, these cases all involved an ex-wife who perceived that there might be good reason for her to be denied full, residential custody, thereby losing the benefits of child support and control of the children, as well as, social standing as the best parent. In all but one case, the fathers had moved out of the house, thereby giving the wife control of the children and an open opportunity for coaching and convincing the children. Parental alienation of the children was pervasive. In the William Smith case, the allegations surrounded an incident alleged to have occurred while he was out of the country. When he refused to be coerced into leaving his home, his wife removed herself and the children, first to a shelter, then out of the country.

In all cases, the allegation was made to some agency that dealt with social services and, by extension, child protective services.

The allegations were made by the ex-wife and assumed to be true by the social worker, who then set in motion interviews and therapies to support and substantiate the charge. Not once could I find evidence of an objective investigation to seek facts from all parties involved before therapy was begun. Not once were collateral interviews effected. In all cases, the accused, the husband, was the last to know anything was going on. When interviews, physical examinations, videotapes, doll sessions, and therapies all occurred without his knowledge, culminating in an allegation that sometimes leads to criminal charges, as well as stiff sanctioning in family court, it is no wonder that the falsely accused begins to feel he is the victim of a conspiracy.

In three of the cases studied, it is clear that the accused did not initially have the benefit of adequate or competent counsel or an attorney familiar with the ramifications of a SAID syndrome case. Even an experienced divorce attorney who has not come face to face with this issue, who has not educated himself into the machinations and ramifications of such a case, may flounder under the weight of defending false allegations of child sexual abuse. In Rick's case, on the advice of the public defender that he plead no contest to physical abuse charges in the interest of diffusing the sexual abuse charge, there were far-reaching negative ramifications for Rick and his three children. In Mark's case, the fact that his own attorney suggested he had no choice but to agree to the unreasonable demands of his wife's attorney has resulted in untold emotional damage for his middle son and a lengthy and expensive battle to regain any kind of access to and relationship with his three children.

In my own case, a reliable civil attorney simply did not have the background and expertise to deal with the criminal charges of child sexual abuse. A competent and effective criminal attorney didn't have the expertise to successfully carry the battle back through the family courts.

In all cases studied, the criminal charges of child sexual abuse were dropped or the father was acquitted. However, in all cases, the allegations stood in family court and, based on testimony of social workers and agency-selected therapists, the father was either denied access to his children, or provided extremely limited and supervised visitation. In all cases, the children were ordered by the court to continue in therapy, and the father was ordered to enter therapy as an alleged abuser, in spite of never having been found guilty in criminal court, in spite of the fact that they repeatedly and steadfastly maintained their innocence of the charges. In all cases, the evaluations of video tapes by child psychologists have routinely identified the leading and coercive questions used to gain a child's testimony. In all cases, benign psychological and psychosexual evaluations and summaries regarding the alleged perpetrator have either been summarily ignored or have led to requests for further evaluation by state-selected psychologists, who could be counted on to provide an evaluation to support the allegations of child sexual abuse. In all cases, there is serious doubt that the events of the last several years have, in fact, been in the best interest of the children.

There are a number of things to be aware of if you are to protect yourself from false allegations of child sexual abuse and a potential abuser and a number of questions you can ask that may indicate what is coming.

- Has the marriage been stormy?

- What are the benefits derived by your ex-wife if she can win sole custody?

- Is there another man in the picture?

- Does your ex-wife have any reason to believe she might have difficulty proving herself the best parent?

- If there has been a history of animosity and lack of cooperation throughout the divorce and/or custody battle, are you suddenly being treated in a more cooperative manner?

- Has she ever brought an accusation or threatened to bring an accusation against anyone else?

The following explores the many facets and complexities of the individuals, professionals, agencies, and systems involved when an allegation of child sexual abuse is leveled as well as outlining the characteristics of the SAID syndrome.

6.

The Accused

How do you describe the feeling, the reaction, of being accused of sexually abusing your own child? There are a myriad of emotions, all negative. One of the first realizations you have is that, in spite of the premise upon which our justice system is supposed to be based, when it comes to this allegation, you are presumed guilty. Immediately. Period. The abhorrence with which sexual offenses against children are viewed fills the majority of the population with righteous indignation toward the accused, even before any evidence has been presented. Logic is replaced by the ideology that children cannot be mistaken regarding disclosures of abuse and must be protected at all costs, even if those costs equate to desecration of the family.

In cases of child sexual abuse, hearsay evidence from doctors and nurses, whom you will probably never see, from social workers and the accusing parent, is commonly used to circumvent the unreliability and short memories of children. Because no one is in favor of child abuse and everyone wants to do their part for the children, there has been a steady erosion of the accuseds' rights to confront accusers and a corresponding rise in the use of hearsay evidence. Since there is rarely actual physical evidence of child sexual abuse, the accused finds himself fighting a phantom, a ghost. Given the current trend of believing that children don't lie, any allegation, even based on hearsay, is assumed to be valid.

All of these facts don't change the way you, the accused, feel. In reality, being labeled an abuser may produce many of the personality characteristics later cited as the causes of child abuse-anger, bitterness, and defensiveness.

Waiting is the worst. And the waiting breeds questions that never seem to have answers. One individual, accused of abusing his 2-year-old daughter, even began questioning himself. Could he have scratched her the last time he bathed her? Did she have an irritation he should have noticed, something that caused her to scratch herself? The emotions engendered by false accusations of child sexual abuse are endless and devastating. Sleep is forever elusive, night terror becomes commonplace, and depression is a constant companion. Rarely is there any support to be found within the community and rarely is there any sympathy for the falsely accused. The frustration and anger increase every day, affecting you and your children. The realization that winning in one court doesn't mean winning in another makes the ordeal seem to go on forever. Throughout it all, you must bear the title "abuser," until you prove otherwise, if you can. Disorientation, denial, shock, confusion, anxiety, and disbelief are constant. Lack of concentration is a chronic problem, exceeded only by the frustration of being denied the right to see your children.

During this battle, understand that numerous negative emotions are going to become a part of your everyday life. Disorientation, denial, confusion, and depression become normal day-to-day feelings. Often the shock felt by the accused makes concentration difficult, if not impossible, while they try to deal with the anxiety and disbelief. Some contemplate and even commit suicide.

The temptation to give up can be strong. You can't see your child, you can't get any information about the charges, the evidence, the test results, or current events. Your ex-wife seems to win on all fronts, using evidence that is patently untrue, evidence that has been fabricated, and cannot be disproved. Even when evidence is disproved, it doesn't seem to matter. The state is paying her legal fees, evaluation, and therapy fees, while you are footing the bills for your attorney, court costs, child support, and seemingly never-ending psychological and psychosexual tests to prove your innocence. The paranoia begins to overtake your common sense and your ability to function in your best interest and the children's. Everything seems so hopeless that, sooner or later, every victim of a false accusation asks the same question: *What have I done to deserve this?*

There is a grieving process that is an ongoing part of this fight against false allegations of child sexual abuse. Your children have been taken from you. If a child had died, there would be a period of grieving, a period that would end when the fact of death had been accepted. However, the child is still alive, and only artificial circumstances, circumstances over which you seem to have no control, are separating you from your child, resulting in a roller coaster of grief, sadness, hope, despair, anger, frustration, and bitterness. Accept that grief is an inherent part of the process, as are anger and resentment. You grieve for the time lost with your child; you grieve for the important milestones that you are missing; you grieve for yourself and your loneliness, and you grieve for your child and his or her current circumstances. Since the battle against false allegations is an on-going process with no immediate end in sight, there is no finality, no way to put closure to the grief and no way to say, "This will be over in two weeks."

When Mark was accused of molesting his son, he found he was unable to focus on anything but the false accusation and the results of the same. He was humiliated and wanted only to run away, seeking self-imposed isolation, and sinking into a deep depression. As a result of his emotions, Mark experienced severe headaches, stomach disorders, high cholesterol, and a host of other stress-related disorders. He became obsessed with concern for his children, the loss of his children, and his personal future. This obsession and the attendant physical problems led to the loss of a highly successful business he had been running for a number of years.

One individual we spoke with was fighting for custody against a wife who had a history of drinking and drug use, a promiscuous sex life, and was physically abusive of the children. He knew what she was and what her problems were. Whether he could have proved her unfit in court, whether a judge would have believed him was beside the point. She knew what she was, and she knew that no judge in his right mind would give her custody, so she resorted to desperate means. Ken Pearson, a paralegal, who works in defending against false allegations of sexual abuse, states that, in his experience, many of the women who make false allegations have something pretty terrible to hide, a knowledge that they are not, in fact, fit to have custody of their children.

Gather a support system to get you through this period. Friends, relatives, lawyers, mental health specialists, and victims' support groups. The process of working through and disproving a false allegation of child sexual abuse is a long, draining, lonely process, and you will need ongoing support for those times of frustration, depression, and weariness. You will spend most of your time feeling (and often acting) defensive, fighting the unfair social stigma that says, "If he was accused, something must have happened." You don't need someone to tell you what to do, so much as you need someone to listen, to hold your hand, to pat you on the shoulder, and encourage you to keep on pushing, keep on working toward the day when your children will be yours again.

Self-imposed isolation is a natural reaction, a method of avoiding embarrassment and hiding the shame you feel about the fact that anyone could even consider accusing you of such a heinous crime. Draw strength from your support groups, get out in the world and try to function as a part of it. In addition, isolation is hard on the mental and emotional system, and you need all the positives you can get at this point, to allow you to meet and deal with the myriad issues of the allegation in a mature, controlled, sustained manner.

In addition to your personal support group, find an organized support group such as Victims of Child Abuse Laws (VOCAL), at 1-800-745-8778. I urge you to locate a group that can give you not only moral support, but often provides resources of which you may be unaware. Most important, please believe you are not alone in this situation. Others have been there and are there today. We know the questions and doubts you have, the emotions you are encountering, and the frustrations that seem to mount on a daily basis. We are aware of the questions you are asking, questions like the following:

- How did it happen?

- How can my relationship with my child be terminated without an investigation?

- Don't my constitutional rights protect me from indiscriminate and irresponsible governmental intervention?

- How could this situation take so long to be resolved?

- Will I succumb, or will I prevail?

Be prepared to deal with a host of negative emotions, recognize that depression, grief, anger, frustration, and confusion are an inherent part of your reaction to the accusation leveled against you. The critical issue, if you are dealing with false allegations of child sexual abuse, is to maintain your innocence, locate a competent and experienced attorney, be prepared to spend a great deal of money, find a local support group, and find a consultant to assist you with your battle. This writer can help you to help yourself and your children in cases of false abuse accusations.

7.

The Accuser

There was a common thread running through the personalities and actions of the accusing ex-wife in all four case studies examined during the preparation for part of this book. This same dynamic has been identified by scientists studying the machinations of the SAID syndrome and other false abuse cases, also. In several of the cases, accusations of child sexual abuse were used by the accuser against additional individuals, or organizations other than the husband. In my own case, Carla used the threat of a child sexual abuse allegation to avoid payment of tuition fees at a daycare center Diane had been attending. The tuition was refunded, and charges were never formally brought by Carla. In another case, the ex-wife accused not only her husband, but her own stepfather and a cousin of abusing their daughter. Neither incident was ever substantiated or prosecuted. Patti, who accused her stepson of abuse, later accused William of abusing his daughter, but that allegation was never pursued.

In all cases, the allegations were made during the course of a custody dispute, brought by wives who had reason to believe they might need additional support for their claims as custodial parent. In all cases, the custody dispute was acrimonious. In all cases, the ex-wife was in some way involved with another man or other men. In all cases, the wife initially had custody of the child and was in the perfect position to manipulate the child's statements and encourage the child to make and sustain accusations against the father.

A review of the various evaluations done on the accusing parent shows many common personality traits. The evaluation of one accusing ex-wife included the following comments: ". . . is quite capable of anti-social behavior and her MMPI clearly demonstrates a propensity for fabrication. She is an angry woman . . . and very sensitized to sexual abuse."

Dr. Larry Spiegel, a psychologist, was falsely accused of child sexual abuse by his wife. In his 1986 book, *A Question of Innocence,* he points out that the actions of an accuser like his wife are not just extreme examples of revenge, but stem from severe psychological problems. Spiegel's ex-wife perceived herself to be rejected by her husband. A psychological examination indicated that she had admitted to her hatred of her husband, and further indicated that she was quite capable of projecting her own emotional turmoil, doubt, and sexual pathology onto her daughter.

In the case of William Smith in Ohio, his ex-wife had a history of mood swings and depression. Like Marsha, Judy, and Carla, Patti also had a history of relationships with other men during her marriage to William, in this instance, adding William's oldest son to her stable. One evaluation of Patti indicated she was an overly self-confident, energetic, and distinctly defensive individual who was rebellious, willful, and rather impulsive. It also revealed a passive-aggressive personality harboring considerable conflict and tension in the independent-dependent sphere. A psychological test done a year later noted the wife's feelings were similar to psychotic or severely neurotic patients. A third test, administered and scored another year later, indicated that Patti's self-confidence had plummeted; her manifest anxiety level had increased considerably, and her capacity to cope with day-to-day problems had been considerably undermined. She exhibited patanoic indicators. However, the psychologist administering the test, a state appointed doctor, qualified these findings by pointing out that she was under considerable stress as a result of the ongoing custody dispute, indicating that these findings shouldn't be considered in a negative light. That factor is rarely recognized when the accused exhibits such test findings.

In my own case, Carla's psychological evaluation indicated that she chose her answers so as to give a strongly favorable picture of herself. While the psychologist stated that this type of response bias is often seen under such circumstances, it is not necessarily present to such a degree. She denied any anger or hostility, but the results showed it much more likely that she is denying a significant amount of that hostility, not only to others, but to herself. Carla was very defensive, very afraid of exposing her real nature, and, for that reason, the psychologist felt the results of the testing had questionable validity. Although there were many positive character traits identified in the testing, there was indication that Carla would go along in a conforming sort of way while inwardly being quite rebellious. Indirect, rather than direct, anger appeared to be usually expressed, being in general overcontrolled, yet violent or aggressive outbursts may occur. The evaluating psychologist, having been made aware that her biased responses would certainly invalidate much of the data, requested that Carla retake the tests. Carla did not retake the tests, and the psychologist qualified all the test scores and responses with the statement that there was a "need to interpret the test results with the assumption that weak points, problem areas and therefore the clinical scales of the MMPI have been suppressed." Consequently, we had an evaluation that even the professional giving the test said was inaccurate. Other evaluations indicated Carla's use of projection and her elevated K and L scales on the MMPI went along with her display of manipulative and dishonest traits.

In an article by Matthew Miller, published in the *Family Law Commentator*, the writer addressed the issues of child sexual abuse allegations. "Mothers are falsely accusing fathers of sexual abuse or child abuse at an alarmingly increasing rate in order to gain leverage or advantage in custody/visitation disputes . . ." He went on to point out that these women often become obsessed with punishing the ex-husband and using the allegation to gain desired advantages, often losing sight of the effect on the child.

Can a malicious accuser manipulate the system to produce conviction for a false allegation? Unfortunately, given the way the system currently operates, it is all too easy for an individual to manipulate it to his or her benefit, particularly in cases of custody or visitation. An embittered ex-wife, if she knows the system and is capable of any degree of manipulation, will usually find support and belief within the offices of the social workers, case investigators, and therapists. Since she is working with individuals who are prone to believe anything the child says, or anything she tells them the child said about abuse, she's off to an easy start.

The accuser recognizes that deploying the sexual abuse allegation gives her an easy and almost instant win in the custody battle against her ex-husband. The family court system encourages the accusations, since the almost universal result is to deny the accused any access to his children, and assure the ex-wife the ability to further manipulate the child. In addition, she retains child support payments, a strong incentive for some parents. Finally, the accuser will always emerge as the "fit" parent, whether she truly is or not.

Feudal law in the Middle Ages recognized the economic value of the child to its parents, either for purposes of helping in the family business, earning money to be used for support of the family, or, for females, making an advantageous marriage. We consider ourselves to be an enlightened society. Yet, is there not a hint of this economic consideration when bitter custody battles revolve around the issue of child support payments and the changes in lifestyle that may result from support being increased, decreased, or lost altogether because of a change in residential custody?

There are certain characteristics that seem to be consistent throughout the actions and circumstances surrounding false allegations of child sexual abuse within the parameters of a custody dispute, as pointed out in a study done by the Joint Custody Association of Los Angeles, California. The accusing parent commonly exhibits impulse control problems, excessive self-centeredness, strong dependency needs, and poor judgment. Often the individual is overzealous, dishonest, histrionic, or combative. The mother has a need to tell the world about the incident, as opposed to the more common reaction of being secretive and embarrassed. An accusing parent often demands that decision-makers act quickly and is unwilling to consider other possible explanations for the child's statements or behavior. She will insist on being present whenever the child is interviewed and will shop for other professionals who will verify her suspicions and allegations. Regardless of the impact on the child, a mother making false accusations frequently demands the investigation continue, or be intensified. The varied accuser profiles are identified in the next chapter, and chapter sixteen referencing borderline personality disorder.

It is important to be aware of the benefits that accrue to the accusing parent in a custody dispute. The most important is being awarded custody of the child. Even in those instances where both parents have recognized problems and neither parent is clearly better than the other, when allegations of child sexual abuse are present, custody almost always goes to the accusing mother, as occurred in all case studies reviewed for this book.

In my case, the children's mother was deemed "unfit" by the court in its final order of 5 December 1988. However, rather than award custody to me, even where abuse hadn't been supported by the evidence, the court awarded the children to her and assigned Health and Rehabilitative Services (now called DCF-Department of Children and Families) to oversee the lives of the children and the actions of the mother, suggesting or requiring parenting classes for her.

8.

The SAID Syndrome

While almost anyone can be the victim of false allegations of child sexual abuse, more often than not, whenever there has been a breakdown in the family resulting in divorce or separation, the accused is the child's natural father, and the accuser is the mother. Frequently, the allegations have nothing to do with the best interest of the child, but are promulgated in an effort to either satisfy the anger, frustration, or vindictiveness of the mother, to fulfill her requirement to "win" over her husband or ex-husband, or to assure the mother the ongoing income provided by the child support payments.

In 1986, Dr. Gordon J. Blush and Karol L. Ross presented their study, prepared for fellow professionals in the field of child advocacy, dealing with the Sexual Allegations In Divorce (SAID) syndrome. In this study, Blush and Ross pointed out that sexual allegations made within the framework of a divorced or divorcing family environment need to be addressed in a different way than sexual abuse allegations made within a non-divorcing family. The study was done in a family services clinic, which served as a diagnostic agency within a circuit court. Primary in the evaluation process were cases in which custody and visitation problems existed, involving minor children. It is common, when dealing with the two parents in a divorcing family situation, to find that each parent wants to present the other parent in the least complimentary manner possible. Each parent wishes to establish that he or she is the best choice for custodial parent, and this is accomplished by placing the other parent in a negative light. Unfortunately, over recent years, allegations of sexual impropriety are being heard more frequently in custody disputes. This type of allegation results in the alleged perpetrator not only fighting a custody issue, but finding him/herself in a position where access to the minor child can be terminated without due process of any type. The individual is completely excluded from his or her children's lives and, in addition, suffers the social stigma of the allegation and often has to contend with felony charges within the criminal court system.

The sad thing about allegations of child sexual abuse is that once accused, the alleged perpetrator finds himself in the position of being guilty until proven innocent, a statement in direct conflict with the basis of our country's judicial system and beliefs. This position is strengthened by the actions and activities of the various social agencies that become involved when such an allegation occurs. In many instances, cases are systematically built on a false allegation that, through manipulation of facts and children's testimony, can create damning "evidence." Several papers presented by expert psychiatrists and psychologists over the last fifteen years have pointed to the strong potential for false allegations of child sexual abuse within the framework of a divorcing family, particularly when there is a dispute over custody and/or visitation rights.

An article in the Denver Post on 9 April 1989, referred to studies done by Dr. Richard Gardner of New Jersey in regard to the SAID syndrome, which found numerous instances in which children had been brainwashed, and conditioned by one parent in an acrimonious divorce to accuse the other parent of sexual abuse. Blush and Ross caution that child sexual abuse allegations should be viewed within the context of the entire family dynamic, to determine whether there may be more involved than concern for the child by the accusing parent. According to their study, there are six "red flags" which should form the focus of investigating the allegations. While these are not conclusive indicators of a SAID case, they are valid clues to the possibility of such a situation. The six red flags to be observed are:

- Evidence of a family on the verge of marital breakup;

- Divorce proceedings already in process;

- Divorce proceedings that have been unsuccessfully in progress for some time;

- Unresolved visitation or custody problems;

- Unresolved money issues related to the divorce in process;

- Involvement of either or both parents in ongoing relationships with others.

Any one of these circumstances may provide a clue that the allegations are a part of the SAID syndrome. In each of the cases studied for this book, as well as in my own case, three or more of these "flags" were in evidence, yet none of these considerations were addressed in the consideration of the allegations leveled against me or the other accused fathers. Too often, agencies involved in the investigation of allegations of child sexual abuse are, in fact, therapeutic in nature as opposed to investigative. Treatment of the involved child is begun before the cause of the child's action or alleged action is investigated. If more social agency employees were required to be aware of the SAID syndrome and its effects, there would be fewer lengthy and expensive court cases crowding our judicial system calendars, most of which have no basis. As a consequence, these agencies and courts would be better able to pursue true child-abuse cases involving legitimate allegations. In the interest of avoiding false allegations, as well as anticipating such, it is important to note that Blush and Ross identified personality types that may well bring such allegations against an ex-husband or soon-to-be ex-husband. In the first profile, the individual may present herself as a fearful person, believing she is the victim of manipulation, coercion, physical, social, or sexual abuse in the marriage. She tends to see men as a physical threat, a means of economic retribution, or people who do not understand the physical safety and psychological needs of children. In the second profile, the ex-wife manifests the characteristics of the "justified vindicator." This individual is a hostile, vindictive, and dominant female, who often becomes insistent that formal legal measures be taken immediately-not waiting for reasonable proof of the allegation. This personality often appeals to experts in both the mental health and legal communities and often has concurrent criminal action pending alongside her domestic legal action. The third pattern is that of an accuser who is potentially psychotic. Although rare, these individuals are functioning in a borderline reality in which what they want to believe, in order to protect their current status, is clearer to them than what is actually occurring.

Regardless of the profile exhibited by the accusing female, in all cases her emotional basis of appeal can be very convincing and misleading to the inexperienced or well-intentioned professional. For those reasons, the "red flag" considerations need to be incorporated in any investigation of child sexual abuse occurring during the course of divorce/custody hearings.

In those infrequent cases where the accusing parent is the male, the personality is usually found to be intellectually rigid, with a significant need to be "right;" often, he has been hypercritical of his wife throughout the marriage and exhibits a number of "nitpicking" examples of her unfitness as a mother. In the instance of such a male accuser, the allegations are generally against the male(s) with whom the mother has become involved, rather than directly against the mother. The accusations against the mother generally involve her leaving the children in inappropriate or incompetent care or generally placing them in an "at risk" situation at home. Children involved in these situations typically occupy the key position in the adversarial struggle. Parents, who cannot, or will not communicate directly with each other, communicate through the child, thereby providing the child with a part of their adult insight, feelings, and information. Children in this position often evolve into miniature dictators at a very early age, given the ability to manipulate and control both parents because of their knowledge and insight. Younger children tend to align their requirements and their emotional allegiance with the dominant or custodial parent and frequently mirror that parent's descriptions or feelings concerning a situation. Children in these situations often reflect one or more of the following behaviors:

- Giving responses that appear to be rehearsed, coached, or conditioned.

- During interviews, initiating conversation by quoting the same phrases as those used by the controlling parent who presented the complaint.

- Using verbal descriptions inappropriate to their age, with no demonstrated practical comprehension of the meaning.

- Offering spontaneous and automatic reports of the act(s) perpetrated upon them, without any direct questions being asked to solicit this information.

- Offering inconsistencies in various aspects of the reported incident(s), such as the specifics (who, what, where, when), frequency (once or twice, exaggerated to numerous times) and subjective perceptions of the experience (very frightened, not scared, hurt, not hurt).

- Lacking the appearance of a traumatized individual, from an emotional and behavioral standpoint.

It is important to note that Blush and Ross found that as children approached adolescence and developed into their teenage years, they developed a more vindictive agenda. Whereas young children tend to mimic the dominant parent, adolescents develop their own requirements and desires, often built around getting or not getting their own way. In cases of allegations of child sexual abuse where the red flags of a potential SAID syndrome situation are present, it is also important to consider the general personality profile of the alleged male perpetrator, as the characteristics exhibited by a victim of the SAID syndrome are similar to those of individuals who actually do engage in sexual abuse of children.

Typically, the following characteristics may be demonstrated by the alleged perpetrator:

- An inadequate personality, with marked passive and dependent features;

- A socially naive perception of the adult world;

- Evidence of a caretaker role taken toward the female during courtship and early marriage;

- A need to "earn" love by yielding to the wants and demands of the spouse.

Because of these characteristics, this type of male typically finds himself in a relationship with a more dominant female. Further, the male victim is puzzled and at a loss to explain what has happened to him. He may be unable to effectively or appropriately respond to the allegations of the spouse, the children or other adults drawn into this situation. The allegations, in effect, create a relatively helpless and ineffective individual, whose lack of direct or assertive response may give the appearances of guilt. Because of this-the similarities between the typical male victim of false allegations and the individual actually guilty of inappropriate sexual behavior-it is critical that the overall home and family situation be closely reviewed for indications of the red flags of the SAID syndrome.

In the early 1980s, when Dr. Mel Guyer started the Family and Law Program at the Child and Adolescent Psychiatric Hospital in Ann Arbor, about 7 percent of the two hundred-plus divorce custody cases studied each year included allegations of sexual abuse. He says that now 30 percent of the custody cases include such allegations, and he believes that 70 percent of those alleged abuses never occurred.

In divorce-custody disputes, child sexual abuse has become the accusation of choice. Many psychologists who evaluate such cases for the courts estimate that from a third to half of the cases they deal with include this allegation, and they believe most of these claims are unfounded. An allegation of child sexual abuse is so powerful and so effective, others may encourage the wife to consider it as a valid and conclusive weapon. Dr. Guyer, who is an attorney as well as a psychologist, suggests a possible scenario:

> Suppose you have an attorney who knows his reputation and income depends on winning cases. He's not hired to do what's best for kids. He knows that success, for him, is getting custody for the woman. So, he sits down and takes a very careful history of the marriage, asking some very pointed questions. Does their father ever bathe the child? Have you ever noticed anything inappropriate? Does he put the child to bed and linger in the child's room?

By asking those types of questions, he can lead the client to think in a certain way. Actions that once seemed tender in a happy home seem suspect, once a couple is separated or divorced. The parent, in the privacy of her own home, actually does the first interview. While I don't know what occurs when the parent arrives home, I can imagine her questioning the child about what he or she does while they're at daddy's house. Normal child care activities suddenly become distorted to possible acts of sexual inappropriateness, when placed in improper perspective by a spouse who is not objective or impartial, but who most likely is under stress and possibly bitter.

It is important to note that the professionals within the social agencies can also be victims of the SAID syndrome, if the red flags are not considered. Many times, the accusing parent immediately takes the child to a therapist or some other intervention specialist and reports the child has been sexually abused. The professional receives information that, because of legal and social implications, takes on great importance. The original introduction to the case is within a limited and biased environment, and too often the professional responds immediately to the presenting parent's report. Since most intervention professionals are trained to believe children and accept what they have to say regarding sexual abuse, these professionals become potential victims by accepting what the child or accusing parent has to say at face value. There is the additional fact that professionals, who do not call in suspected child abuse, face serious trouble for failure to report. According to the Federal Child Abuse Prevention and Treatment Act, and state laws, nationally, mandated reporters, such as doctors, nurses, police officers, teachers, and youth care workers, who fail to report any reasonable suspicion of alleged child abuse or neglect can be criminally and professionally sanctioned.

As pointed out by attorney Robert Pope, most children are natural mimics. Therefore, the question of whether or not innocent children are capable of lying is somewhat rhetorical. We teach children to speak by repeating to them, over and over, a word or a phrase, until they can mimic that word. Why then, is it so difficult to accept the possibility that a vindictive accuser may coach the very small child by repeating to them an accusing phrase? The child is certainly not lying intentionally, only repeating words which have earned him or her positive rewards. Once the accusation is made, social workers further this cycle by asking questions that will lead to accusing answers because of what the child has been told. When the child provides the expected response, they are told that is "very good." When the child does not provide the expected response, it is assumed that he/she isn't paying attention, and the question is repeated until the expected response is forthcoming, at which time the child is again praised. It is often upon this defective manner of reporting and investigating that the guilt or innocence of an individual is determined.

Based on the child's report and the standard methods of intervention, therapy, and investigation, "facts" are created which shape the entire situation. This results in social and legal agencies accepting a created reality as truth. Once a professional opinion has been formed by a therapist, that individual is generally reluctant to change his or her perception. Because of the effect of professional opinions and the credence attached to them, it is critical that every effort be made to accurately assess the overall situation in the initial stages. Because of the legal and social ramifications, as well as the long-term effect on the entire family, it is important to investigate the possibility of divorce and family dysfunction leading to false allegations of child sexual abuse before assuming actual abuse occurred. Blush and Ross point out that one or more the following situations indicates a need to investigate the possibility of the SAID syndrome:

- The allegation surfaces after separation, and legal action for divorce has begun;

- The family has a history of dysfunction, with unresolved divorce conflict;

- The personality pattern of the female parent tends to be that of the hysterical personality;

- The personality pattern of the male parent tends to be passive-dependent;

- The child is a female, under the age of eight, who shows behavioral patterns of verbal exaggeration, excessive willingness to indict, inappropriate affective responses and inconsistencies;

- The allegation is communicated by the custodial parent, usually the mother;

- The mother takes the child to an *"expert"* for further examination, assessment, or treatment.

At this point, the expert often communicates to a court or other authority a concern and/or confirmation of apparent sexual abuse, usually identifying the father as perpetrator. The court typically reacts in what it considers a responsible manner, suspending or terminating visitation, foreclosing custodial arguments or, in some way, limiting the child-parent interaction after allegations are recorded, or criminal charges are filed. More and more, the courts are relying on the behavioral and social science community for recommendations in protecting the best interest of the child. If the professionals providing these recommendations are not familiar with the SAID syndrome, and are more interested in therapy than in investigation, rarely will the accused perpetrator receive just and equitable treatment, and rarely will the courts find in favor of that individual.

Too often, social workers have not familiarized themselves with the indications and ramifications of the SAID syndrome and are using information, methodologies, and approaches that were valid when the bulk of child sexual abuse cases were of an incestuous nature, where the major concern was that the child might not admit to the abuse, that the mother wouldn't believe her husband was capable of such an act, and everyone wanted to hold the family together. Today, the majority of false allegations are occurring in divorce situations where a bitter custody battle is being waged and child support and social status are important issues. The theory that a child would deny the abuse in the interest of holding the family together is no longer necessarily valid. The child may be denying the abuse because, quite simply, it never occurred.

Many agencies continue to use the methodology and percepts of the *Child Sexual Abuse Accommodation Syndrome,* published by Dr. Roland Summit in the early eighties. A review of the five components of this theory indicates that this methodology is based on cases where the issue is incest, far different from the SAID syndrome cases currently reaching epidemic proportions. Moreover, states like Florida—see *Hadden v. Florida,* 690 So. 2d 573, 574, 575 (1997), are not accepting Summit's Accommodation Syndrome as meeting the Frye test as general acceptable science in a forensic setting (see Appendix F).

9.

The Victim

An alleged victim of child sexual abuse, whose father successfully fought the allegations and was awarded sole custody of his children, made several telling statements in an interview she granted me for this book.

> They need to be aware that it hurts the kids the most. The mothers think they're hurting the other parent, but they're really not, they're hurting the kids. It hurts the parents a little bit, but that's not going to stop them from living. They're already grown-up, they know the facts of life and stuff. The kids don't really have a way to know what's going on and that basically destroys a part of their life and I think that's wrong.

Matilda was five years old when her mother used false allegations of child sexual abuse, citing instances of oral sex involving Matilda and her sisters, to block her father's motion for a change of custody. Now an adult, Matilda lived with her father until she reached the age of majority and, in the interest of other children who are or may be potential victims of false allegations brought during a custody battle, she agreed to speak out about her feelings. We asked Matilda, more or less as an expert witness speaking in the true best interest of the children, for her feelings, her opinions, her thoughts on the issue of false allegations of child sexual abuse, and its effects on the children involved. Matilda's messages to mothers, fathers, social workers, and mental health care professionals are probably more valid and more valuable than the most learned dissertation on this subject from a degree-bearing specialist. "Basically, the mothers or fathers-whoever thinks about making false allegations-tell them to think twice. It's a stupid thing to do, and it hurts. It hurts more and different people than they know."

In Matilda's case, not only did the allegations cause questions and, in fact, fear of her father, but Matilda truly dislikes her mother because of the lies that involved her entire family. There is a rift between Matilda and her sisters, and Matilda doesn't know if it will ever be healed. She doesn't trust women in general although, fortunately, she is close to her step-mom who has, over the past eight years, proven herself to be a person deserving of trust and respect. Matilda's trust in authority figures has been seriously undermined, partly by the fact that the counselors and therapists-people with authority-worked with her mother to perpetuate the lies.

As a result of the lengthy, consistent, and intense attempts to substantiate her mother's accusations, Matilda knows a permanent seed of doubt has been planted. Although she sincerely loves and trusts her father, Matilda admits that a doubt will always be there. She doesn't think the question of whether it happened or didn't happen will ever go away and is learning to accept that this is something she may always have to deal with in her life.

> Tell the fathers to talk to their kids. Not directly about that, but about things that are related, like how not to lie and how to tell a truth from a lie. Try to have fun with the kids so they can tell the truth from a lie, don't let them be able to have ideas planted in their heads by other people . . . Fight for your kids, but don't say bad things to them about their mom. My dad didn't say bad stuff about Mom. I think; if he had, it would have made me mad and I would have hated him as much as I hate my mom now . . . Tell the mothers it's wrong. They're teaching the kids bad values, bad thoughts . . . destroying their trust.

Today, Matilda says she's very careful with whom she is friendly. Lying is totally abhorrent to Matilda, and what a person is like "inside" is critical to her. Because of her mother's allegations and the actions of primarily female social and mental health care workers, Matilda readily admits that she doesn't hold women in very high regard and frequently wishes she were a man. She feels most women need to make themselves worth something and would like to have more respect for herself than most women seem to have. "Tell the caseworkers, counselors, and therapists not to take sides. They do take sides, all the time—the mother's side. Don't tell the kids what happened or what to do. Don't dwell on the accusations. Listen to the kids and help them deal with it, and work with them. Don't act like another parent. You're supposed to be a friend, someone to help us . . ."

In Matilda's case, she says she felt like it was her against the world-against her mother who was, in fact, physically and emotionally abusive to the girls; against her father, whom she hadn't seen for four and a half years and couldn't remember; against the social workers and therapists, who kept asking the same questions, repeating the same accusations, raising the same issues, and questioning her dad's actions. "Why, she asks, would people keep asking these questions? They kept repeating over and over and finally, I thought, My God, maybe he did do that, and I don't remember. What's a kid supposed to think? Even though you don't remember, and you don't know that it happened, it gets planted. The doubt, the question is there. It makes me sick . . ."

We asked Matilda what it felt like to be in the middle, to know her parents were fighting over her.

> We see in our minds that our parents are in a fight, they're trying to get back at each other and you think they're fighting to get custody of you just to try to get back at one another more than they're fighting because they want you in their home. We really didn't know if they were fighting because they really wanted us with them, or fighting just to fight each other. It's stupid . . . When Dad won, we thought he'd won against our mother, not a fight for us. . . .

In Matilda's case, even though life was abusive with her mother, the children were truly scared of their father. They hadn't seen him for over four years, as a result of his ex-wife's efforts to discourage and later prevent his custody attempts. Matilda had been a year old when he left home, and the girls had heard nothing good about him. They were the spoils of war, going to a victor about whom they knew nothing except what their mother had told them.

Matilda's mother fought to regain custody of the children after they moved in with their dad. Matilda's recollection of that period is that she and her sisters felt their parents were still fighting each other, and which they, the kids, were simply the rope in an ongoing tug of war. Unfortunately, Matilda's situation is no more unique or unusual than the four case studies presented at the beginning of this book.

Because of their age and vulnerability, the children find themselves being manipulated by a number of different, and often unfamiliar, adults. The accuser often brings in a host of supporting witnesses from agencies, hospitals, and schools and uses various means to substantiate the claim. Children can be trained to say various things, which may or may not be true, as a result of either direct teaching or subtle teaching through reinforcement such as verbal responses and encouragement, body movement, and facial expressions. Discussions of the incident between the child and mother, the child and friends, or other family members can serve as an effective learning process, reinforcing the child's knowledge and recital of a contrived event.

As a general rule, children seek to give the answers they think are desired, rather than deal with facts that may get negative reactions. Through the use of facial expression, body movement, or verbal responses, an interviewer can make it plain what type of answer gains approval and what gains disapproval. A strongly biased interviewer can shape a child's response by reinforcing the child with smiles, hugs, and "good girl" statements when the answers are what the interviewer wants to hear. Children placed in this situation become pawns in a game that they don't understand; a game they shouldn't be expected to understand, let alone be forced to play. It is not unusual, in divorce situations, to find one parent pitted against the other, often making negative remarks and accusations in front of the children. In these instances, children are torn between loving both parents, wanting to be loyal to both parents, and wanting to please both parents. In the case of child sexual abuse, the accusing parent has made it clear that the other parent is bad and is to be blamed. Today, most courts include standard admonishments in their final divorce judgments that neither parent denigrate the other in front of the children.

A false allegation of child sexual abuse places a child in an intolerable situation: They don't want to hurt daddy; they don't want to lie; they don't want to disappoint mommy or make her angry. Placing a child in this position is itself child abuse at its worst.

Children are easily coached and easily manipulated, especially when they are emotionally and physically dependent upon the accusing parent for all their needs. During the course of an investigation of child sexual abuse, the child is expected to go through the same questions and exercises, time after time to satisfy everyone's requirements for testimony. By the time the child has been exposed to the same round of questions and the same round of coaching over a period of weeks, it is not difficult to convince the child that the incident actually occurred. He or she has a tape recorder going in his or her mind, giving the responses that people want to hear and receiving the praise they've come to expect for being "a good girl and helping us so much." Even though he or she may not be convinced, the question, the doubt is planted and will remain throughout his or her life, as Matilda has pointed out.

In the Colorado case, all three of Rick's children were placed in therapy and "treated" for sexual and physical abuse, starting as soon as Marsha made the allegation. These children became victims of the system and victims of their mother's vengeance, not victims of child sexual abuse. They were and still are thoroughly confused. They were separated from their father, denied any contact at all, and are now having to learn to know him again. They have a stepfather whom they are required to call "dad," while instructed to refer to Rick by his first name. They don't understand their mother's attitude and are trying to cope with what she did. Meantime, they have been treated like victims and made to feel like victims, losing much of their childhood trust, dreams, and pleasures in the process.

Forcing a child to lie, or to accuse a parent whom they love, may well cause permanent and irreparable harm to the child who is, in all probability, unable to cope with the situation. We recognize that the adult who has been accused has tremendous difficulty accepting and adjusting to the accusation. Why can't we recognize what the situation is doing to the young child?

The Connecticut Bar Association's Guidelines for Courts and Counsel states, in connection with custody cases, "counsel should act to move the proceedings toward conclusion as speedily as possible, since undue delay in the resolution of the custody or visitation dispute is rarely in the best interest of the child. The minor will suffer more than any of the adults as a consequence of the anxiety of uncertainty." Unfortunately, it seems that few social service workers, prosecutors, or family court judges, in Connecticut or anywhere else, appreciate the validity and importance of this directive.

In cases involving allegations of child sexual abuse, where the allegations are made by one parent against the other, the case customarily deteriorates into a series of interviews of the minor child and attempts by the accuser to introduce hearsay statements into evidence.

We are routinely asked to believe that children do not lie, or cannot be mistaken. Research has indicated that, in cases of divorce and custody disputes, the child is often affected by the psychological functioning of the accusing adult and adult agendas, which impose their ideas upon the children, making the children pawns and victims of the directive adult, who is using the allegations and the child as a weapon. And, because the accusing adult is oft the temporary custodial parent, too, Bowlby's Attachment (mother-love) Theory is relevant, too. It wasn't until the 1970s that psychologist's Rutter and Lamb proved that child-paternal attachments were as pertinent as child-maternal attachments. A. Matthew Miller, in an article in the *Family Law Commentator*, made the following comments: "Too often the child is the innocent victim of the failure of the marriage and becomes a mere pawn between parents competing for the love and loyalty of the child. . . . Unfortunately, a custodial/residential mother with vengeful attitudes may perceive the child's relationship with the father as the only means of getting even."

A child usually reflects the emotional responses of the adult with whom the child resides. Children encode and retrieve information messaged to them firsthand. A child's ambivalent feelings for the noncustodial parent may well be the result of the influence of the custodial parent, or the child's emotional perception of that parent's feeling for the noncustodial parent. The child's need to please and be loved by and accepted by the custodial parent creates a dependency or identification with that parent. Rarely is testimony of the mother, child, or social services people carefully reviewed to determine the extent, if any, of the mother's bias, interests, or anger. As it currently operates, the system encourages manipulation of the child by the custodial parent, provides support for the accuser, and is an effective aid in assuring maternal custody. Recent 1998 figures point to mother winning custody 85.1 percent of the time.

What happens when the allegation is proven false? The child has probably still been subjected to endless interrogation and often sexual abuse therapy that is confusing and probably emotionally damaging. He or she may have been taught the role of victim. A young child has probably learned a great deal about explicit and deviant sexual behavior long before he or she would normally have had that type of exposure.

Too many social workers and mental health care workers approach an interview with the belief that if the child said it or the mother said the child said it, then it must be true-the child has been molested. The child is given positive feedback when he or she provides the sought-for an-swers, i.e., say "yes" and mommy is proud of you. Negative feedback and contradictions result from his/her denial of any abuse. Say "no" and the child is asked, "Is this one of the yucky secrets? Is this a scary secret? Were you told not to talk about this?"

If a child says he was abused, he's telling the truth. If he says he wasn't, he's lying; he's in denial. This seems to be the theory practiced by many social workers. This belief is clearly documented in *The Real World of Child Interrogations*, Underwager and Wakefield, 1990.

Social workers and mental health workers can "train" a child to believe he or she was molested. If the child continues to maintain that nothing happened, they may say that other children say it did. They may attempt conjecture: "Do you think it might have happened?" They may use anatomically correct dolls, or other props and ask the child to pretend something happened and to show them how it happened. They have now given the child an opportunity to play or fantasize. If that child is at all interested in the enlarged genital areas of the anatomically correct dolls, they have proof of molestation.

The potential of harm for the children involved in these cases was recognized over fifteen years ago. In January 1978, the National Center on Child Abuse and Neglect published the following statements in the federal register: "Sexual abuse of children, especially in cases of incest, is perhaps one of the least understood and, consequently most mishandled forms of child mistreatment . . . There is often as much harm done to the child by the system's handling of the case as the trauma associated with the abuse . . . care must be exercised, lest the very social intervention employed produce the very outcomes that are feared."

The theory that children don't lie about sexual abuse, because they haven't the knowledge or experience to create such claims, totally ignores the fact that children can be taught to parrot almost anything and coached to relate stories both true and false. This is, unfortunately, why they are such valuable tools when guided by a manipulative parent and assisted by overzealous and untrained social workers. The child is the victim of the system. The prosecutor in Larry Spiegel's case made the following statement regarding the validity of his daughter's statement: "If you ask a child the right questions, you get the truth." More accurately, in cases of false allegations involving young children, if you ask the "right" questions, leading questions, closed-ended questions, you can get the answers you want.

A child who is being used by a parent as a pawn in the game of custody and child support is daily and hourly subjected to the obsessions and attitudes of that parent as well as to the questions and attitudes of the therapist, who will generally operate from the assumption that the child has been abused. Over a period of time, this type of exposure results in the child either becoming convinced that he or she was, in fact, abused, that something bad happened when they were with daddy, or the child carrying forever the question, the doubt, about what really did or didn't happen, as we have seen with Matilda.

In the case of Mark Doe in Texas, not only was his son subjected to therapy for nonexistent abuse, but one of the conditions of his divorce settlement was that his son be placed in a state-approved institution, totally removed from his family, for intensive evaluation and therapy. Mark had a choice: he could agree to the hospitalization of his son, or the psychologist for the state would recommend that all three of his children be placed in foster homes. Although the charges of sexual abuse had been dismissed, he was placed in a situation of forcing all of his children into a completely foreign environment or going along with the requirement of therapy for himself and hospitalization for his son. The child, being placed in an institution designed to treat disturbed adolescent or prepubescent children at the age of three, became an extreme victim of the manipulations of his wife's attorney and the state social services system.

In reviewing Mark Doe's case and the actions and activities of the therapists and hospital involved, Dr. Underwager and Hollida Wakefield, M.A., made the following comment: "When a non-abused child is treated by adults as if the child had been abused and adult pressure and influence is used to produce statements from a child about events that did not happen, this is an assault upon the child's ability to distinguish reality from unreality."

In instances where the child becomes caught up in the agency system, his or her denial may well lead to some well-intentioned but misguided social worker interpreting his play, his dreams, or his behavior on his behalf, depicting that he is, indeed, an abused child. If he continues to deny the abuse, the child will be given more "counseling." One father, charged with child sexual abuse when he attempted to gain custody of his 3-year-old daughter now has supervised visitation, eight hours, every other week. The judge, in ruling on the case, concluded there was insufficient evidence of abuse, but suggested that the girl had been conditioned to fear her father by months of therapy. He ordered the therapy ended. At a recent visitation, the little girl leaned over from her coloring book and whispered, "You put your penis in my bottom."

"No, I didn't, darling," he responded.

"Mama says. We talk about it at home a lot." With that statement, his daughter turned back to her coloring book and nothing more was said.

During a psychological evaluation of another 3-year-old, following several months of therapy for alleged child abuse that had elicited more and more sophisticated and wide-ranging admissions from the child, the psychologist at the University of Michigan Family and Law Program made the following observation. "This 'therapy,' although meant to be helpful, has been continually sexually stimulating to her. Each of these charges is the product of continuing interviews and therapy and who knows what." In referring to use of the dolls to determine what had happened, he pointed out that children are curious as well as suggestible and compliant, especially with an adult whom they seek to please.

In the William Smith case, the victimization of the children was ongoing. These two children were old enough to realize what was happening and, as they have grown older, have steadfastly denied any wrongdoing on the part of either their stepbrother or their father. In spite of psychological examinations and recommendations to the contrary, the children remain in their mother's custody. Both children are totally baffled by the fact that they must live with their mother and are not allowed to see their father. They are confused by the fact that their mother is lying; they have told everyone that their mother is lying and how she told them to lie, yet no one listens to these two small voices.

In this instance, while there was no physical abuse, Dr. Hill of Ross Associates pointed out that the emotional abuse of having to tell lies, to select one parent over the other, and to experience an ongoing uncertainty about their future home and lifestyle may have serious effects on their future mental health. She expressed concern about the lengthy court process to which they were being subjected and the conflicting messages they were receiving from their mother and numerous "helping" professionals who were attempting to manipulate the court system for their own vested interests.

In a review of the children's psychological well being, done two years after the allegations were made by their mother against their stepbrother and, subsequently, their father, Dr. Janice Hill of Ross Associates included the following statements:

> Beginning with the Women Together Shelter experience, Janice and Johnny have been subjected to numerous inter-

views, physical and mental status examinations with police, physicians, psychiatrists, clinical social workers, psychologists, attorneys and victim advocates. While such investigations may have originated in the best interest of these children, and should have addressed the original complaint of sexual abuse and custody, unfortunately the legal complexity of this case, the numerous vested interests of the parents and the "helping" professionals have resulted in doing further damage to the emotional well-being of these two children. In fact, the Guardian indicated on 8 August 1985 that this therapist's report was essential to the Court's Award of Custody. To date, however, the therapeutic findings of this therapist have not been requested, in spite of well over one and one-half years of consistent and intensive therapeutic involvement with these children.

To summarize, Johnny and Janice Smith have been subjected to a series of traumatic events:

1. Disruption of their intact family

2. Changes in temporary custody, living environments, academic opportunities

3. Intensive and intrusive investigations of alleged sexual abuse by multiple social service, law enforcement, and civil justice systems personnel

4. Parental indoctrination to falsely accuse family members of these serious charges

5. Parental pressure to establish family loyalty and, most importantly

6. Child protection service providers, both social services and legal services, exacerbated their emotional well-being rather than protect it.

"It is imperative, then, that a speedy resolution to the custody issue be enacted to truly and finally serve in the best interest of these children. Continued prolongation of this matter on the part of the court would represent a travesty of justice and simply, but tragically, demonstrate to these minor children that our system to protect and assist children is woefully inept ... Finally, the best interests of these children could indeed best be served when they are given the opportunity to speak for themselves to the greater authority of the court."

A psychological evaluation was done at the University of Michigan Family and Law Program, involving Bernie, his ex-wife, and their 3-year-old daughter. Because of an innocent question asked by the ex-wife during a medical examination, the doctor reported to social services that she suspected possible sexual abuse, and charges had been filed by the agency. His daughter had been put in sexual abuse therapy for several months to allow her to "deal with" and "provide information about" the alleged abuse. Over a period of months, the child had reportedly alleged a variety of instances of sexual abuse. At the end of over five hours of evaluation, the psychologist made the following observation: "This 'therapy,' although meant to be helpful, has been continually sexually stimulating to her." He noted the escalating allegations. "Each of these charges is the product of continuing interviews and therapy and who knows what. This evaluator sincerely doubts any of the . . . acts took place, let alone all of them." He also criticized the continued use of anatomically correct dolls in her therapy. "It is important to remember that children are curious. Children are suggestible and compliant, especially with a parent and those adults whom they seek to please and protect."

The preceding evaluations indicate that there may be long term ramifications to the children as a result of being involved in the allegations, the investigation and the almost automatic therapy process. Matilda can tell us clearly that these fears are well founded:

> I'd had more sex education by the time I was six than you can imagine. With the help of the dolls, I could name every part of the body. They spent all that time talking about it and they'd bring out the little dolls and point to the parts of the body and stuff . . . And now it's several years later and Matilda should be dating boys and giggling with other girls and exploring the natural curiosity we all experience during our teenage years regarding sex and its fascinating mysteries. Instead, Matilda could probably teach her peers almost anything they want to know.

> . . . I don't like anything that has to do with sex. I mean, people talk and they say how great it is and I'm, like . . . Yuck!

The physical and emotional effects upon a true victim of sexual abuse are enormous. We have yet to fully comprehend the emotional, mental, and sociological effects upon a child who is coerced into playing the victim of a false allegation of child sexual abuse. Can we, as parents, social workers, mental health care professionals, attorneys, judges, legislators, and caring adults in the general population justify continuing experimentation with our children to find the answers? Matilda's comments clearly illustrate that it is the children who are the true victims of false allegations of child sexual abuse. The agencies and mental health workers win; the attorney's win; one of the parent's wins. The children always lose.

10.

The Dolls

As Matilda pointed out in the preceding interview, children who are alleged victims of sexual abuse receive an extensive sex education, most frequently with the aid of what social workers refer to as "anatomically correct" dolls. Too frequently, the responses and behaviors elicited in interviews using these dolls are presented to the courts by social workers and child protection team workers as "evidence" of child sexual abuse. There are a number of problems inherent in the use of these dolls as a diagnostic tool.

The Dolls

The dolls are generally twenty to twenty-five inches in length. Pubic hair is simulated with dark embroidery or synthetic fur. The breasts of the mature female doll protrude and both the boy and man dolls have penises, often disproportionately large in the dolls provided by some manufacturers. All of the dolls have representations of oral and anal openings and the female dolls include a representation of the pubic area and vaginal openings. The dolls are designed so the penis fits into any of these openings. The doll family used in most investigation and therapy generally includes a mature male and female doll and a boy and girl doll, the latter having no pubic hair nor protruding breasts. All are dressed in clothing that is easy to remove. There is no standardization of the dolls' design, some are purchased from various toy manufacturers and some are handmade, nor is there any established standard procedure for using the dolls in investigation or for conducting interviews or play sessions with the dolls.

A serious problem with the standard doll family provided in the interrogations is that it appears to represent a typical nuclear family: mother, father, one boy, and one girl. However, particularly in SAID Syndrome cases, the child is frequently dealing with a nontypical family. There may well be mommy, daddy, mommy's boyfriend(s) or second husband, daddy's girlfriend(s) or wife. There are usually no dolls to represent these additional figures. In one of the case studies we examined, the mother had remarried, and the children were instructed to call their stepfather "Daddy," while referring to their natural father by his given name, Rick. In the doll session, there were a number of negative references from the youngest boy referring to "Daddy." The social worker attributed all these negative responses as being directed toward Rick. Rick's attorney asked how the social worker could be sure which man the child was really referring to, given the child had only one male doll to select from and play with.

Scientific Validity of Anatomically Complete Dolls

In the October 1986 issue of *Trial Talk,* M.J. Phillippus, a psychologist, and Glen V. Koch, a psychiatrist, addressed the use of anatomically exaggerated dolls and their validity in determining sexual abuse. They point out that anatomical dolls, complete but not correct, are manufactured by a variety of companies with no standards applicable. One manufacturer claims, "They may be used diagnostically to help determine whether incest or molestation has occurred." Without the application of standards, both Drs. Phillippus and Koch contend this is a completely false statement.

The dolls are sold by toy manufacturers, not by standard psychological test distributors. They have been developed excluding the standards set forth in test development by the American Psychological Association (APA). The APA requires that psychological tests are carefully restricted, a licensed psychologist must be a member of APA, and he or she must file a request form before purchasing a standardized test. The doll manufacturers sell their dolls to anyone requesting them and then provide expensive seminars to explain their use. The dolls are then used by social workers and child protection team personnel, who may have no professional expertise in the areas of child play, child development, or diagnostic techniques and standards. Unqualified personnel using nonstandard tests are in violation of the tenets of APA. Many judges and trial lawyers seem to be unaware of this. In addition, the dolls do not meet the Frye test or Daubert factors (see Appendix F) for forensic admissibility as set forth by the APA.

Anatomically complete and exaggerated dolls were originally used as educational toys in child psychology classes and schools and as therapeutic aids in helping sexually abused children learn to deal with their experiences. Today, instead of being used for their intended purpose, as therapeutic tools, they are being used as diagnostic tools by individuals who are often lacking in education and expertise in the area of child interrogation and have little, if any, knowledge of the projection-provoking properties of toys. Anatomical dolls are gross disfigurements of the human condition. And, there is no data suggesting that same dolls represent actual persons in a child's life. Yet, in alleged child sex cases involving young children, the world of guided imagery, make-believe, and real life drama in the courtroom is not too far apart.

Children and Toys

A doll is a toy. Giving a young child a toy is an invitation to play, to fantasize, to engage in make-believe. As pointed out by Underwager and Wakefield in the book *The Real World of Child Interrogations,* children's play involves fantasy, pretend, and imagination. The anatomical dolls are routinely used with young and very young children as a means of overcoming their lack of verbal abilities. Yet, research evidence on this issue suggests that children do not reliably distinguish between fantasy and reality until approximately age seven or eight.

A child is naturally curious. The dolls he or she is accustomed to playing with do not have breasts, a penis, or pubic hair and, in most cases, children have not been much exposed to those parts of the human anatomy. Phillippus and Koch state it is normal for a child between the ages of three and four to be interested in sex and elimination organs, and that the incidence of genital self-stimulation in children of that age is generally high.

Although videotaped interviews with the anatomically complete dolls are often offered as evidence in cases of alleged child sexual abuse, the way a child plays with dolls has not been proven to be indicative of real life. If a child throws a doll on the floor, do we assume that the child throws his or her baby sister on the floor? If a child twists an arm or leg around and around to see if it comes off, do we assume that he twists his brother's arm in the same manner? Dr. T.F. Naumann (1985) pointed out that it is natural for young children to touch and manipulate parts of any toy, as well as, to mouth protruding parts of a toy. Yet, if a child touches the pubic area of a child doll or the penis of the man doll, social workers and child protection workers often view this as proof of the child having been exposed to these actions. In the use of the anatomical dolls, child's play may not be treated as play. Too often, interviewing adults believe they can invite a child to play, to fantasize, to enter a game of "let's pretend," and then use the child's play as evidence of reality.

The Dolls as Diagnostic Tools

The use of dolls and play sessions is based on the assumption that children who have been sexually abused will demonstrate sexual behavior with the dolls that will not be exhibited when non-abused children are exposed to the same dolls. This theory has been proven false by scientific research. In a paper published by the Institute for Psychological Therapies (IPT) William McIver II, Ralph Underwager, and Hollida Wakefield explored the characteristics of the dolls and documented the use of the anatomically correct dolls with both abused and non-abused children in a controlled study. Fifty non-abused children and ten abused children were led through identical exposures and interviews involving the anatomically correct dolls. The average age of the children was four years. In this study, there were no significant differences between the abused and non-abused children's spontaneous behavior and comments when interacting with the dolls. Sixty-two percent of the non-abused children and 50 percent of the abused children placed the dolls in clear sexual positions and/or played with the dolls in an overtly aggressive manner. Their play activities included placing one doll on top of another in the missionary position and placing the male doll's penis into the oral, anal, and vaginal openings of the dolls. Fifty percent of the non-abused children and 40 percent of the abused children made spontaneous comments, such as, "He did something naughty," "(He) jumped on his bed," and "Daddy went poopy on my head."

A study done by Canadian researcher Dr. R.M. Gabriel (1985) and a report to the American Academy of Child Psychiatry in 1986 both supported McIver, et al.'s, findings that there is little difference in the reaction and activities between abused and non-abused children when exposed to the dolls. Gabriel observed nineteen non-abused children who were exposed to the dolls and to other toys. About half of the children showed interest in the genitals of the dolls and manipulated them. Many of the children exhibited behavior and actions that could have been viewed as indicative of likely sexual abuse if one were in the process of attempting to prove such an allegation. Gabriel stated that, "On the evidence of the dolls alone, when used as part of a 'fishing expedition' exercise, the suspect will almost always be found guilty, especially if the examiner is already biased in that direction."

In the study by Jensen, Realmuto, and Wescoe, which involved both abused and non-abused children, reported at the American Academy of Child Psychiatry, some of the non-abused children got the highest rating of "very suspicious," while some of the abused children got ratings of "no suspicion of abuse." Research has also shown that the assumptions that children will identify the dolls as male or female based on genitals, and use the dolls to symbolize actual people in their lives, is unfounded. The McIver, et al., study found that most young children were unable to identify the dolls as males or females on the basis of primary sexual characteristics. Only 15 percent of the children related the dolls to people in their lives. Herbert, et al., (1987) also found that young children show an inability to identify gender on the basis of the symbolic genitalia.

Sivan, Schor, Koeppl, and Noble (1988) found that, overall, the anatomical dolls are of little interest to children, and they do not spontaneously choose to play with them. The Herbert et al. study showed that the interrogator had to direct the children to approach the dolls. None initiated undressing the dolls, although all accepted the direction of the interrogator to undress them.

Despite their wide use by social workers and child protection team members, there is not, to date, any empirical data that support their validity as a diagnostic tool. Not only are the anatomically complete dolls not of standard design, there are no protocols, standards, or norms established or followed for methods of interviewing and interpreting the responses and activities of the children involved. In addition to the non-standardization of the dolls, the procedures used by social services personnel are inherently suspect, according to Dr. Naumann (1987). Not only are few social workers qualified psychologists, but they usually approach the interview with a plethora of previous information from doctors, relatives, neighbors, and the accuser, which could cause the worker to be biased and to have a set of preconceived notions as to what to expect. Thus, the objectivity, which is imperative in an interview of this nature, is seriously compromised.

The dolls are not generally accepted in the scientific community, and it is the conclusion of McIver, et al., that nothing obtained from their use should ever be admitted as evidence in a legal setting. A California appeals court ruled in 1987 that the use of the dolls was not supported by scientific evidence, and their use did not meet the Frye test for admissibility. Testimony based on the use of the dolls was therefore ruled inadmissible (*Law Week*, 1987). Recently, the highest court in Holland ruled that evidence gained using the dolls could not be admitted into court, unless the judge could explain why the objections to the dolls did not apply in the specific case being reviewed.

Validity of Evidence

There are a number of questions and concerns regarding the validity of information gained in play sessions with the anatomically complete dolls, questions not only of interpretation, but of legality. Louis Kiefer (1989), an east coast attorney, points out that if a child is competent to testify-having the ability to receive correct impressions and to recollect and narrate intelligently, the dolls are unnecessary. If the child is incompetent to testify, how does one deem that child's actions with dolls are credible or competent evidence?

Young children do not understand, cognitively speaking, the adult concept of a lie or of justice, and it is unreasonable to expect them to grasp the concept in the time during which the interview is held. It is also important to discover what children can say without lying. In one case reviewed by Kiefer, the child was absolutely certain she had never lied. On cross-examination, she admitted to fibbing, unable to see this as a problem. One must establish what is and is not permissible behavior, i.e., telling lies versus "fibbing" versus "telling stories," a somewhat daunting task.

It must be remembered that the child has been invited to play, not to document an event that has actually happened. In a child's mind, make-believe stories are not lies. Many children believe in Santa Claus and the Tooth Fairy. If the interviewer has helps create the "story" by asking questions, the child often believes this is part of the game.

The Interview

Several issues make the use of information gained in doll session interviews questionable, i.e., the manner in which the interview is conducted, the behavior of the interviewer, and the suggestibility of young children. Psychologists and researchers note that children easily are led to model or imitate adults, and normally seek to provide actions and statements that engender positive reinforcement and approval. Underwager and Wakefield have reviewed numerous videotapes and interview transcripts in which the social worker or child protection team worker has been extremely active in the play session process, asking leading questions, pointing to and touching the "private parts" of the doll and repeating a question numerous times, until the sought-for answer is given.

There are numerous examples of adults modeling behavior that impacts the child's reactions and activities. During the course of the interview, the interviewer may repeatedly touch the genital areas of the dolls, reinforcing the child's curiosity regarding the new and unknown toy. The child will likely follow the adult's example. A statement such as, "Let's pretend this is daddy, and this is you," invites the child to play make-believe. The interviewer then places the dolls in sexually explicit positions or strokes the private parts of the body. Following the interviewer's lead, the child learns to do the same. In the case of false allegations, a child with nothing to report will report nothing. This may be deemed as failure on the part of the interviewer, who wants to save this child, having already determined in his or her own mind that the child has been abused, based on information provided by the accuser.

It was noted in several of the studies cited in this chapter that children rarely selected the anatomically complete dolls as the toy of choice, but had to be encouraged or directed by the interviewer to play with them. During the course of an actual doll session interviews, children are not allowed to put the dolls aside, but are required by the interviewer to continue playing with them.

Many doll session interviews contain a large number of leading and closed ended (yes-no) questions and a high degree of reinforcement for desired or expected behavior or responses. Children are highly suggestible and easily led. Analysis of the questions asked and the manner in which they are asked is necessary before establishing the level of credibility attached to the responses. Different kinds of questions will elicit different responses from a child. An open-ended question calls for spontaneous, free recall. "What happened?" might be the question asked of a crying child. If there were no response, the question might be made more specific, "Did you fall down?" The questioner has now begun providing potential answers to the cause of distress. The question can be further altered to provide the child with a potential explanation, as in, "Did Bobby push you down?"

A child's memory via free recall may be quite accurate, especially if captured by Statement Validity Analysis (SVA) and/or Content Based Criterion Analysis (CBCA). However, a response of "nothing" may not be acceptable, if the interviewer believes that the child has been the victim of abuse. Therefore, the interviewer who receives no definitive response regarding sexual abuse may become more active in the interview, advancing to leading questions in an effort to garner information or evidence. The younger the child, the fewer memories they have, the fewer events they remember. The less a child remembers, the more he or she can be misled by leading questions containing suggested answers.

In his book, *The Battle and the Backlash,* Hechler asked Lawrence Daly, a former detective with King County (Washington) Department of Public Safety, whether with a young child, it was sometimes necessary to ask what might be considered leading questions to get the story or an account of the case.

Daly responded, "You do. But, I'm talking about where you pick up the doll, an anatomically correct doll, and you say, 'Did your Daddy touch you here? Did your Daddy touch you here?' You can talk to the child and say, 'Are these your feet? Is this your nose? What do you call this? What do you call this? Do you call this anything?' "

"But, as soon as you suggest, the child responds because they think that you want that answer. It is a suggestive type thing, so you have to be careful. But, you can lead the kid a little bit. 'Were you in the bedroom with your Daddy?' Well, if Daddy didn't do anything wrong in the bedroom, the next question's going to be, 'Did anything happen in the bedroom?' That way you can lead, but you don't say, 'Did Daddy touch you there in the bedroom?' " Unfortunately, that is exactly the type of question too often used by interviewers using anatomically exaggerated dolls.

In addition, the interviewer may provide positive reinforcement when the child provides desired information. For example, such statements as, "Good girl, you've helped us so much," in response to questions such as, "Daddy touched you here, didn't he?" suggests to a child what type of behavior is expected and rewarded. In addition, repetition of a question that includes the suggested answer will eventually elicit a positive response. Often, denial of the abuse or sexually inappropriate behavior results in questions about the validity of the denial, such as, "Are you sure?" or, "Did he tell you not to talk about it?" When a child is repeatedly subjected to interviews or therapy geared toward identifying or treating suspected sexual abuse, the child is taught, through modeling and questions and reinforcement, to believe something happened, as was the case with Matilda.

In the McIver, et al., study, six of the non-abused and one of the abused children were intentionally asked leading questions in conjunction with modeling and reinforcing behavior by the interviewer, questions such as, "Can you show me?" and, "How else could they go together?" All but one child responded by performing the behaviors that were cued or modeled and reinforced by the interviewer. As the interview progressed, the children demonstrated and produced more and more behaviors. Although only one of the children in this group had actually been abused, six of the seven children demonstrated hitting, punching, cunnilingus, fellatio, anal and vaginal intercourse, and the mommy doll sitting on the boy doll's face. In the real world of child interrogation, children are pressured to interact with the dolls until the desired behavior is elicited. They must frequently be encouraged, sometimes almost forced, to initiate play with the dolls. Questions are not asked once and then dropped if the child does not respond as desired. Children are not permitted to put the dolls aside in favor of a preferred activity.

The Interviewer

It has been suggested that, when using the dolls, the interviewer should be unaware of who has been accused and exactly what type of abuse has occurred, in the interest of avoiding leading questions, modeling, suggestions, and prompting which would influence the child. Rarely is this protocol followed. Interviews with the dolls are most frequently conducted by social workers and child protection team workers, individuals with only undergraduate degrees or less, whose education in the use of the dolls has consisted of one or two weekend seminars or a four-hour in-service training program. These individuals set themselves up as expert witnesses and their opinions and recommendations are accepted and "rubber stamped" by prosecutors and judges.

Mental health professionals generally interpret non-responses as responses of affirmation. If a child does not respond to a question about sexual abuse, it is assumed the child is either ashamed or denying it. Since denial is unhealthy, interrogation continues until a response is elicited that can be interpreted as an admission of abuse so the child can be treated. In the event the adult believes there has been abuse, and the child says "no," the adult may assume the child is keeping it a secret or was told to keep it a secret by the alleged perpetrator. Now the adult must press the child into telling the secret so the child can be saved. If a child answers "no," the questioning continues; the denials are often ignored until the desired affirmation is obtained. It is interesting to note that those who most strongly assert that children don't lie are the very individuals who believe that when a child says "no" to questions of sexual abuse, he or she is not telling the truth about the incident.

Accusations of child sexual abuse are often based on a child's response to an adult's question, not to an actual accusation or statement made by the child. The normal course of events is for an adult to suspect abuse, usually because of a change in behavior, and to question the child. The next step is to contact the police or the social services agency. The first contact is usually a social worker, who hears the adult's account of what they think might have happened. Frequently, this account becomes a statement of fact to the social worker that now feels responsible for substantiating the claim so they can act to save the child.

The first interview with the child rarely is electronically recorded, only summarized. Thus, there is no indication of what type of questions were asked, whether or not there were repeated denials prior to the affirmation of abuse, or whether the child's accusation was the result of answering suggestive questions or making a free statement. Where audio or video tapes have been reviewed, it has often been found that the interview reports are wrong regarding what the child actually said and what the interviewer actually said. The summary may simply state the opinion of the interviewer, based on his or her recollection of the final outcome of questioning. In many of the interviews observed by McIver, et al., the interviewer told the child to pretend or imagine. The child did. The interviewer then concluded that the resulting behavior showed that real events happened. The interviewer, now believing abuse took place, continued the interrogation, talking to the child about what started out as pretend behavior but is now represented to the child as real, i.e., "Remember when you told me Daddy did . . ." In this progression, a child may be taught to believe and subjectively experience as real what started out as a response to the adult's invitation to pretend (see chapter 14 and "guided imagery").

11.

The Agencies

The headlines in *The Florida Times-Union* on 11 November 1990, read: "HRS Investigator Finds Baby with Eyes Black, No Clothes and a Tail." The *Florida Today* headlines were: "Accused Child-abusers Explain Princess is a Pet."

The Times-Union article began, "James and Mary Seay were surprised yesterday when a state welfare official came to their Westside Jacksonville home to investigate a child-abuse report involving their eighth-month-old baby, Princess. Princess, after all, is their pet raccoon. The articles went on to explain that the Department of Health and Rehabilitative Services (DHRS) had received reports that the Seay's were picking up Princess by the neck and locking her in a bathroom. The Seay's introduced the raccoon, and the investigator talked with their veterinarian. Although the call was obviously a prank, Seay said the investigator told her the agency would have to continue checking to see if the couple has a human baby and that she and her husband would be listed on the HRS central child-abuse registry until the investigation was completed. The middle-aged couple was ordered by other HRS workers to come in the following week for child-abuse counseling. Mrs. Seay, the mother of three teenagers, commented, "I'm just disgusted. This isn't going to be over until Princess is eighteen."

There are many caring and competent individuals involved in social services and mental health care across the country, professionals who are educated and experienced in child cognitive development, child pathology, and child interrogation. Unfortunately, due to heavy case loads and frequent turnover in personnel, many agencies are either understaffed or are staffed by individuals who do not have adequate training or expertise to qualify them for the authoritative role they have in areas of child-abuse and, specifically, child sexual abuse allegations. In recent years, people have begun to question the effectiveness and competence of these agencies, their policies, procedures, and personnel. In his book, *A Question of Innocence*, Dr. Larry Spiegel, who was falsely accused of abusing his daughter, relates the following incident:

I was working with a couple in my clinical practice who had a 3½-year-old girl. One evening, as a consequence of a series of events, the mother created such a disturbance that the police and Department of Youth and Family Services (DYFS) were called. My business card was on the bulletin board in their apartment, so the police called my office. I went there immediately.

When I arrived, the DYFS worker was preparing papers to remove the child from the home. I interceded and volunteered to take the child to her relatives out of state, rather than have her placed in a foster home. The DYFS worker said he would check on that, but the child would have to spend the night in a foster home. The following day, I sent Janeen to the DYFS headquarters to request that the child be released into my custody and flown to her relatives in Detroit. As incredible as it sounds, this same agency which pressed child molestation against me-charges which were still pending in court-released this child into my custody. I received a letter from DYFS a few days later, thanking me for my help. Need I say more about the credibility and competence of this agency?

Ken Pearson tells about his experience with the agency charged to protect innocent children at-risk of abuse. His wife had filed for divorce and full custody when their youngest child was a year old. Facing a court that had no interest in what he had to say, Ken didn't fight the decree. However, he later received a call from the state supervisor of welfare, telling him horror stories about what his wife was doing to his children and her treatment of them, insinuating that if Ken were any kind of father, he would do something about the situation.

Ken questioned the social worker. "You're telling me I'm a terrible father because I'm not doing anything about this. Let me ask you a question. If I come up with the money to launch a custody fight and go in there after the kids, will you or someone from the agency appear in court, testify to what she's been doing with the kids, and tell the court she shouldn't have those kids, and I should?"

The supervisor's response was short and simple. "Why, no, we can't do that."

Anyone who is dealing with a false allegation of child sexual abuse is most likely associated with some sort of state agency like DHRS (now called DCF-Department of Children and Families), an agency that believes itself to be acting in the best interest of children. Whether called Health and Human Services (HHS), Department of Social Services (DSS), Children's Services Department (CSD), State Rehabilitative Services

(SRS), or some other name, there is a state agency that was originally designed to protect children and families. Unfortunately, their mindset regarding the protection and reunification of families is secondary. Many of these agencies have some sort of abuse hot line, a toll-free telephone number that individuals can call to report child-abuse of any type, often with complete anonymity. This agency, whatever its name, is going to be involved, and probably in control, before you ever know you've been accused. An allegation of child sexual abuse, whether false or factual, whether placed by an anonymous caller or by an ex-wife, is usually made to the county or state social services agency and sets in motion a relatively standard chain of events.

First the child will undergo a medical examination to determine whether there is physical evidence of sexual abuse. With young children, rarely is there any such evidence. Next, the child is interviewed by a social worker or perhaps a police investigator. Subsequent steps vary, depending on the outcome or perceived outcome of that interview. If the child denies the allegations, the next step is often therapy, based on the assumption that the child is too young to understand or too frightened to talk about the experience. This "therapy" may well continue until the allegation can be substantiated.

Many of the agencies dealing with allegations of child sexual abuse include what are called "Child Protection Teams," composed of persons representing mental health, social work, medical, legal, and law enforcement disciplines. To date, there is no empirical data to support the conviction that multi-disciplinary teams are more effective or that they increase accuracy of conclusions. Teams are a medical concept, not a criminal law evidence-gathering body (Schultz, 1989).

There are four types of teams: the hospital-based team (as in my own case), the state consultation team, the rural team, and the treatment team. The hospital team is where most criminal charges of child-abuse are initiated and evolve. Most often it will be a hospital-based team that makes the initial decision that causes further interventions and actions of the state, calling in prosecutors, therapists, etc. The team approach has some inherent problems, including being so large it bogs down, has power struggles within the team ranks, and has differing definitions of child-abuse laws among team members. In cases of alleged sexual abuse of young children, there is rarely any medical evidence of penetration. Except for reporting "excited utterances" of alleged victims at the time of the medical exam, pediatricians' opinions of psychological factors are no more valid than layman's. A physician's opinion or report, when there are no physical findings but a statement, is made that abuse is "consistent with," must be treated cautiously (see Appendix H). Too often child protection team members tend to give more credence and credibility to medical opinion (versus medical evidence) than may be warranted.

During the trial of a young man accused of molesting children at the Manhattan Ranch Pre-School in California, one of the witnesses for the prosecution was an examining physician, a pediatrician at County Harbor General Hospital. She testified that she had examined one of the child witnesses and that her findings were "consistent with sexual abuse." During cross-examination, the attorney asked the pediatrician if she ever reported findings "inconsistent with sexual abuse." The pediatrician said she never used those words, "because there are no findings inconsistent with sexual abuse." This statement then leads to the conclusion that, if there is no finding inconsistent with sexual abuse, anything or nothing can be diagnosed as evidence of sexual abuse.

Depending on the attitude and urgency of the accuser, the attitude and ambition of the involved social services agency, the direction of the therapy, and conclusions drawn from various interviews, a complaint may be filed with the district attorney's office as the next step. Unfortunately, the accused is rarely aware of all this activity and has no idea of the case being built against him until most, if not all, of these steps have been accomplished. By the time I was aware of the initial allegations, my daughter had already had a medical examination at a local hospital and had been interviewed by social services and a police officer. By the time I was aware of the second set of allegations, she had gone through another series of these examinations. These interviews were conducted by social services, the child protection team (who had interviewed her using the anatomically correct dolls), a police detective, and a therapist.

Before the father in the Colorado case study became aware of his ex-wife's allegations at the time of his arrest, all three of his children had been receiving therapy through social services for sexual abuse and DSS had filed a complaint with the district attorney's office. Mark Doe was advised of the allegations against him immediately prior to the family court hearing that was to determine custody. Again, his children had been undergoing social services directed therapy for sexual abuse without his knowledge.

Once the social services agency has determined that, in its opinion, sexual abuse has occurred, it will usually file a petition for dependency (also, called CHIPS or CHINA Petition) in juvenile or family court. In the case of allegations made by the ex-wife or soon to be ex-wife, the petition routinely recommends that the mother receive residential custody, the accused father denied any access to the children, at least for the time being. The children receive counseling and therapy for sexual abuse, and the father enters and completes counseling and therapy as an abuser, before any consideration is given to his visitation or parenting time with the children. In many cases, these recommendations are made before the social worker has even met or talked with the accused father. In cases of sexual child abuse allegations against fathers, stepfathers, or paramours, mothers find themselves accused of "failure to protect" in juvenile court, if they believe in the man's innocence. Divorces can follow.

Rick's experience in Colorado was not unusual for a father falsely accused of abusing his children. In spite of his ex-wife's recantation and Rick's steadfast pleas of innocence, the family court accepted the opinion of the social services agency that the children exhibited behavior consistent with abuse victims and followed the agency's recommendations. Rick was not allowed to see his children until the required counseling and therapy for him had been completed.

The agency-selected therapist advised Rick that he would have to admit to sexually abusing his daughter before he could even attend therapy sessions. He refused to admit to something he hadn't done and requested another therapist. The second therapist selected by DSS was the same one who had filed the accusations against him and who was a good friend of his ex-wife. Unable to trust her, he also refused this therapist and was caught in a catch-22. It appeared that unless he admitted to something he hadn't done, he wouldn't be able to meet the conditions required to see his children.

In a separate case in the state of Colorado, where false allegations were made by the ex-wife during a divorce and custody battle, the two young children and the ex-wife were interviewed by the Department of Social Services. The caseworker's impressions and recommendations were presented as an expert evaluation to the family court. Her report stated that she believed that the child had been sexually abused and that the child presented an advanced knowledge of adult sexual activity. To her knowledge, there had not been any other form of exposure for the child, other than what was described by the children. Therefore, she respectfully recommended that the court honor the filing of a dependency petition on behalf of this child. In addition, it was recommended that the physical custody of both children be placed with their mother. Furthermore, this worker recommended that a protective order be issued disallowing physical or verbal contact with the children and their mother by the father. She felt it essential that further investigation and evaluation of the child be done before the father be allowed contact with the child. The court accepted this individual's evaluation and recommendation and acted as requested, although there had been no professional psychological evaluations done, the father in this case had never been evaluated or even interviewed, and the children had been treated as abuse victims before the allegations were ever substantiated.

Currently, social workers and mental health care workers within the agencies have a tremendous amount of authority, their opinions are considered as fact, their credibility viewed as unassailable, unimpeachable, and their recommendations considered expert testimony and rubber-stamped by prosecutors and judges, in spite of evidence to the contrary.

More and more studies, investigations and case evaluations are showing that the falsely accused are truly the ones being abused by the social
services agencies and the family courts. Over the past several years, many
of the agencies responsible for handling child-abuse allegations have grown
into unmanageable bureaucracies, with almost absolute authority over the
alleged victim and the alleged perpetrator. Frequently understaffed by
individuals who are expected to handle investigative duties for which they
have never been trained, the agencies and their employees are, nonetheless, often considered expert witnesses when it comes time to make a
determination of custody and guilt in juvenile, family, and criminal court
(the 3-ring circus). Many social workers, investigating allegations of child
sexual abuse and making determinations of probable guilt, are totally
unfamiliar with the SAID syndrome and its ramifications. Many have
little education or expertise in the areas of child-abuse detection and
prevention or child developmental psychology.

The results of such an approach and the application of such a method
are far reaching. First, we have a system so overburdened with false
allegations that we don't have the time or energy to do a good job with
cases where there is real evidence of abuse. Next, we have children being
trained to believe something has happened in such a way they can't tell
if it happened or not, as we saw with Mary. The long-term ramifications
of this on the children have yet to be determined, but the potential
consequences cannot be considered innocuous or inconsequential. The
lives of the falsely accused are left in ruins regardless of the outcome of
any criminal proceedings or eventual proof of innocence. Finally, we
suffer a lack of resources for promoting adequate prosecution of the guilty
and adequate protection of the innocence. Too often, social workers and
child protection team members go into the investigative interview with
the belief-for whatever reason-that the child has been molested and that
their mission is to substantiate that belief in such a way that the family
and criminal courts will act in what the worker has determined to be the
best interest of the child. Two things occur as a result of this. First, the
worker may act as a therapist, instead of an investigator, determined to
treat the child. In this case, the child receives strong positive feedback if
he or she says that something happened and negative feedback, contradictions of his or her statements, or encouragement to revise the responses, if he or she denies the abuse.

One individual who was the victim of incest during her childhood,
told Hechler, during the course of an interview for his book, that a child
doesn't need "treatment." A child needs solutions, options, an ear to
listen, or a caring person. How often do the social services agencies get
involved in "treating" the child before they have even established the
basis of the symptoms, symptoms that have often been relayed by another
adult? How often are investigators acting as therapists before they have

completed their investigation? Mary provided an excellent suggestion for social workers: "Listen to the kids and help them to deal with it. Don't act like another parent; you're supposed to be a friend, someone to help." In Mary's opinion, the social workers did more harm than good, continuing to push for indications of abuse and raising questions in her mind about what might have happened, despite her repeated denial of abuse from her father. Is this *in loco parentis* (the state as the parent), it takes a village, mindset, truly in children's best interests?

Larry Spiegel, a psychologist, author, and victim of false allegations of child abuse, argues that much of the problem resides within the social services agencies. He identified specific issues of concern: a system geared to believe abuse charges, lack of proper training to investigate and assess the charges, the ease with which children can be led by social workers during interviews and investigation, the anonymous reporting system, and the convenience of an abuse charge in a custody battle.

Unfortunately, most state agencies that deal in the areas of child protection are primarily autonomous, with little if any supervision from or accountability to anyone. While they can remove children from a home and file a charge without presenting any evidence, they cannot be held personally responsible for their actions; governmental sovereign immunity under the Eleventh Amendment protects them. Much of their information and many of their records are exempt from the Freedom of Information and Public Records Acts, making it difficult for the accused and his/her attorney to obtain necessary CPS documents.

There is often no clear line of command or reporting requirements. The attorney general, public advocate, director of courts, and governor's office exercise no supervision over these child protection agencies, which have awesome powers. In addition, under the aegis of the state, the interests of the accuser, law enforcement, child protection, allied mental health, and prosecutorial personnel are advanced and protected. Only recently have some states enacted new laws, sanctioning ex-spouses who knowingly and maliciously file false allegations, making it at least a second-degree misdemeanor. In Florida, the same is a third degree felony.

Today's system for responding to allegations of child sexual abuse is one that in the majority of cases exacts no negative consequences for the individual filing false allegations. An allegation, true or false, immediately elicits interest, attention, emotional and financial support, and legal and investigative services for the accuser and claimed victim. An accused parent's rights are not uniformly and consistently protected, as interrogation by the child protection team of the alleged child victim is often not preceded by informing you of your rights, and the presence of your attorney may not be permitted. You may be admonished that if you do not execute a written waiver of rights, you must be guilty since if you are innocent, you have nothing to worry about. There is nothing further from the truth. Moreover, the naïve accused can be induced into submitting to police-directed polygraphs, often tilted on the side of finding deception.

There is the potential for a great deal of monetary reward for those individuals involved in identifying and even more money in treating victims of abuse. An allegation of child sexual abuse inevitably results in evaluations of the alleged perpetrator, the accuser, and the children, as well as required therapy for the children and usually for the alleged perpetrator throughout the process of determining whether abuse has even occurred. The social workers file cases that result in receipt of grant money. State and federal money received by these agencies is dependent on the number of cases they have filed. Once an accusation has been made, and the social worker assigns it credibility by placing it on file, the agency has its numbers, and the individual can be placed on the central abuse registry blacklist. Florida and Georgia are the only two states which do not have abuse registry blacklists.

To substantiate the case, the child is sent to a doctor for a physical examination, and put through psychological evaluations. The psychologist is paid by the state on a per-case or per-child basis and, because they are involved in this type of work, become eligible for grants and contract work, themselves. Some medical, psychological, and social work professionals appear to have developed large practices by providing affirmation and support of accusations. In some areas, individuals of this nature have been clearly identified and are routinely used by county or state authorities dealing with alleged child sexual abuse. These physicians and psychological agencies can be relied upon to determine that there has been abuse, regardless of the evidence or testimony or lack thereof, as evidenced in the testimony in the California case.

In the William Smith case, an agency-selected physician examined Janice and Johnny, who had allegedly been abused by their stepbrother. In a handwritten note, the physician stated, "Janice exhibited vaginal irritation and stretching of rectal opening, Johnny exhibited reddened throat, end of penis irritated, stretching of rectal opening." While these symptoms may be indicative of abuse, the examination identifying those conditions occurred five months after the allegation was reported.

Professionals who do not develop a history of affirmative support may be informally blacklisted. There is also the danger of professionals who are ready to come to premature closure with minimal information and leap to the conviction that a child has been abused and requires immediate counseling. A premature and swift closure by a mental health professional on an opinion that abuse occurred is recognized as one of the hallmarks of a false allegation (Klajner-Diamon, Wehrspann & Steinhauer, 1987; Wakefield & Underwager, 1988).

What is most frightening is that often the individuals involved in the case believe they know what happened and work in a heady atmosphere of sincerity and moral righteousness. The prosecutor believes he has charged a guilty man; the social workers believe they have protected a child from more harm; the psychologists believe they have successfully spotted the key signs of abuse; the jury believes, or at least says, that it can be objective and impartial; and the judge, deeming the case indeterminable, errs on the side of caution, doing what he thinks "best for the child."

Almost all prosecutors and social workers claim that statements by children about abuse carry some sort of inherent credibility. However, statistics compiled and released by the American Human Association refute this contention. As of 1978, more than 65 percent of all reports of suspected child maltreatment, involving over 750 cases per year, turned out to be unfounded. Of 328 sexual abuse cases studied by Underwager and Wakefield over a period of five years, 39 percent were divorce and custody cases. Of those cases that were adjudicated, it was determined by the legal system that in 79 percent of the cases, there had been no abuse (Wakefield & Underwager, 1989). Another separate study indicated that of each 576 sexual abuse allegations, approximately 267 may be false allegations or very questionable, usually described as "unfounded" (Young, 1985).

There is some feeling of paranoia within the social services agencies. What if they close a case erroneously, and there are additional allegations afterward? It will appear they don't know their business. For this reason, cases are often kept open even after the initial investigation indicates no abuse. The child continues to be watched, perhaps sent to more therapy, while restrictions on visitation remain. In this case, the agency isn't protecting the child. It is actually abusing the rights of the child and the parent while protecting itself.

The policies and procedures of these agencies need to be closely and carefully reviewed, while the competency and capability of the social and mental health care officials is questioned. Agency workers need to be educated in the basics of the SAID syndrome and have a standard list of investigative questions to be answered before making the automatic assumption of guilt. If the family is not intact, if there are divorce proceedings or a custody battle in process, or if visitation rights are an issue, the investigator needs to establish several facts. Who filed the initial complaint and why? What professionals evaluated the child and when? If the complaint came from the ex-spouse, were other relatives, neighbors, and friends contacted and interviewed? No one suggests that all social workers and psychologists lead children to confess. But, there is no one size fits all protocol for interviewing children in suspected abuse cases, no rules insisting that all members of the family, including the accused, be interviewed before an evaluator decides the validity of the allegation. Because the stakes are so high, many critics say that inexperienced and poorly trained interviewers are dangerous and that the ramifications of their interview techniques cannot be considered inconsequential or innocuous.

In his book, *The Battle and the Backlash*, Hechler quotes Michael Sands, a Sacramento defense attorney who has handled at least fifty sexual molestation cases over the past twenty years, "The fact of the matter is that we have documented that the so-called experts-and this includes cops, and the psychologists, and the sex molest support teams-do not do an objective job of questioning the kid. They slant these kids, some of them. I'm not saying everyone."

Often, interviews conducted by therapists and social workers include techniques that are intrusive and suggestive, tainting the interview and rendering the information unreliable and unethical. Leroy Schultz studied child protection workers and presents the following profile: self-righteous, unwilling to admit mistakes, lacking in ethics, naive about children, willing to use hearsay evidence, likely to conduct one-sided investigations, and blind to contradictory input ("The Social Worker and the Sexually Abused Minor: Where are We Going?" 1985). Several recent studies lead to some disturbing conclusions. Child protection workers often appear determined to find evidence of wrongdoing in order to make them look good. Promotions are sometimes given to police officers who have a good record of convictions. An increased case-load allows social workers and state agencies to cry for more funds, more staff, and greater authority over families, child care workers, and teachers. Child protection has fostered and exacerbated an already litigious society.

In their defense, the number of cases assigned to individual workers may have a strongly negative effect on the ability to properly and thoroughly investigate allegations. However, too often, the job performance of all those involved in the "investigation" of these allegations is measured by the number of "wins" they have in suspension of parental rights. In addition, few social workers are trained in the art of investigation; more often, their background and education are in the therapeutic treatment of abused individuals. While therapy is certainly necessary in cases of abuse, it needs to be separated from the initial investigative process. Therapy may lead to reinforcement of fiction, causing the child to become convinced the abuse is a fact, since positive reinforcement of expected behavior and actions is what children are taught to respond to. Accordingly, the child in this situation begins to think he or she has actually been abused. Most social workers have little or no training in the use of the dolls, which are standard equipment for many child protection teams. A social worker usually has a collection of information from the ex-wife, doctors, perhaps relatives, teachers, or neighbors, which would cause him/her to be biased and have a set of preconceived notions as to what to expect from a child suspected to have been abused. Researchers at Case Western Reserve University School of Medicine state that the objectivity of the interviewer is imperative, and advocate that the interviewer receive no prior information relative to abuse and be told only the child's name and his/her birth date.

Schultz (1989) reported on a survey done in 1986, where one hundred questionnaires were completed by individuals who had been acquitted of false allegations made in ten states. Forty-four percent of the respondents felt the social worker was unskilled in investigation of the suspect and in child victim interviewing. Sixteen percent felt the social worker was biased in favor of the charge before the investigation ever took place, what Stephen Ceci, Ph.D., calls "confirmatory bias" (see chapter 14). Eight percent felt no warrant would have been issued if the first interrogation of the alleged child victim and suspect had been videotaped.

The following issues were raised in a motion to amend motion for rehearing, filed by my attorney, that pointed out flaws, inconsistencies, and errors in testimony allowed, hearsay testimony heard and allowed, and denial of constitutional rights to face and cross-examine the witnesses against me. HRS and child protection team personnel have been often known to draw erroneous conclusions, to use interview and other techniques not scientifically reliable, to use unproven protocols or go outside established guidelines, to unintentionally lead children to desired answers and actions, to fail to examine, explain, or rule out other causes for what they and others observed, and to draw conclusions from incomplete or suspect data. In addition to these issues, the motion raised a number of questions about the videotaped interview with Diane, the child protection team coordinator and the anatomically complete dolls. Why did the videotape have obvious gaps? What happened during those gaps?

On the tape, the child protection team interviewer refers to a prior interview and session with the dolls. What happened during those prior interviews and doll sessions? Who conducted them? How long did they last? What methods, protocols, and techniques were used? Were they reliable? Were they faithfully followed? Was Diane coached or led, intentionally or unintentionally? How many times was her performance practiced before the video was made? What other explanations exist to account for Diane's behavior on the videotape? Could she, in fact, have been trying to demonstrate innocent or appropriate behavior? Innocent behavior that with the misinterpretation or contrivance of HRS-DCF and CPT was made to appear inappropriate?

It is interesting to note that, during the course of the Colorado case, the county social services agency failed miserably in a management audit conducted after the County Board of Commissioners received numerous complaints from citizens. The county officials recommended a review by an outside agency of all child-abuse and -neglect cases handled by that department, to determine if they were handled properly. Unfortunately, that review was never carried out. However, the county social services chief found the staff was not adequately trained, had not been properly supervised or directed, and the record keeping was inadequate. He also determined that few of the social workers involved in the child-abuse cases were qualified for the work they were doing.

Ken Pearson is personally aware of the flaws within the social services system. Shortly after his conversation with the social services agency in Wisconsin, Ken learned of the Father's Right's Movement and filed for custody of his three children. His wife's response was allegations of inappropriate sexual conduct that, although nebulous, were sufficient in the Midwest at the time to create trouble.

12.

The Courts

The following quotations are taken from the *Liberator*, June 1990:

Judge J. L., Houston County, GA:

I feel that everything else being equal, that there is no substitute for a mother, and custody of this child is awarded to the mother.

Judge R. J. N., Douglas County, GA:

I ain't never seen the calves follow the bull, they always follow the heifer, therefore I always give custody to the mamas.

Judge I. J., Fulton County, GA:

Many things change, but some things don't change, and children belong with their mothers, especially younger children.

Judge R. W., Gwinnette County, GA:

I don't believe in joint custody and won't order it. Since both parents are equal, I have no choice but to award custody based upon traditional gender factors, and therefore award sole custody to the mother.

Rep. D. G., Macon, GA:

A bad mama is better than no mama at all.

Judge R. F., Cobb County GA: (When confronted with direct evidence of adultery by the mother and the exposure of the child to the mother's conduct)

These are the eighties, and that type of behavior is more accepted now.

While these attitudes are not shared by all who serve in our judicial system, these quotations unfortunately represent the prevailing attitude in many of the family/juvenile courts across the country. In spite of the age of liberation and much-touted equality of the sexes, when it comes to children, mothers, and gender bias, it appears that our judicial system is not particularly enlightened. The aforementioned judicial remarks go beyond giving custody to the mother because the child is of "judicial tender years." Fortunately, for those advocates of the 'best parent is *both* parents,' the 'tender years' doctrine has been replaced by the 'best interests' standard.

Consistently, the case studies reviewed for this book have shown clear indications that neither parent is the perfect parent and that both parents may have some difficulty in the area of proper or adequate parenting skills. However, even when the mother needs assistance from social services and requires parenting classes, it is usually the mother who receives custody and parenting assistance, rather than the father, even when there is no proof or validation of abuse on his part. In Mark Doe's case, the children were placed in the mother's custody, despite the fact that her live-in boyfriend had a documented history of child sexual abuse, and the criminal charges against Mr. Doe had been dropped. In my case, the children were placed with their mother, who had been proven, in court, to be an unfit parent. Child sexual abuse cases can involve one or all of five basic court arenas. Our judicial system provides for more than one type of court, and the individual facing allegations of child sexual abuse may well end up fighting on multiple fronts, battling prejudicial judges, biased social and mental health workers, hearsay evidence, and laws that act to his detriment. Each court has a specific purpose, a designated area of authority. Be aware that the findings of one court may have no effect on the findings of another. Findings of DSS might be different from the courts.

The family or juvenile court deals with the settling of custody disputes, visitation rights, and determination of the restriction or removal of parental rights. The criminal courts hold trials, sometimes based on an indictment brought against the alleged abuser by a grand jury. Civil suits are filed in state and/or federal court to recover compensatory and punitive damages. The appellate court rules on appeals of a criminal court decision or family/juvenile court ruling. Not only can this system require pursuit of charges on more than one front, it may well mean the necessity of retaining more than one attorney. A lawyer who is skilled in the battles of the trial court, where juries must be convinced and arguments prepared and presented to meet the trial court's official and unofficial protocol, may be totally ineffective in a family court or judge's chamber and vice versa. The time frames and procedures adhered to in civil court and federal court are not the same as those outlined for family or criminal court. An attorney without the experience and expertise required in the particular arena in which you are doing battle can do as much harm as good.

The juvenile court system dawned at the very end of the nineteenth century and remains with us today. This movement was not spearheaded by lawyers, but by social workers who envisioned an environment of informality and intimacy that gathered all kinds of evidence. Matters of due process and parental rights took on a new meaning within the juvenile justice system; the court's authority was to include determination of the child's welfare and what was in the best interest of the child. A major purpose was to remove the juvenile court from the rigid procedure of the criminal court, thus eliminating the requirement for due process. The family or juvenile court has a great deal of power. Within our judicial system, these courts often seem to operate differently under the burden of determining the validity of child sexual abuse allegations. In my research, the presumption of innocence appears to be ignored. The right of the accused to face his accuser is brushed aside, in the best interest of the children. Hearsay evidence, usually disallowed in the criminal courts, is sufficient to separate a father from his children for the rest of his life in juvenile court. Interview results, involving anatomical dolls, are often admissible based on jurisdiction and relied upon by the social service workers who present the information as expert witnesses in spite of the fact that there is no research to support the validity or credibility of information garnered through the use of the dolls, and that same does not comport with legal admissibility requirements under the Daubert-Frye case law (see Appendix F).

The standard of proof in family court is lower than in the criminal courts, which require evidence "beyond a reasonable doubt." Family courts require only that a case be proved *prima facie*, by a "preponderance of the evidence" or by "51 percent." Hearsay testimony-an out of court statement that is not made under oath, that is repeated by someone to whom the statement was made and that cannot be cross-examined in the courtroom-is allowed in the family or juvenile court systems. In the latter, if a child is adjudicated dependent or abused, an accuseds' parental rights are in jeopardy. DSS must prove in juvenile court by clear and convincing evidence, which can be tantamount to a parents noncompliance with a caseplan, in order to terminate a parent's rights to his or her children. According to the 1997 federal law signed by President Clinton, the Adoption and Safe Families Act (ASFA), parents have one year from the time of adjudication of dependency to substantially comply with the caseplan from DSS or face the possibility of termination.

These courts often have an unstated agenda for doing something about child abuse. If an objective review of the validity and credibility of hearsay statements were to be instituted, it could well result in the defendant having a better than even chance of prevailing. This, however, would produce a result that is inconsistent with "doing something." The family courts, in cases where there is no definite right or wrong conclusion, i.e., the case is deemed "indeterminable," will always err on the side of caution, protecting the child from any possible harm. Unfortunately, family courts are often not taken seriously by many in the judicial system, primarily because of the lack of experience and expertise exhibited by many of the attorneys, the social workers who offer testimony, and even the judges who sit on the bench. Given the autonomy of the social service agencies and the looseness of requirements in family court when it comes to solid evidence, it often appears the scales of justice may be tipped in the direction of the accuser, particularly if that accuser is an adult who has the opportunity and motive to influence a very young child's actions and speech.

Doctors and other professionals whose reports are used by the prosecution are often not available for cross-examination during juvenile dependency hearings. Videotapes that have never been seen by the accused, or his attorney, or the court, may be entered as evidence by the social services agency and are accepted by the court. For this reason, fighting false allegations in the juvenile courts is often more frustrating, more difficult, and more time consuming than fighting charges in criminal court. Throughout my lengthy ordeal, all motions, orders, and restrictions placed on me were based on hearsay evidence. The only evidence used to support findings was from the court recording of proceedings of a dependency hearing, hearsay testimony by an HRS worker referring to a video tape of a child interrogation. No admissible evidence was produced at any time, by any party, at any hearing, to prove by a preponderance of the evidence that my daughter was ever sexually abused or that I was the perpetrator. In actuality, we proved by a preponderance of the evidence my innocence, and the lack of substance to my former wife's allegations.

A further problem often encountered in family courts is the fact that the key or primary witnesses may be social workers with little experience in investigation or courtroom procedures. While we recognize that there are many competent and caring professionals in these fields, there are also many social workers who are not only inexperienced, but overworked and undertrained. This may be due, in large part, to the high turnover in the social service agencies that results from burnout, frustration, low pay, and limited resources. While police officers, who may be called as witnesses, are trained investigators, few of them are knowledgeable or experienced in interviewing young children, or in areas of child development. These witnesses make it difficult for the defense attorney to identify the basic causes, motives, and actions that may be crucial to an objective rendering of a decision by a relatively inexperienced judge.

Law guardians, legal representatives for minors, were not developed until the early 1960s. These attorneys *ad Litem* are supposed to serve in the best interests of the children, but time constraints and other outside factors often prohibit this. In custody and visitation disputes, guardians *ad Litem* (GALs) often become involved, especially where there are allegations of abuse, as in SAID syndrome cases. These individuals are volunteers, attorneys, or psychologists trained by social service workers and appointed by the family/juvenile court judge. Their function is to protect the best interests of the children and to act as mediators for the ex-spouses or adversarial parties. One of the functions often served by the GAL is to act as supervisor in cases of restricted, supervised visitation.

As seen in the cases presented in this book, and others reviewed for additional information, the GAL often enters a case with the belief that abuse has occurred. Prior to meeting the accused parent, he or she usually has interviewed the social workers involved in the case, the child protection team workers who conducted the interrogation, and the accusing parent. Although these volunteers often possess the common sense necessary to cope with the day-to-day aspects of supervision, they usually have no psychological education or expertise. Nonetheless, their opinions and recommendations regarding the accused and the children are frequently rubber-stamped by judges in the family courts.

Some states like Tennessee involve Court Appointed Special Advocates (CASA) in child dependency cases. According to information disseminated to this writer CASAs, in general, appear to be more objective than GALs. The court monitor system places family advocates in the juvenile and family courtrooms and reports observations to the media, giving judges incentive to pay more attention to the needs of the family. The Naples, Florida Victims Of Child Abuse Laws (VOCAL) court monitor, or court watch program, reported that after two months, judges were expecting HRS-DCF to back up their recommendations.

Court monitors are volunteers. To institute a court monitor program, call or write to your juvenile judges' office and explain the situation. For example, "I represent (organization name, such as DADS, Mothers Without Custody, or VOCAL) that helps families having problems. We understand that the hearings are open unless a child victim will be testifying. We want to begin visiting in the courtrooms during hearings as friends of the court. What is the procedure you want us to follow?"

Once you know how the court wishes to proceed, the volunteers can begin their work. Each court monitor should be provided with identifying badges. Monitors should show up at the proper time, properly attired, with pencil and clipboard for taking copious notes. A prepared checklist is recommended, as the hearings proceed at a rapid rate. Monitors should follow mandated procedures, observing mandates regarding no talking during sessions and such. Weekly reports, with no names included, are sent to the media.

There are several advantages to considering the court monitor program. First, families get a better shot at judicial justice while the organization(s) sponsoring the program gain more understanding of the judicial processes. This program provides an opportunity to observe which attorneys are working to protect their clients' rights and allows an insight into which HRS personnel, GALs, doctors, etc., are more vigorous in their prosecution of families.

In cases of child sexual abuse, the allegations sometimes result in criminal charges being filed, either by the accusing parent or through the agency doing the investigation and therapy, with the state attorney's office determining the extent and severity of the charges. One of the first problems in being faced with criminal charges of child sexual abuse is the fact that, again, the presumption of innocence doesn't seem to apply. The burden of proof almost immediately shifts to the accused, as opposed to the dictates of our judicial system and the premise of "innocent until proven guilty."

Indictment by a grand jury on criminal charges is accomplished by the prosecutor presenting his case. Only the prosecutor determines what evidence is to be presented and only the prosecutor is present, not the accused, nor his attorneys. Be aware that the prosecutor enters information at his discretion, especially when facing the grand jury in an attempt to get an indictment. In Spiegel's case, four certifications verifying the events of the weekend of alleged abuse were never shown to the grand jury. A letter from the physician, stating that his examination under no circumstances revealed any evidence of child abuse, was never presented. The psychological certification, provided by the doctor seeing Speigel's ex-wife for psychological counseling, was withheld. That certification stated that she had indicated to the psychologist that she had spent two days convincing her daughter to hate her daddy, that she had talked at length about her family's hatred of Larry Spiegel, and indicated that the ex-wife was capable of projecting her own emotional turmoil, doubt, and sexual pathology to her daughter.

In the Smith case in Ohio, the attending psychologist was available to testify at the hearing regarding temporary custody and visitation of Janice and Johnny. Since referral from the state social services agency, the psychologist had seen the children over a period of twenty months for purposes of ongoing counseling and monitoring the progress of the children. She had seen each child twenty-six times on a weekly basis. The judge in the case determined there would be no witnesses, other than a social worker and the agency appointed physician, both witnesses for Mrs. Smith. Worse, he ordered that the children be removed from Mr. Smith's home and live with Mrs. Smith until the trial, having only visitation with Mr. Smith. The children's psychologist expressed concern over the one-sided nature of the judge, stating it would seem more reasonable to hear from professionals on both sides regarding the children's well-being. The best interests of the children were not served by precluding Mr. Smith from presenting any of his witnesses or experts.

A civil court law suit may be filed to recover damages for the alleged victim, the child, *next friend*. In this day of lawsuits for almost any reason, a number of individuals are liable to end up in civil court, including doctors who do not report suspected abuse or exhibit malpractice, social workers who abruptly remove children from their homes (sometimes to foster care where actual physical or sexual abuse occurs), public officials for improper investigation, and the accuser on grounds of slander and libel. The accused may find himself facing a suit in civil court, seeking long-term damages for the emotional and psychological pain and suffering of the alleged victim, invasion of privacy, wrongful torts, etc. The alleged perpetrator may file a civil suit in state and/or federal court to reclaim damages resulting from the false allegation. And finally, once a father attains at least joint custody, should he notice that the child suffers emotionally and/or physically in the future, he can file a suit on behalf of the child. This is called a "next friend" lawsuit.

Any appeal of a trial judge's decision must be taken to the appellate court for further hearing and decision. This is also the avenue to pursue when appealing rulings in family court. One has thirty days to appeal a lower trial court order. This appeal involves filing a Notice to Appeal and having the party who is the appellee served with that notice. The appeals process is a slow, grinding procedure. The appeals courts are inundated with what are termed "trivial" appeals, coercing justices to skim by bona fide appeals rendering them injustices. Ninety-five percent of all domestic appeals heard by the appellate courts in Florida are ruled *Per Curiam* Affirmed (PCA), meaning that the appellate court has reaffirmed the lower court or trial court decision and the appellant loses. Moreover, the appellate courts usually do not even render an opinion with their PCA order. There is a threefold reason for this lack of opinion:

1) The appellate courts are inundated with cases and just don't have the time to devote to your appeal;
2) For reasons of politics and prestige, the higher court doesn't like to "muddy the waters" by overturning a lower court's decision;
3) If the appellate court does render an opinion along with their PCA order, it allows the appellant information that can be used to appeal that order to the state supreme court. A PCA, accompanied by no opinion, usually will not be heard by the higher court.

When an appellant appeals a trial court order, the appellant or his attorney must file an initial brief. The brief can be no longer than fifty pages and it must incorporate statements of the facts, arguments to be made, cited authorities, state statute codes, any errors made, and appellant's conclusions of law. Of course, the appellee can answer with an answer brief on the merits, or lack of same, of the appellant brief and the case.

Sometimes, it behooves an appellant to coax a nonprofit organization like the Children's Rights Council (CRC, 1-800-787-KIDS) to intervene and file an *Amicus Curiae,* friend of the court, brief, also. If one receives a PCA ruling from the appellate court, the next steps you may take include a Motion for Rehearing, a Rehearing *En Banc* (heard by entire panel of judges), or a Motion for Certification and Petition for *Writ of Certiorari* in trying to go to the Supreme Court. Sometimes at the appellate court level attorneys file *writs of mandamus,* or mandate, requesting the higher court to compel the lower court to reverse a previous order.

Federal court is the arena to which the falsely accused may turn when lodging complaints regarding a violation of one's civil and constitutional rights under color of state law. When one sues in federal court for injustices that occurred in the midst of a SAID syndrome case, one is alleging that he or she was denied "due process of law." One would be alleging that, in the context of the SAID syndrome case, the child protection team and/or the former wife did not act in good faith and/or that the child protection team acted *ultra vires,* beyond their reasonable authority, and/or that DSS was negligent or derelict of their duties as child protectors.

Forty-two U.S.C. 1983 is a very meaningful federal section being utilized by victims of SAID syndrome cases today. I sued my former wife and the HRS under this section, in combination with alleged deprivations of my Sixth and Fourteenth Amendment rights. The gist of 42 U.S.C. 1983 is that the plaintiff must show cause that the defendant(s) acted beyond their reasonable authority "under color of state law." Be aware that the federal courts, like the appellate courts, are inundated with a heavy caseload. Again, it's hurry up and wait and seems that justice may be denied, not just delayed. Federal rulings can be appealed to a higher federal court or even to the U.S. Supreme Court. One must be aware that the Abstention Doctrine, or *res judicata/collateral estoppel* arguments in a motion to dismiss by the defendant can disallow an equitable relief claim to be heard in federal court, if same has already been litigated in state family court . Also, the social services agencies will cling to the Eleventh Amendment in federal court, claiming that they have sovereign, absolute immunity. Finally, one must be cautious and diligent and seek and hire an attorney competent in that particular court arena (see Appendix C). In most states, the criminal and family courts have independent functions. Even after the alleged abuser is acquitted in criminal court, the accusing parent can file motions in family court to restrict or prevent visitation for the accused. The family court is obligated to decide in the best interest of the child, based upon its own hearings and/or trial. Victims of false accusations seldom realize that, in spite of their acquittal at other levels, the family court hearings are necessary before they have their parental rights reinstated, including the right to see their children.

Issues of custody or managing conservator and visitation are determined separately from issues of criminal guilt. Never attempt to predict what a family court judge will do, and never expect them to provide reasons or explanations concerning their orders. Bear in mind, the agencies and the courts need to cover their backs and make sure that they can justify their actions and their budgets. So what if they appear to lose the case in the criminal court? Because of the different requirements in family court, the accused may well be deemed guilty of abuse there and prevented from seeing his children. Thus, the agency is vindicated in the charges brought against the alleged perpetrator and in their demand for a court hearing regarding the child's welfare.

Bill Dodd, a Miami electrician, has been in and out of court for six years, trying to restore his visitation rights. In 1986, his ex-wife accused him of molesting his daughter. The police cleared Dodd of the charges, and he won a 350 thousand dollar slander judgment against his ex-wife. But a family court judge still cut off all contact between father and daughter, ruling there was a "probability of abuse."

In SAID syndrome cases, the majority of the battles will be fought in the family or juvenile court, in an effort to resolve the issues of custody and visitation. It is critical that you locate and retain an attorney well versed in these issues, knowledgeable about SAID cases, and familiar with the policies, politics, and procedures of family court (see Appendices C&D). An uninformed or incompetent attorney can cost you the right to see your children for years, perhaps forever. In one case study, the accused's attorney advised him to plea bargain, pleading no contest to a charge of physical abuse. The juvenile court used that plea to forbid the father any contact with his children, even thought the criminal charges had been dropped and his ex-wife had admitted to concocting the allegations.

In another case, an attorney who was inexperienced in the area of child sexual abuse allegations, recommended that his client accept a plea bargain offer that included admitting to sexual contact with his 3-year-old daughter in the interest of obtaining a deferred prosecution. If the client would admit to the allegation, he would receive two years probation and criminal charges would be dropped. However, this action would give the family court all the ammunition it needed to forbid him to ever see his kids again. Today the same accused would be *required* to register as a sex offender with the police for the rest of his life under Megan's Law.

In the Mark Doe case, an inexperienced attorney advised Mark that he had no alternative but to meet the ultimatum issued by his ex-wife's attorney in requiring him to admit his son to an institution. There are numerous instances where the rights of the accused are ignored. The Confrontation Clause is meant to aid in the truth-finding process and protect the right to cross-examine one's accusers. The Constitution requires that a person who has been accused by another has a right to confront his accuser in the flesh, and not through an alternate or substitute. In addressing the problems of an adult substituting for a child witness, a unanimous panel of the North Carolina Court of Appeals stated that where the witness is the principal accuser and the only person, except for the defendant, to have firsthand knowledge of the crime and related events, the appointment of an alternate might deprive the jury of crucial facts which only the witness knows and might reveal in cross-examination.

In 1988, the United States Supreme Court identified a two-part test for determining when the Confrontation Clause must yield to admissibility of hearsay statements. "The proponent (1) must show the necessity for using the hearsay declaration, i.e., the unavailability of the witness, and (2) must demonstrate the inherent trustworthiness of the declaration." Unavailability occurs when the prosecution has made a "good faith effort" to obtain a witness's presence at trial but has failed. While there may be a number of reasons for unavailability, such as the witness's refusal to testify, memory loss, or death of the witness, in the context of child abuse, several courts have held that a child declared incompetent to testify is unavailable with this ruling. This rationale raises one very important question: if a child is incompetent to testify (i.e., he lacks the prerequisites to be a witness), how can his hearsay statements be said to be trustworthy enough to satisfy the trustworthiness requirement of the ruling?

Because no one is in favor of child abuse and everyone wants to do their part for children, there has been a steady erosion of the accused's right to confront his accuser and a corresponding rise in the use of hearsay. There is an ongoing controversy surrounding the right of the accused to face his accuser and the potential emotional damage to a child witness. Justice Scalia explained the Confrontation Clause in the opinion, *Coy v. Iowa*, supra, 866, "It is always more difficult to tell a lie about a person 'to his face' than behind his back . . . That face-to-face presence may, unfortunately, upset the truthful rape victim or abused child; but by the same token, it may confound and undo the false accuser or reveal the child coached by a malevolent adult." Where analysis of the trustworthiness of hearsay statements is involved, two troubling questions arise: 1) How does a judicial finding of incompetency reflect on the child's hearsay statement? 2) When the statements are a result of some pseudo-scientific procedure, such as a child's play with so-called "anatomically correct" dolls, are those statements accurate and inherently trustworthy?

A young child is called to the stand and, after examination by both attorneys, is ruled incompetent by the judge, based on the child's lack of ability to communicate effectively and not understanding the difference between truth and falsehood. Is it right to then presume that the story the child related to a doctor or social worker six months ago is inherently trustworthy and satisfies the dictates of the Confrontation Clause? If the term "unavailability" is used to show the child's inability to appreciate the truth, it is difficult to credit anything the child has said earlier as inherently trustworthy. Does a statement made by an incompetent child witness become competent or trustworthy because an adult repeats that statement? The declarant's competency is a precondition to admission of his hearsay statements, as are other testimonial qualifications. Child competency and hearsay relevancy hearings are a necessity for an alleged perpetrator involved in a SAID case. These hearings can be made reality by the accused's attorney via motions, and will usually be heard by the juvenile court judge, for they are incorporated as dependency proceedings.

The purpose of a trial is to discover the truth. Unfortunately, it may instead become a crusade to get a conviction, manipulate the witnesses, and distort the facts for the good of the client. This is too often true of both the prosecutor and the defending attorney, who may feel they have to fight fire with fire. What seems to be lost in the shuffle of legal moves and strategies are the child, the defendant, their emotions, and mental health.

In an article in the *Denver Post* on 9 April 1989, James Selkin made the following statement, "The many people I have known who have been falsely accused of sexual abuse of a child have all agreed that the American justice system, for them, proved a sham. It did not result in the restoration of their reputation, their livelihood, or their good name."

Under the heading "search for truth," perhaps the truth to be recognized is that often a lawyer, whether prosecuting or defending, does not, in fact, want the court or jury to reach a sound, educated result or even guess, if it is not in the best interest of his particular client. Where, then, is the best interest of the child truly considered, protected, and defended?

13.

A Critical Review

In several of the case studies reviewed for this book, the individuals involved provided us with a number of evaluations and analyses that were done during the course of their attempts to regain at least visitation rights, if not custody rights, during and after the divorce. Many of the evaluations were done by objective, third party professionals, who documented the situations that had evolved during the divorce and subsequent custody battle. These evaluations, which included review of previous documentation, covered, not only the psychological conditions of all parties involved, but also the therapies applied, the interviewing techniques used, and the overall scope of events. While much of the information actually identifies problems and suggests solutions, it is important to see what qualified professionals have to say about the manner in which many alleged child sexual abuse situations are handled.

The issues raised and the points made in the following evaluations come from professionals in the fields of child development and child sexual abuse, professionals who are recognized nationally and, in some cases, internationally as experts in their fields. These evaluations serve to indicate the many problems existing in our current approach to resolving allegations of child sexual abuse and underscore the necessity of properly qualifying and training all social workers who deal with these allegations. They also sound a warning to anyone falsely accused, a warning to secure adequate counsel, to attempt to prohibit therapy and continuing interrogations, to seek expert, outside evaluations, and to constantly and consistently assert your innocence, maintain contact with your children, and be aware of the people, policies, and procedures against which you are fighting.

Dr. Ralph Underwager and Hollida Wakefield were asked to do objective, third-party evaluations of the doll interview with Diane Tong and the psychological evaluation done by the court appointed psychiatrist in the William Smith case. Presented below is the transcript from Diane's doll interview, including the actions of Diane and the interviewer, followed by excerpts from the Underwager and Wakefield evaluation of that interview. Diane was interviewed by a Child Protection Team coordinator and the interview was videotaped. As is usually the case, the interview took place in the child protection team offices, an environment unfamiliar to the child.

Interviewer: Can you remember what my name is? Why don't you sit over here so you can look at me better and look at the camera, too. [Interviewer changes positions with Diane] Okay, you sit right over here. Okay. There. Remember what my name is?

Diane: [nods]

Interviewer: Hmmm? What's my name? Hmmm? Do you remember? [Diane shrugs] Should I tell you again? My name is Susan. And what's your name?

Diane: Diane.

Interviewer: Diane? And how old are you?

Diane: Three and a half.

Interviewer: Three and a half. That's a big girl. And where do you live?

Diane: [no response]

Interviewer: Hmmm?

Diane: I don't live.

Interviewer: You don't live?

Diane: No. My daddy do.

Interviewer: Oh.

Diane: Dean do.

Interviewer: Oh, oh. Is that your daddy's name? What's your mommy's name?

Diane: Carla.

Interviewer: Oh, that's a pretty name. How about your brother? [Diane squirms, wiggles, and looks around, moving away] Diane, I want you to sit right here, okay. What's your brother's name?

Diane: Kit.

Interviewer: Okay, Diane, the reason why we're going to talk on the floor this time is so that you don't have to keep talking to people all the time, okay?

Diane: (Unintelligible)

Interviewer: Well, we're going to talk one more time about what happened this morning, and it's going to be on this camera so that other people can see it later, okay?

Diane: [nods]

Interviewer: And I'm going to bring these-the dolls-down here again, okay? We'll put them down here this time. Do you want to name the dolls?

Diane: Yeah.

Interviewer: Okay, what's this doll's name?

Diane: [Points to man doll] Dean Tong.

Interviewer: Uh, okay. And what's this doll's name?

Diane: Diane.

Interviewer: Diane, what a pretty name.

Diane: Diane Cook.

Interviewer: What's her last name?

Diane: Diane Cook.

Interviewer: Oh, okay. Okay. Now, Remember where we were when we talked about this before, what room that we were in?

Diane: [nods]

Interviewer: What room was, did that happen in?

Diane: [shrugs]

Interviewer: Hmmm? What were you getting ready to do?

Diane: [shrugs]

Interviewer: Was it daytime or nighttime?

Diane: The nighttime.

Interviewer: Nighttime. So what did Diane have on?

Diane: [points at doll] These on.

Interviewer: Okay. [picks up doll] Do you want to show me again. Okay, you can show me with the Diane doll what she had on. Was she sitting up, or was she laying down?

Diane: Laying down.

Interviewer: Okay. Want to lay her down?

Diane: [nods] [Interviewer helps arrange doll.]

Interviewer: Her arms move, you have to kind of press her legs down, that's right. Were her arms down?

Diane: [nods]

Interviewer: Okay. Now you show me what she had on.

Diane: [Removes the dolls shoes. Looks at interviewer and points to doll's stomach]

Interviewer: What, what with this?

Diane: With these.

Interviewer: Okay, you take them off. I'll hold her down so she doesn't move. Is that elastic kind of tight? I think if you go like this, boy, she's a big (garbled). There.

Diane: [points at doll]

Interviewer: Okay. This is Diane, and you have to, is she sleeping?

Diane: [nods]

Interviewer: Okay. Now, who is this again?

Diane: Dean Tong.

Interviewer: Okay. What did Dean Tong have on? Hmmm? What did he have on?

Diane: This.

Interviewer: Okay, and this is like-what do you call that?

Diane: A shirt.

Interviewer: A shirt. What do you call these?

Diane: Pants.

Interviewer: Okay. Do-what about these?

Diane: Shoes.

Interviewer: Shoes. And he had those on, okay. Why don't you show me then what happened.

Diane: There's a pee-pee and butt.

Interviewer: Oh, there is? Which one's her pee-pee? [Repositions doll]

Diane: [points]

Interviewer: That one? And where's, and where's the butt?

Diane: [points]

Interviewer: That one there, okay. Okay, you show me with the Dean doll what happened.

Diane: [takes Dean doll's hand, places it on the Diane doll's crotch] He put her, his, his finger in there. [Laughter and talking in background]

Interviewer: Okay. Anything else?

Diane: Put his finger in there.

Interviewer: Anything else?

Diane: And I started crying.

Interviewer: Oh no, 'cause that didn't feel good. Any other thing that happened?

Diane: Him used other fingers.

Interviewer: Used other fingers?

Diane: [nods]

Interviewer: Okay, you can show me again with other fingers. [Holds Dean doll] Okay. Like that. What about anything else?

Diane: I don't know.

Interviewer: Okay. Did any other parts touch the Diane doll? Touch Diane here?

Diane: [nods]

Interviewer: Okay. You can show me that. Okay, but any other parts that Dean touched Diane with. Can you show me . . .

Diane: [referring to male doll] What's in here?

Interviewer: Hmmm?

Diane: What's in here?

Interviewer: Well, did Dean have his pants zippered, or unzipped?

Diane: Zippered.

Interviewer: Okay, then we'll leave it like that. Okay. You can tell me anything else, is there anything else that the Dean doll did?

Diane: [shrugs]

Interviewer: Hmmm?

Diane: [shrugs]

Interviewer: You can show me.

Diane: [begins undressing doll] What's in there?

Interviewer: Hmmm? I don't know. What is in there? What's in there? What's that called?

Diane: I don't know.

Interviewer: You don't know.

Diane: [shakes head]

Interviewer: Have you ever seen that before?

Diane: No.

Interviewer: Okay, then we better close that back up, right? Okay. Can you get that? There, okay. Now, did Dean do anything else to Diane? [Touches girl doll's lower stomach] Anything else, touch her anywhere, bad touches? What?

Diane: [shrugs]

Interviewer: Hmmm?

Diane: [shrugs]

Interviewer: Any other parts of Dean? [Interviewer holds male doll's hand, then sits male doll up between her and Diane]

Diane: [shakes head]

Interviewer: Sure?

Diane: Uh uh [shakes head]. I got to put those back on.

Interviewer: Okay, okay, if you want to put those back on. Okay. Thank you, Diane. At this point, the interviewer stands and starts toward the camera. The camera is turned off, then back on.

Interviewer: [walks on-camera] Okay. Diane, one more thing, another thing I wanted to ask about is this morning, [picks up male doll] you talked to me about something else that Dean did to you. Do you remember any parts of the, any other parts of his body that he put on you? Hmmm?

Diane: [referring to doll] This is the pee-pee and this is the butt.

Interviewer: Right, okay. Do you remember this? This morning when you showed me that Dean put his mouth on Diane?

Diane: [nods] [There is more background noise of talking and laughter]

Interviewer: Can you show me that again?

Diane: [nods, takes dolls]

Interviewer: Let's lie her back down again like she was. [Interviewer positions doll] Okay. Okay.

Diane: [shows dolls]

Interviewer: What part of his body is that, Diane?

Diane: I don't know.

Interviewer: What, do you know what part of the body this is?

Diane: [nods]

Interviewer: What is it?

Diane: A mouth.

Interviewer: So is that the part of the body?

Diane: [nods]

Interviewer: Okay. Can you show it one more time?

Diane: [nods]

Interviewer: Okay. [Moves dolls closer to Diane] With the, with his mouth. Okay, you going to show me again?

Diane: [nods] [Moves male doll so face covers the crotch of the girl doll]

Interviewer: Okay. That's all?

Diane: [nods]

Interviewer: Okay, well you've been a real good girl, and you've helped me a lot. Okay?

Diane: [nods]

Interviewer: Okay, now you can dress the doll. Let me give you her clothes, Okay.

Diane: I can't do this.

Interviewer: Oh, okay, I can. I can help you.

Once again, the camera is turned off, then on. The interviewer is sitting beside her desk and identifies herself and her agency, as well as, Diane, the child's age, the location of the office, and the date and time.

The actual tape of the above interview was reviewed and analyzed by Dr. Ralph Underwager, Hollida Wakefield, and the research staff of the Institute for Psychological Therapies, recognized professional experts in the field of child sexual abuse and sexual offenders. The analysis showed that the interviewer was three times as active as the child, providing 76 percent of the total statements in the interview. Sixty-four percent of the interview, or almost two thirds of the adult actions, were comprised of leading questions, closed questions, modeling, pressure and/or reward type behavior or questions, paraphrasing of the child's statements by the interviewer, and use of anatomically correct dolls. All of these behaviors have been found to introduce error in the information elicited during such an interview.

The analysis stated that this was the thirty-seventh such analysis of interviews. The interviewer in the Tong analysis asked slightly fewer questions of the child, but used anatomically correct dolls twice as much as interviewers in previous studies. The child responded with more affirmations and provided more descriptive statements than children in previous studies. This is not alarming since the sheer volume of pointed instructions and questions used by the interviewer in conjunction with the use of the dolls may have served to keep the child focused on the task of responding at a very high rate.

The concluding paragraph of the letter that accompanied the analysis bears consideration. "In this particular case, it is clear that this is not the first interview of Diane. The interviewer reminds the child about when they talked about this before. When the dolls are brought out and the interviewer asks, 'What is this doll's name?' Diane immediately replies, 'Dean Tong.' Children, particularly those as young as Diane was in this interview, simply do not spontaneously use the dolls to signify actual people in their lives. Diane's readiness to label the dolls as her and Dean, and to demonstrate with the dolls, indicates that she has been taught to do this in an earlier interview. This earlier, undocumented interview was likely much more leading and suggestive even than this one."

This videotape was admitted as evidence and viewed by the family court judge, who subsequently determined that I should not be allowed visitation with my children. The obvious references to previous interviews were ignored. ("We're going to talk one more time;" "Remember where we were when we talked about this before?;" "Do you want to show me again?"). When questioning failed to elicit the desired response-exhibits of abuse-the interviewer left the area, and the camera was turned off for an undetermined period of time. When the interviewer returned, the first statement included, "This morning you talked to me about something else that Dean did to you." When there was no response from Diane, the interviewer asked, "Do you remember this morning when you showed me that Dean put his mouth on Diane?" After nine attempts to focus Diane, the interviewer succeeded in having Diane position the dolls to indicate the man doll touching the girl doll with his mouth.

The next two evaluations were done in connection with the Smith case. The first is a comprehensive evaluation of the myriad events involved in the case, done by Dr. Rice of Loyola University. The second evaluation, done by Underwager and Wakefield, applies to the conclusions of the agency-appointed psychologist, who is referred to as Dr. Nelson, presented as evidence in the Smith case. In preparing her evaluation, Dr. Rice used an extensive series of tests and interviews, in an attempt to determine an objective and positive resolution to the ongoing custody problems and their effects on the two children. Dr. Rice's evaluation included the following statements and information, "In a city prideful of its clinic health resources, with a child protection agency funded by federal and state tax dollars, the appalling mismanagement of this case of alleged sex abuse is worth a review to evaluate the competence of the so-called professional experts."

> 10/29/84 The teacher acted appropriately in reporting the allegations made by Mrs. Smith, which required investigation within twenty-four hours for the safety of the children.

11/2/84 It was three days later when Ms. L. interviewed Patricia and the children. If, as she stated in a letter to Mr. Smith, she suspected venereal disease or physical damage, why did she not take them immediately to a hospital emergency room, as is routine and mandatory? Why did she not state if she is a state licensed social worker or give her degree or use the official stationary of the county HSA? Why wait six days for a physical examination? This is highly incompetent professional behavior.

11/4/84 The memo from the M.D. is grossly medically deficient for a physical exam. Why were none of the following done, given the allegations of fellatio and rape: throat examination, throat culture, no mention of hymen, no culture or microscopic slide for vaginal irritation, no rape kit and procedure followed. The date of the alleged abuse was not noted. The stretching of rectal opening is a normal function of human beings for bowel movements. If anal intercourse was suspected, why no anal fissures and no cultures taken? If Johnny had a reddened throat and irritated penis, why were no cultures taken, nor photos taken for court?

11/9/84 The two-paragraph "report" by the psychologist is a professional disgrace. No description of the children is given, no quotations of what each child saw as a problem. "Sustained emotional disturbance" needs careful qualification, as it could be related to the setting, the way the interviewer behaved, the separation from home and their father. In December, this same psychologist gave Patricia an MMPI to complete at home. This is malpractice.

11/12/84 Audiotape with children made by CPT with leading and misleading interrogation.

11/16/84 William was having standard "tickle time" before putting children to bed. Patricia accused him of this being sexual abuse and hit him over the head with heel of shoe. Both children remember the incident. He called police.

12/3/84 William's son indicted for criminal sex abuse, arraigned, and released on fifty thousand dollars bail, with help from English relatives in raising money.

12/24/84 Patricia withdrew about ten thousand dollars cash from personal and business accounts, moved herself and the children into a state-supported battered women's shelter. There were no formal charges of battering made against husband. The shelter's criteria for eligibility and accountability should be examined, since this was more than an overnight emergency stay.

12/27/84 Patricia filed for divorce and custody.

01/4/85 Ms. L. of HHS alleged William sexually abused both children. No repeat medical report or psychological evaluation was done for children. Competence was again in question.

William filed counterclaims for divorce and child custody. Guardian *ad-Litem* appointed. William expressed concern for abduction as passports were missing. Why did guardian fail to respond?

1/12/85 Patricia moved into duplex.

1/20/85 Patricia approached William at concert box office about clothes, beds, and toys, which he took over to apartment. They dined and made love.

1/22/85 Patricia told him not to visit. William felt hopeless, despondent, and suicidal. He began to take pills, but stopped himself and called her. She called police to check on him. After police, Patricia invited William for dinner, and afterwards they made love. The next day Patricia tried to contact her stepson at his lodgings, but only talked to landlord's daughter.

1/23/85 Patricia called England and talked for forty-three minutes to her mother. Then told a local woman friend she was going to London via Toronto.

1/24/85 Patricia kidnapped Janice and Johnny to England, in spite of court custody and guardian-ad-litem. In London, filed for and was granted child custody by falsely alleging her stepson was found guilty of sex abuse in Ohio. Children became wards of court in Britain.

1/25/85 William called England when he found the duplex deserted. Grandmother lied about their presence in her home. William informed local police.

2/5/85 William received summons to be in England 3/4/85 for hearing. Tried to talk to his children in England, but was unable to do so because of interference from Patricia's family.

3/85 A lieutenant with the Ohio police wrote Patricia about leaving unlawfully with children and her availability for the local case against her stepson. She requested expenses for return be paid and police agreed. She tried to cash a two thousand dollar check, but check bounced. Wrote to friend with keys and parking ticket for Toronto airport, requesting her Honda be fetched.

3/6/85 Guardian-ad-Litem issued affidavit for return of Janice and Johnny to Ohio. Two full months of non-protective guardianship of the children entrusted to her makes it questionable whether this lady is competent or involved enough to deserve this trust.

3/12/85 William went to England, eventually managed to see children with police guard present. Reassured children and said he was trying to get them back home. Returned to U.S. via Toronto where, with police help, the keys and the card, he picked up the Honda.

3/12/85 Ohio Public Prosecutor heard from Patricia that she would not return. He dropped case against stepson as *Nolle Prosequi.*

4/1/85 William went to England, certain he could regain children who were feloniously kidnapped, only to learn British courts could disregard U.S. jurisdiction. Tried to get help from social services to see children and managed a one-hour supervised visit. Children could not leave England.

6/14/85 William asked children if they truly wanted to return to U.S. They flew to the U.S. and immediately reported to police.

6/19/85 The appointed social worker for case recommended counseling for children with Ross Agency.

9/85 Patricia returned to U.S.

9/16/85 Court ruled neither parent was to remove the children from that jurisdiction.

9/27/85 William took MMPI with J. M. and Patricia repeated previous MMPI with Ross. Visitation conflicts continued.

11/8/85 Court ordered William to pay five hundred twenty dollars a month child support to Patricia, despite the fact the children were living with him.

1/27/86 Patricia submitted an affidavit stating William is violent to children. Both children deny statement.

2/1/86 Dr. Nelson's highly biased interpretation of MMPI's showing blatant skew towards minimizing Patricia's pathology. Innuendos given about William with condemnatory, non-applicable opinions were added, as if Nelson were jury, judge, and prosecutor. Technically this is called negative counter-transference to William and positive to attractive young Patricia. Peer review recommended.

3/27/86 Children's psychologist protested to Ohio court authorities that hearings were improper. No response from courts or guardian *ad-Litem*. Custody established as twelve days mother, two days father.

6/25/86 Both children evaluated by Professor Alice Carl, Uni. of Ariz. Her opinion was that the children were not molested by their father, and she considered him a good candidate for custodial parent. She did not see Patricia.

11/3/86 In a clash with her mother, Janice yelled at her about making them lie. Patricia tried to smother Janice with one hand over her mouth and the other holding Janice's hands on her knee. When Janice asked her father what would happen if she died, he questioned her concern and learned of the above incident. He filed a police report, due to his concern for the safety of the two children if Patricia became desperate about the discovery of her perjury and brainwashing of the children.

11/8/86 Janice wrote a letter to police to give to judge so they could return to their father.

11/22/86 Children sent to Loyola Medical School for evaluation by Dr. Rice.

During the course of the evaluation, two hours of videotaped interviews were done, which are available to police, the DA, judge, and other officials and consultants. Dr. Rice points out that "the failure of inept agency mental health professionals" to be even aware that there was a possibility of false allegations is highlighted. Agency personnel behaved as if they subjectively believed (without corroboration or hard evidence, such as confession by the accused, genital injury, venereal disease, pregnancy, or pornographic materials) that, if an accusation is raised, the innocent but accused person must therefore be guilty. The finger of blame was arbitrarily taken as a verdict of guilty. The agency arrogantly preempted the justice system and, in so doing, abused their power and neglected their own task by being totally incompetent as primary data-gatherers.

Dr. Rice pointed out that the chronological outline makes a critique possible. Childcare workers must be trained to have equal suspicion of untruth as well as truth in child molestation allegation cases. They need training in child development and child pathology to learn that children can be tricked or trained to lie by adults-parents; professionals whom they wish to please or whom they fear-that children can be misled to believe non-truths or to say them. If they were to receive proper and adequate training, professionals then could be open-minded and objective enough to become true guardians and protectors of both the children's rights and the family.

Dr. Rice goes on to state the Smith case shows gross insensitivity by workers to both the children and the integrity of their family. There is no record of a family session with father, mother, and children together— why not? William's son was in jail, so this was not a case where perpetrator and child must be kept apart. The father was accused much later, and almost as an afterthought, by his wife. It seems clear the agency women were polarized pro-Patricia and anti-William, therefore antifamily and not in the best interests of the children. If these were well trained, child sex abuse professionals, they should immediately have been alert to the fact that false sex abuse allegations to obtain sole custody are epidemic in divorce cases as was mentioned by American Enterprise Institute legal scholar and attorney Douglas Besharov, former director of National Center on Child Abuse and Neglect, many years ago.

Instead of providing exploration, investigation, objectivity, and assistance to the children and family, these HSS workers became antagonists. In reading their documents, Dr. Rice found gross investigative incompetence and misuse of the power entrusted by well-meaning child-abuse laws. There is a question, requiring local investigation, as to whether Patricia was advised by agency personnel to "train" the children in the hotel about what to say about their stepbrother's alleged abuse in order to "make a case." The children stated repeatedly that he had not sexually molested them, that Patricia had told them to lie about it. Dr. Rice concluded, "Real molestation must not be missed. False allegations must not be supported."

In his evaluation of Dr. Nelson's conclusion, Dr. Underwager first notes out that it is less than ideal to review testing information without having the raw test data (answer sheets, profile sheets, Rorschach protocol, and scoring sheets). He states that this is the first case in which they've been involved where the attorney was unable to gain access to the case notes, MMPI scores, children's drawings, etc. Many of the issues raised in this evaluation paralleled concerns expressed by Dr. Rice, who recommended a peer review of Nelson's report. The evaluation further points out that Nelson's performance was in violation of Principle One of the Ethical Code and cites the following as not meeting acceptable standards for a psychologist to follow:

> (1) The MMPI's were sent home with Mr. & Mrs. Smith and his report did not so state. MMPI's are to be administered in a standardized or controlled environment, particularly in forensic situations.

> (2) Dr. Nelson interprets information from the diagnostic interviews with a bias toward interpreting observations about

Mr. Smith much more negatively. He appears to have concluded early on that Mrs. Smith's version of history and events was more factual than Mr. Smith's, but provides no support for this assumption. He states that Mr. Smith presented information "with a distinctly personal bias" and says nothing comparable about Mrs. Smith. He states Mr. Smith omitted, denied, or dismissed pertinent details, but makes no such comment about Mrs. Smith. He makes no mention of Mrs. Smith taking the children to England against court order, but refers to their return as Mr. Smith spiriting them away. He says she hasn't seen the children, but neglects to state the reason is that she chose not to abide by the court order that she visit them. He states that Mrs. Smith's negative description of Mr. Smith is born out by test data, but his description of her is not.

(3) Dr. Nelson misrepresents procedures and techniques that do not meet criteria for tests by describing them as tests and offering interpretations based on the non-tests. Animals and Three Wishes are not tests in any sense of the term as defined by the American Psychological Association (APA). There is no empirical evidence to support any of the interpretations of the children's drawings made by Dr. Nelson.

(4) Dr. Nelson's bias is evident in the interpretation of the MMPI's for Mr. & Mrs. Smith. Although we (Underwager and Wakefield) were not provided the test data, it is an over-interpretation, in referring to a within-normal-limits profile, to state that the individual has a "highly assertive and domineering style." In his testimony, Nelson states that Mr. Smith is willful, doesn't play the game right and that he suspects that the indications of the test scores lead him to believe that Mr. Smith's dominance characteristics have led him to be autocratic. The MMPI Supplementary Scale Manual states that the title "dominance" may be partially misleading, in that the scale reflects taking charge of one's own life more than bossiness. Dr. Nelson characterizes Mr. Smith as an inductive thinker, when in fact neither the MMPI nor the California Psychological Inventory (CPI) measure thinking styles. The CPI is not a measurement of pathology, but a measure of one's strength and sociability.

(5) The statements and conclusions about the children's anxiety are grossly overstated in terms of the data he presents. Again, we do not have the test data, but doubt his interpretations will be supported by that data. He reports the children said nothing indicating problems with their father, generally

answering questions with "I don't know." The use of drawings to form conclusions is totally inappropriate. On the basis of the drawings and his interpretation of them, he recommended the children be removed from their father's home and live with their mother.

(6) Dr. Nelson's recommendations are not supported by the data he reports. He states he could not evaluate interaction between Mrs. Smith and children because of recent separation, but depends upon what the agency therapist tells him about Mrs. Smith. However, he makes no attempt to communicate with the children's psychologist, who has been seeing the children regularly for over a year. He states that the children's interactions with Mr. Smith were positive and appropriate. He minimizes the fact that Mrs. Smith has not been seeing the children according to the court-ordered schedule and implies in an affidavit that Mr. Smith or someone has been denying Mrs. Smith access to the children.

(7) Dr. Nelson appears biased against Mr. Smith, inflating psychopathology on Mr. Smith's part, and minimizing or ignoring problems with Mrs. Smith. He acknowledges he doesn't like Mr. Smith, but denies letting this affect his judgment.

(8) Dr. Nelson did not attempt to contact the children's psychologist in order to gather information before forming an opinion. Further, he recommended the children receive treatment from the agency therapist, despite the fact they were, and had been, receiving therapy from a child psychologist. Later, without ever contacting their current psychologist, he recommended their therapy with her be terminated. Underwager believes this violates Principle 7, Professional Relationships.

Dr. Nelson states that the agency therapist is the only professional who really had an open relationship with the children, ignoring the fact that they had been consistently open with the child psychologist about their concerns and desires.

(9) Dr. Nelson misstates the ethical principles and standards in refusing to provide Mr. Smith's counsel with copies of raw test data. The APA provides that raw psychological data is released only with the written consent of the user or his or her legal representative. Mr. Smith's attorney certainly qualifies as his legal representative.

In the Mark Doe case in Texas, critiques were done by Underwager and Wakefield of reports issued by the psychologist and the therapist of the Texas CPS and by a mental health counselor at the mental health clinic in which Bill was placed. The following issues were raised in that evaluation.

The Interview:

The videotaped interview with Bill did not meet accepted standards of how such interviews should be conducted. The questions were leading and the interviewer coercive. It was clear that Bill had previously been exposed to the dolls and to similar questions. In spite of the rehearsal, his responses were confusing and not credible. Over 62 percent of the interviewer behaviors fell into potentially error-inducing categories such as closed questions, pressure, rewarding/reinforcing responses, modeling, use of aids, and paraphrasing. There was no recognition given to the acrimonious custody battle in progress. In addition, there was no recognition of the fact that Bill was not toilet-trained, and his father cleaned his genitals whenever he had an accident.

The Therapist:

No case notes were kept-this is contrary to accepted standards of care and practice. There was over-interpretation of observed behaviors in the absence of empirical support and premature conclusions of alleged abuse. This therapist provides a purely speculative and subjective opinion that depends entirely on her perceptions, biases, and observational skills, with no research reports or child development literature to support her assertions. Using play behavior to support perceptions and conclusions is not acceptable. When adults invite children to engage in play, they invite them to engage in fantasy and pretend behaviors. Research indicates that children who are involved in divorce/custody battles often exhibit behavior problems, but this is not even considered in determining Bill's behavioral problems.

The Psychologist:

There were questions about the competency and training of this psychologist in providing psychological services of the nature she did for the Doe family. Her transcript did not indicate any clinical experience, did not correspond to any APA approved programs for applied specialties, did not show any clerkships or internships or supervised training in any applied activity. It appeared to the evaluator that the total number of credit hours completed (seventy-five) was slightly more than half the credit hours required by APA approved programs.

By the time this psychologist saw Mark, she had already seen Bill several times and had concluded that Mark had sexually and physically abused him. With this conclusion, she interpreted Mark's tests as pathologically as possible. She concluded his "obsessive-compulsive tendencies, high defensiveness, and intense need to control ... his rigidly defensive posture does not adequately bind the underlying anxiety and trepidation of doing poorly." Nowhere is this supported by empirical data, nowhere does she indicate the tests were not all performed under supervision and nowhere does she give any allowance for the situation in which Mark Doe found himself at the time of testing.

The interpretations of the Rorschach were personal, subjective, and idiosyncratic interpretations. Examination of the actual responses yielded absolutely no evidence for interpreting his Rorschach as pathological, yet she saw "an undercurrent of anxiety, unrequited love, and cloaked sexuality . . . difficulty with relating appropriately to others . . . polymorphous perverse orientation to the environment . . . fantasies (that may include) homosexual, bisexual, and exhibitionist feelings . . . hostility toward women."

It appears likely that, from other evidence, she had already made up her mind that Bill was abused by Mark, and his behavior was interpreted in terms of this. It should be noted that a premature and swift closure by a mental health professional on an opinion that abuse occurred is recognized as one of the hallmarks of a false allegation (Klajner-Diamon, Wehrspann & Steinhauer, 1987; Wakefield & Underwager, 1988). While the psychologist recognized the stress of the acrimonious divorce as causing problems for Norman, she concluded that Bill's problems were due to his being sexually and physically abused, most likely by his father.

On her recommendation, Bill was hospitalized in an institution designed to treat disturbed adolescent or prepubescent children. He was the youngest there and was exposed to children and therapies more advanced than his age. Hospital notes suggest that the statements about abuse by his father were encouraged and reinforced in the hospital.

The Mental Health Institution:

The diagnosis, after three months of observation and treatment, does not meet the diagnostic criteria of DSM-III-R. Bill was not toilet-trained at the age of three years, yet was diagnosed as having encopresis (which cannot be diagnosed before age four) and enuresis (which cannot be diagnosed prior to age five). However, because of the diagnosis, an inordinate amount of attention was given to soiling and wetting. This attention (a reward) reinforced the possibility of repeated instances. It appears that, once the decision was made that Bill was abused by his father, the observations, interpretations, and diagnoses were made with the goal of supporting that conclusion.

Studies by Underwager and Wakefield indicate that when a non-abused child is treated by adults as if the child had been abused, and adult pressure and influence is used to produce statements from a child about events that did not happen, this is an assault upon the child's ability to distinguish reality from unreality. Throughout the videotaped interview done with Bill, the interviewer had to repeatedly ask questions to get the desired responses. When desired responses were finally attained, and the interviewer tried to confirm them, Bill responded with "I don't know." Using the anatomical dolls, the interviewer routinely touched or pointed to the "private parts" of the doll when asking where daddy had touched Bill. At the end of the interview, when asked if he told the truth or a lie, Bill said, "A lie." He repeated this assertion three times.

14.

Fighting Back False Accusations of Child Abuse

Well-meaning, well-intentioned child abuse reporting laws have ignited a backlash within our child protection system, and society. Only during the last three decades has child abuse been recognized as a serious national problem, and, with that recognition came federal funding, new legislation, and greater public awareness, including enhanced media attention. In 1973, the US Congress passed what came to be known as the Child Abuse Prevention and Treatment Act, or The Mondale Act, which established the National Center on Child Abuse and Neglect (NCCAN), and authorized at least twenty million dollars per year for research, professional conferences, training, and demonstration programs. Laws regulating the reporting and investigation of suspected child abuse cases were enacted, making it mandatory for certain professionals to report any reasonable suspicions of abuse. Failure to report brought stiff penalties, including criminal sanctions, against those who did not do so. These same professionals, nurses, doctors, youth care workers, police officers, et al, were granted immunity upon reporting, so long as their reports were made in good faith. This boon in reported cases of alleged child abuse and neglect took on a life of its own. Toll-free reporting child abuse hotlines became open invitations to malicious slander. According to a published report from the National Child Abuse and Neglect Data System in *Child Maltreatment 1998*, out of two million investigated reports of alleged child abuse and neglect, 57.2 percent of all cases were closed as *unsubstantiated*.

What was meant by giving protection to people who might be afraid of reporting abuse, has become a means to perpetuate multimillion dollar grants, support federal foster care facilities, gain custody of children in divorce suits, seek revenge, treat children for abuses that never happened, and decimate families. Meanwhile, many cases of actual child neglect, physical abuse, and even sexual abuse are not being reported or properly investigated, because they're buried under the deluge of unfounded reports.

In America, child protection is governed by an *in loco parentis*, or the state is the parent, mindset. This *It Takes A Village* ideology has put children, homeschoolers, teachers, and families, at risk. According to Dr. C. Henry Kempe, author of *The Battered Child*, children are state property. Kempe pushed for home health visitors for families to identify preschool children in jeopardy. According to him, natural parents were more dangerous to their children than strangers despite national statistics that state the opposite. It wasn't surprising that Hillary Clinton gave kudos to Kempe in her book, and former President Clinton reauthorized the Mondale Act in 1996, in Public Law 104-235. Considering the ideology of our child protection system that children are never mistaken regarding abuse disclosures and must be protected at *all* costs, it's no wonder that today's families must be forewarned as well as forearmed.

There are more reasons for today's accused innocents to fight back unfounded allegations of child abuse and clear their names than ever before. The Adoption and SAFE Families Act of 1997 (ASFA), Public Law 105-89, signed into law by former President Clinton, moves children out of foster homes into permanent homes more quickly. Those parents whose children are adjudicated dependent (i.e., abused, neglected, or abandoned) in juvenile (dependency) family court have one year to substantially comply with a governmental case plan if their family is to be reunified. If substantial compliance is not met at the time of the second six-month judicial review hearing, the children can be placed for adoption. Child Protective Services' "reasonable efforts" attempts at family preservation are deemed moot if chronic abuse, sexual abuse, assault, or other aggravating factors were reasons for adjudication. Moreover, CPS can use a parents' past (criminal conviction or adjudication of dependency) against him or her in the future, what is now termed prospective or future abuse or neglect. Megan's Law, coined after a young girl, Megan Kanka, was ruthlessly raped and killed in New Jersey, is another obstacle to those wrongly convicted of sexual child abuse. He who pleads *nolo contendre* or no contest, or is convicted, in an alleged criminal child sexual abuse case, must register with the local authorities as a sexual predator. If innocent, that stigma alone can be enough to cause one to attempt suicide.

Given the zeal with which child abuse cases are prosecuted in juvenile, family, and criminal courts in America, it is incumbent upon the accused to land a swift and aggressive counter attack. Once accused, now is not the time to vacillate, skimp on your resources, or do something foolish. Now is the time to possess a clear mind, reconstruct events in your mind as you recall them in the form of a timeline, a written dated chronology, and retain an experienced, informed trial attorney (see Appendices C&D). Depending upon which courts you're fighting accusations in, e.g., you could be litigating in the three-ring circus (juvenile,

family, and criminal court), dictates your eventual selection o.
It may be necessary to retain more than one lawyer because o.
titude of court fronts you're fighting. You would be best serveq
one very experienced lawyer who can handle the dependency, cus
and/or felony court cases, or in the alternative, retain a local well .
spected attorney along with an expert attorney from out of state, *pro ha.*
vice.

Since the accused and his or her attorney are the last to be, or are
never privy to, details of alleged child abuse charges, it's necessary one
knows how to obtain copies of documents germane to your case. A
simple "Request for Production of Documents" can be filed with both the
CPS Department and Court. If that fails, counsel is advised to file a
Motion to Compel Production of Documents with the court. And, if that
fails, counsel can request an *In Camera* review by the court of the sought
after documents citing the case of *Pennsylvania v. Ritchie*, 107 S. Ct. 989,
480 U.S. 39 (1987). In criminal cases of alleged sexual child abuse, whereby
the accused has been arrested for probable cause only, but not yet formally charged, it may be difficult, if not impossible, to obtain a video or
audio of the child's intake interview.

Most states' child protection teams include Child Advocacy Centers
(CAC) that are responsible for interviewing alleged child victims of sexual
abuse. These CACs are child friendly, designed to accommodate children who are suspected of being victimized and traumatized. At first
blush, CACs do not appear to be objective assessment centers, whereby
a child is an *alleged victim* of sexual abuse by an *alleged perpetrator*. Typically, CAC team workers will interview alleged child victims of sexual
abuse via anatomically detailed dolls, puppets, drawings, or using other
aids. Typically, CAC team workers err in false accusations cases because
of confirmatory bias mindset, whereby they have a preconceived notion
that abuse already happened. Their substandard interview methods and
protocols induce source misattributions errors, whereby they misattributed
children's benign stories with actual pathology or targeted the wrong
alleged perpetrator, perhaps because they didn't conduct collateral interviews. It's incumbent upon your attorney to know that not all interviews
of alleged child sex abuse victims are done by the book. Young children
are very suggestible and impressionable. They can be easily influenced
and led to give incorrect answers. While their responses may appear on
the surface to be credible, many times they're inaccurate. CPS, CAC,
and police detectives are not supposed to incorporate leading and suggestive questions into their child interviews. But they do. The same are not
supposed to use reinforced behavior, e.g., good girl, but they do. They're
not supposed to use closed-ended questions (yes-no), but open-ended
questions, asking for free narrative, spontaneous replies, but they do.
They're not supposed to use anatomically detailed dolls or other play

therapies for diagnostic purposes, unless the child is pre-verbal, but they do. They're not supposed to use scripting, whereby repetitive interviews foster desired responses, but they do. They're not supposed to taint an interview by bad-mouthing the accused in front of the child, using stereotype induction, or what I refer to as "accused alienation syndrome," but they do. They're not supposed to use guided imagery, a technique that is potentially suggestive as it goads children to pretend imagined events, but they do. Clearly, interviewer response and confirmatory bias, coupled with suggestive interviewing techniques promote source misattributions and source monitoring errors among young children.

In 1998, Psychologists Sternberg, Lamb, Esplin, et al., published a study at the National Institute of Child Health and Human Development that attempted to improve the interviewing skills of social workers in alleged child sex abuse cases. Termed a "Structured Protocol to Improve the Quality of Investigative Interviews," Esplin, et al, recommended Statement Validity Analysis and other free recall prompting methods to extract better information from the mouths of babes, leading to better case resolutions.

I recommend that all electronically recorded child interviews, audio or video or transcripts, be sent for forensic analysis. In other words, all documented child interviews should be analyzed for the presence or absence of open-ended versus closed-ended questions, specific versus forced-response questions, leading and suggestive questions, reinforced behavior, use of dolls, props, or other aids, etc. A leading research firm that analyzes child interviews and generates raw data and reports from the same is the Institute for Psychological Therapies in Northfield, Minnesota at 507-645-8881. In rare situations where CPS made tapes are thought to be electronically altered or doctored, Joel Charles out of Coral Springs, Florida at 954-752-5465, is a tape analysis expert, and has testified for the defense in many high profile state and federal court cases.

There is a growing corpus of empirical research suggesting that alleged child sex interviews be conducted by Content Based Criterion Analysis-Statement Validity Analysis (CBCA-SVA) (Steller and Kohnken, 1989), and not the Garven, et al., Suggestiveness, Influence, Reinforcement, Removal (SIRR) from direct experience model. The aforementioned CBCA-SVA model interview assumes that an account based on memory of an actual event differs in content and quality from accounts that are based on fabricated, learned, or suggested memory. The procedure requires a complete statement obtained as soon after a child has disclosed an incident. The interview must contain statements of the child's free volition. The interview is taped and later transcribed for scientific analysis. The CBCA-SVA model interview targets five constituent groups: general characteristics, specific contents, peculiarities of content, motivation-related content, and offense-specific elements. Studies have shown that older children, twelve to fourteen, produce more specific content than younger children using open-ended questions and requesting free dialogue. Younger children do provide accurate information even to closed-ended and specific, but non-leading, questions.

According to the published manual of the National Center for the Prosecution of Child Abuse, "During the interview process, the interviewer must remain open-minded and try not to be influenced by any preconceived ideas . . . As an interviewer you must remain open, neutral, and objective, and beware of any reactions which could be interpreted as reinforcing certain responses . . . Avoid leading questions . . . Never threaten or try to force a reluctant child to talk or continue an interview."

The following guidelines are suggested for interviewers:

- Interviewers should decide at the planning stage how they will approach the interview and tailor it to the individual child. In other words, what types of questions will be asked; what prompts, and what verbal affirmations will be used?
- The rapport stage needs to be carefully considered and implemented;
- Interviewers should continue to use as few leading questions as possible;
- Interviewers should increase their use of open-ended questions, particularly with older children;
- Interviewers should feel comfortable using specific yet non-leading questions with younger children;
- Interviewers should pay careful attention to the child's age before they begin the process;
- Interviewers should be monitored, professionally speaking, concerning their interview practices.

As noted, the scientific research indicates that suggestive interviewing procedures can lead young children to give false reports of real-life experiences, including erroneous claims about interactions involving physical contact between an adult and a child. The same research shows that few young children would fabricate detailed claims of bizarre sexual abuse in response to one or two mildly leading questions; it usually takes more than a single false suggestion to get children to adopt false beliefs (Ceci & Bruck, 1995). In addition to children committing source misattributions errors, professionals in the child abuse field do so, too. Many social workers and therapists respond to allegations of child sexual play with a consistent-with-sexual-abuse mindset. It is normal for young children to play doctor and touch their private parts (Gagnon, 1985; Friedrich, et al., 1997). If the child's sexual curiosity is excessive, it may not be due to sexual abuse. It may be the result of increased anxiety due to the trauma of a separation loss of a parent. Hence, another possible source misattribution error. False accusations of physical child abuse can occur in cases of Osteogenesis Imperfecta (OI), a hereditary condition whereby bones break easily. Most often, child abuse is suspected when the explanation given by the child or parent does not match the injury found by the treating physician. I advise parents in suspected OI cases, cases of unexplained fractures, to consult with a geneticist and orthopedist, to counter the treating physician's findings.

Fighting back false accusations of child abuse requires urgency on part of the accused, resources, competent counsel, a clear strategy, experts, and stamina. The road to victory can be a long and winding one! Normally, it's an education process for the accused's lawyer because trying or litigating false cases is not taught in law school. Occasionally, an experienced lawyer in this genre of law will surface, but it's more the exception than the rule (see Appendix D). Your selection of counsel, the navigator of your ship, will be the most important decision you make in the entire legal process. More often than not, you will not get another bite at the apple, another chance with a new attorney.

Once the accused locates a good attorney, how does the same combat a potentially contaminated interview of an allegedly abused child? In State v. Michaels, 642 A. 2d 1372 (N.J. 1994), the New Jersey Supreme Court stated:

> If the defendant presents *some evidence* that the child's statements were the product of suggestive or coercive interview techniques, then the prosecution must demonstrate by clear and convincing evidence at a pretrial *taint hearing* that, considering the totality of the circumstances surrounding the interviews, the statements or testimony [of the child] retain a degree of reliability sufficient to outweigh the effects of the improper interview techniques. If the prosecution fails to satisfy this burden, then the court must exclude the child's testimony, as well as her prior statements alleging abuse.

Some courts outside New Jersey have occasionally followed the Michaels' decision in requiring taint hearings.

A child competency hearing is another vehicle in which to address an improperly conducted child protection interview. According to Piaget, most children are not deemed competent until age seven or eight, but studies show that children can distinguish reality from fantasy at age two. Thus, the court, itself, *in camera,* or an appointed child psychiatrist, usually makes a finding of whether a child can distinguish between right and wrong, truth and falsehood, good touches and bad touches. This is called competency, and if a child is deemed to be incompetent, his or her testimony is deemed to be inadmissible in court. A motion *in limine* is an effective legal tool used to limit or totally exclude fresh complaint evidence, or evidence adduced via the product of carelessness which doesn't meet applicable scientific standards; e.g., an overly suggestive interview of a three year old, allegedly sexually abused. A hearsay relevancy hearing is a useful defense tactic in determining at pretrial, which out-of-court statements repeated by allegedly abused children to social workers and therapists, are admissible. Offered for the truth of the matter asserted, hearsay is admissible, to some extent, in both juvenile and criminal court proceedings.

There are exceptions to the hearsay rules, which defense lawyers must capitalize on in these types of cases; e.g., Florida statute 90.803 (23), the twenty-third exception to the hearsay rule allows a defendant to challenge the inherent trustworthiness of the child's statements and how these were obtained. According to the landmark case of *Idaho v. Wright*, 497 U.S. 805, 110 S.Ct. 3139, 111 L.Ed. 2d 638 (1990), in criminal cases, a child's statements must bear an *indicia of reliability* and be devoid of contamination before they're admissible as hearsay via a third party. The supreme court of Florida held in *State of Florida v. Townsend*, 635 So. 2d 949 (Fla. 1994), that the competency of a child is a factor that should be considered in determining the trustworthiness, reliability, and thus the admissibility of hearsay statements.

Do everything possible to prevent any further therapy or interviewing that may enforce the child's confusion or belief regarding the abuse allegations. Too often, these activities serve as a teaching tool where modeling, suggestion, and repetition result in a young child *learning* to act the part of victim. Although you or your lawyers are not allowed to be present at the initial CPS interview with the child, the attorney can file a Motion to Suppress Therapies. An alert attorney can prevent conditioning of a child by a zealous Child Protective Investigator (CPI) acting as therapist or vindictive parent by filing responsive pleadings in court.

Psychologist's Julia Hickman and Cecil Reynolds in their abstract *The Effects of False Accusations Upon Children and Families*, state that "false allegations have a variety of effects on children that are detrimental to their development." According to Hickman and Reynolds there are six sources of trauma to a child victim of false accusations:

- The investigative procedures, especially repetitive interviews, are troubling;
- The behavior of the accusing parent may induce trauma in the child;
- The refusal of a delusional accuser who projects her or his own pathology on to a child to recognize and address the same;

- Deprivation of accused parent-child contact past 72 hours is traumatizing;
- Constant high conflict parental litigation, intimidating PAS;
- Treating an alleged child victim prior to an actual finding of abuse may develop a victim mentality and traumatize a child.

I've stressed the importance of children's suggestibility because it is such an important topic when addressing the validity, or lack of sexual child abuse accusations. We know more than we did fifteen years ago. We know it is controversial. We know there is a dearth of knowledge. Obviously, it behooves an accused parent and defense attorney to employ a suggestibility expert in cases of alleged child molestation, where the alleged child victims are twelve to fourteen years or under. Such an expert would be a Ph.D. psychologist with a concentration in cognitive developmental psychology and scores of publications referenced in his or her Curriculum Vitae (CV). I'd recommend Maggie Bruck, Ph.D., Phil Esplin, Ed.D., and John Yuille, Ph.D., as potential forensic experts who are nationally known for their work in children's suggestibility.

The use of mental health experts is a necessary evil when defending unfounded child abuse accusations. As a defendant, you could be embroiled in a combined Sexual Allegations In Divorce-Parental Alienation Syndrome case, requiring you to retain several different mental health experts; e.g. one expert would be knowledgeable in the area of children's suggestibilities and the SAID syndrome, another needed expert would be a psychosexual assessor for the accused, and yet a third required expert would be a Ph.D. custody evaluator knowledgeable in the area of parental alienation. Your experts should possess sterling credentials, and above all, be objective. Thus, it is wise to retain those practitioners who have handled cases for the prosecution as well as the defense. You want your experts to be unimpeachable, to render opinions to a reasonable degree of psychological certainty.

Know your enemy! Your attorney or your attorney's investigator should obtain college transcripts and background information on all of the experts on the other side. That includes the medical doctor, nurse practitioner, psychologist, social worker, guardian-*ad-Litem*, therapist, etc. You may be surprised what you find! Many *experts* are contracted out by state agencies to *validate that child abuse occurred*. Always demand the raw data of psychological tests as well as the written reports. Have your own expert examine these findings. The psychologist for the state may have over-interpreted or misinterpreted the data, and your expert might be able to proffer an affidavit and act as a rebuttal witness.

It's vital that your attorney and experts are on the same page. There must be chemistry between them. The attorney should educate the experts about the law, cross-examination, and determine the significance of testimonies at Frye-Daubert hearings (see Appendix F). The experts should educate your attorney with respect to science and psychology consistent with abuse accusations, and provide to the court their publications that could be admissible under Learned Treatise or via the court taking judicial notice. Obviously, if the experts are *court appointed*, neither the accuser nor accused can prepare, or educate, them beforehand. This writer does not advocate that the accused settle for court appointed experts!

If you are forced to accept evaluations by a court appointed psychologist, ask the following questions: Is your lawyer provided with a copy of the experts CV? Where will the evaluation take place? What tests will be administered? Are the test results affected by any medications you may be taking? Will the accuser be evaluated by the same expert? Will the alleged child victim be evaluated, and, if so, by whom? If a custody evaluation, and abuse allegations have been deemed unfounded, will you be interviewed by the expert in the presence of your children? When can you expect a copy of the report that is furnished to the court?

I will dedicate this next section of the chapter to affording the accused and his, or her attorney, practical advise in countering false child abuse accusations. Don't be a victim of *angry man syndrome*. The most important weapons you have at your disposal for fighting back are your attitude and your presence. You can be your biggest asset, or your worst detriment. It is critical to project a positive attitude and demeanor, especially in front of social workers, therapists, guardians-*ad-Litem*, and judges. Coming across to governmental officials who would like nothing more than to keep your children from you, as an abrasive person, is legal suicide. Your innocence, or guilt, could be dictated by how you are perceived by these same governmental officials. An angry man is seen by them as being unable to control his actions, and probably capable of unacceptable behavior. While it is *normal* to feel frustrated and upset with the workings of our legal system, do *not* display these feelings in court.

It is imperative that you develop the ability to control your emotions and project a picture of calm, caring, cooperative interest. Cooperate with the social workers and child protection team workers, while recognizing that their goal is to build a case against you. Displays of bad temper, impatience, or anger, will inevitably place you in a poor light and cause negative comparisons of you with the custodial parent. Be congenial, but firm! Be courteous in dealing with prosecutors and judges. In formal settings, such as the courtroom, a professional appearance in slacks and a jacket and an attitude of cooperation and calm will do much to convince a judge that he or she is viewing an average, intelligent, *normal* individual, who respects the court.

In a nutshell, here are Tong's Tips:

* Recognize you're in for the fight of your life;
* Become familiar with the SAID and Parental Alienation Syndromes;
* Find the necessary resources;
* Retain *expert* legal counsel, and, if necessary, counsel *pro hac vice* *(Appendix C)*;
* Attempt to record all child interviews electronically;
* Attempt to suppress all child therapies until sex abuse has been confirmed;
* Retain independent mental health experts to assess child competency;
* File motions *in limine* to stop potential unscientific methods/evidence;
* Retain an independent forensic pediatrician to refute *consistent-with* findings;
* Consider the need for a consultant to help your attorney assess case strategy;
* Get all depositions typed up;
* Ensure your attorney has experience with *voir dire* of experts;
* Ensure your attorney has experience litigating Daubert-Frye hearings;
* Secure, at least, supervised visits with your child, at the soonest time possible;
* Hold social workers accountable by taking copious notes of interviews;
* If possible, electronically record CPS interviews;
* Do not incriminate yourself . . . if you talk to the enemy it will be used against you in court;
* Do not plea bargain, plead *nolo contendre*, no contest, accept an Alford plea, or *consent* to dependency in juvenile-family court;
* Do not retain any expert, including an attorney, without first perusing their CV;
* Do not be hoovered, or sucked back in, by a delusional accuser;
* Do not waive your constitutional rights, including the right to a speedy trial;
* Do not expect positive results during motion practice . . . be more concerned about the outcome of the war, the trial, not mini-battles;
* Realize that an unfounded finding by CPS could still mean guilt in the eyes of the court;
* Take the necessary tests to prove your innocence (see latter part of this chapter);
* Realize that your dilemma is most probably *not* the fault of your child;

• Do not give up! Your life and that of your child's depends upon you persevering.

Admitting scientifically relative information, such as books, periodicals, videotapes, etc., into evidence, is highly recommended in hotly contested child abuse cases. Called the *Learned Treatise* exception to the hearsay rule under the Federal Rules of Evidence, this is an excellent vehicle for educating judges who are not current on the scientific literature concerning children's suggestibility and memories and parental alienation. In a case of first impression, *Constantino v. Herzog*, 99-7476, the second U.S. Court of Appeals allowed the admissibility of videotapes saying they could be used just as printed material. According to FRE 803 (18), the court accepted a videotape as a learned treatise which was used to impeach the testimony of the plaintiff's expert witness. The court held that the distinction between written materials such as periodicals and videotapes was *overly artificial*. Typically, learned treatise materials are proffered into evidence to attempt to bolster the credibility of an expert's opinion on a case or issue. In matters of alleged child sex abuse, where young children make unsubstantiated claims after scores of contaminated interviews cause them to do so, Dr. Stephen Ceci's authoritative text *Jeopardy in the Courtroom* is an excellent defense reference for admissibility considerations under learned treatise.

Another legal avenue for attorneys to consider is requesting a court *take judicial notice* of scientific publications. Another vehicle used for the purpose of introducing information into evidence, judicial notice alerts the court the materials have met general scientific acceptance criteria. In some protracted child custody cases whereby litigants have filled ten boxes with legal case documents, it is wise to request the court take judicial notice of the case file alleging parental alienation.

Testing is a necessary evil in today's era of no touch rules and he said she said-type accusations. Today a person accused of child abuse could be fighting in juvenile, family, criminal, and administrative (where one's name could be placed on a blacklisted registry of suspected abusers) court, virtually, all at the same time. Because public defenders in criminal cases and court appointed lawyers in juvenile cases are so eager to *plead* their accused clients, and same plea bargains have direct and proximate far-reaching implications on familial relations, it's more important than ever to effect testing. Psychometric instruments and other tests are invaluable tools for assessing the validity, or lack of sexual and physical abuse child abuse accusations facing an accused individual. The rest of this chapter focuses on testing and proving one's innocence when accused of sexual or physical child abuse.

Of paramount concern is the selection of the assessor, the psychologist who will be administering the testing procedures. There are very few skilled psychologists who possess the necessary academic, laboratory, and computer skills to conduct proper forensic psychological and psychosexual assessments of accused individuals. Most assessors are nonobjective with a presumed guilty mindset already established. Attorneys and parents should seek psychological assessors who are affiliated with major universities, have lengthy CVs, and are current with technologically advanced and reliable testing modalities. Realize that your expert must be unimpeachable. If your assessor is, according to *United States v. Addison*, 498 F.2d 741, 744 (D.C.Cir. 1974) "Those most qualified to assess the general validity of a scientific method will have the determinative voice." In other words, your expert should be more credible than the psychologist for the state.

What tests should be administered to accused parents to prove their innocence? Unfortunately, since there are a multitude of tests that assess a wide array of psychological and psychosexual problems, and most lawyers are not trained in psychology, many falsely accused parents avail themselves to irrelevant testing procedures. For example, a divorcing father from Colorado accused of molesting his young daughter after a visitation, recently e-mailed me that he submitted to an MMPI-2, TAT, and Rorschach. Ironically, these three tests are widely used by psychologists to screen for alleged sexual deviancy. But, do they do so?

The Minnesota Multiphasic Personality Inventory (MMPI-2), Thematic Apperception Test (TAT), and Rorschach are commonly misused and misinterpreted. The MMPI-2 is an empirically based, self-reporting assessment of adult psychopathology consisting of approximately 570 true-false questions and covering areas such as defensiveness, depression, paranoia, anger, and low self esteem. Yet, the MMPI-2 contains no scales, clinical, validity, or otherwise, that determines whether or not an individual is a pedophile or sex offender. It's the most widely used psychological instrument, but is often over-interpreted and misinterpreted. The TAT assesses personality through projective technique focusing on dominant drives, emotions, sentiments, attitudes, and conflicts. The accused abuser is shown pictures and asked to make up stories from and about the same. The Rorschach is a projective instrument, too, whereby an accused abuser is shown inkblot cards and supposed to assess the same in timely fashion. Allegedly, one of the blots can determine sexual preference. Yet, there is considerable debate among researchers and clinicians whether projective testing (TAT and Rorschach) per se is scientific or ethical. In fact, astute attorneys should file motions *in limine* citing Frye v. United States, 54 U.S. App. D.C. 293 F. 1013 (1923) suggesting that projective tests do not meet the Frye rule meeting general acceptance criteria in the scientific community (see Appendix F).

An example of misuse of the MMPI-2 by a clinical psychologist follows. Mr. W was administered a full battery of psychosexual tests for allegedly molesting his teenage daughter. His current MMPI-2 results depict an elevated Pd scale, indicating a proclivity toward antisocial behavior. An earlier MMPI-2 administered by Dr. N revealed a similar elevation in the Pd scale, and in relation to alleged sexual abuse with his daughter Dr. N concluded "While there are no psychological tests that I know of that diagnose pedophilia, the protocol produced by Mr. W is consistent with those individuals who have significant impulse control difficulties." The point is, it's unprofessional to conclude a person may possess paraphiliac interests based upon an MMPI-2, without independent corroboration via more specific testing, such as the PPG and ABEL screen. After successful PPG and ABEL screen testing, Mr. W's *independent* psychologist wrote "Mr. W appears to be functioning in a sexual range consistent with that of a male adult with typical sexual response patterns. When all assessment strategies are taken together, it is my professional opinion that Mr. W does not appear to presently meet criteria for a sexual disorder or paraphilia."

There are several tests that an accused abuser can submit to within the confines of a controlled laboratory setting, which for the most part *are* generally accepted in the scientific community, or admissible dependent upon the state, forensically speaking (see Appendix F). Three tests that I champion and tap as excellent yardsticks in assessing one's propensity toward sexual deviancy are the penile plethysmograph (PPG), ABEL screen, and polygraph. In my opinion, and the opinion of several psychologists, if an accused sexual child abuser passes the PPG, ABEL screen, and polygraph, he is innocent.

The penile plethysmograph is a phallometric measurement which attempts to analyze and grade sexual arousal of alleged situational and fixated pedophiles by recording penile circumferential responses via a mercury strain gauge, data recorder, and computer during the presentation of sexual stimuli. The stimuli consist of video and audio depictions of nude male and female children and adults portraying a variety of normal and sexual activities. A complete penile erection is not necessary since it has been documented that smaller degrees of penile engorgement are more accurate and less under the voluntary control of the individual. It is incumbent upon the accused abuser and his attorney to ensure the psychologist uses the PPG for assessments, and not a tool to rule out erectile dysfunction, or for therapy.

Many psychologists who utilize the PPG are members of the Association for the Treatment of Sexual Abusers (ATSA). When used properly, the PPG is also an excellent measure of sexual arousal and preference. Dr. Eugenia Gullick states, The plethysmograph . . . directly measures the outside evidence of sexual arousal. We know, it's established throughout the literature, that when a man becomes sexually aroused, there is engorgement of the penis. It's a direct relationship. We know that when the penis becomes engorged, this indicates sexual arousal. So it's much more akin to a blood pressure measurement. She goes on to claim that, "The plethysmograph has been extensively studied and recently shown to be ninety-five percent accurate in discriminating between individuals who had committed sexual offenses against children and a control group that was randomly drawn from the population."

The PPG has been found to be 100 percent specific (Chaplin, et al., 1995) and 95 percent sensitive (Malcolm, et al., 1993). The PPG has been used in the correct diagnosis of sexual dysfunctions (Annon, 1975; LoPiccolo & Stock, 1986; LoPiccolo, Stewart, & Watkins, 1972). The majority of research on sexual arousal patterns with the PPG has been conducted with sexual offenders (O'Donahue & Plaud, 1994). Thus, many researchers agree that the penile plethysmograph is a reliable and valid means of assessing a male's sexual arousal patterns (Howes, 1995; Maletzky, 1995). It is well documented that there is a strong relationship between a man's pattern of sexual arousal and the probability that he may or will act upon that same arousal. It has also been shown that a lack of sexual arousal to sexually appropriate stimuli can contribute to sexually abusive behavior. Here, treatment of an accused abuser is necessary. Of course, the test cannot indicate whether an individual has or has not committed a specific sexual act with a child. Thus, it cannot predict actual guilt or innocence.

Courts have not formed a consensus on admissibility issues regarding the PPG. The PPG has met considerable confrontation regarding its admissibility in cases across the globe. The ultimate test, however, is the reliability of the theory or process underlying the expert's testimony . . . (*Commonwealth v. Kater*, 388 Mass. 519, 527, 447 N.E. 2d 1990 [1983]). In other words, defense attorneys should not rush to admit the PPG into evidence. They should qualify the tests admittance through the expert's opinion to a reasonable degree of psychological certainty. Since twenty-four of the fifty United States rely on the Daubert test to govern the admissibility of expert testimony and science in court (see Appendix F), the expert's opinion must "have a reliable basis in the knowledge and experience of his discipline." *Daubert v. Merrell Dow Pharmaceuticals*, 113 S.Ct. 2786, 125 L.Ed 2d 469 (1993), see Id. At 113 S.Ct. at 2796.

Most courts are uneducated about the proper role PPG data might play in legal proceedings. *United States v. Powers*, 59 F.3d 1460 (fourth Cir. 1995), looked at the issue of whether PPG results could diagnose or identify an alleged sex offender, rather than addressing reliability and validity issues regarding the capacity of the PPG to predict recidivism. See also *Berthiaume v. Caron*, 142 F.3d 12 (first Cir. 1998), and *Parker v. Dodgion*, 971 P. 2d. 496 (Utah 1998). The test has been widely used and well researched with between five hundred and one thousand studies performed since 1957. In 1995, Howe identified 168 federal, state, and private agencies using the penile plethysmograph.

Another screening test to help rule out an adult's sexual arousal of children and alleged tendency toward pedophilia is the ABEL screen. The ABEL screen, developed by Dr. Gene Abel, is a comprehensive, cognitive measure of sexual interest based on visual reaction time to slide depictions of adult males, adult females, adolescent males, adolescent females, young males, young females, very young males, and very young females. The technique requires no stimuli depicting nudity. The ABEL screen has two components, a computerized assessment of self-reported arousal to the aforementioned slide categories, and a questionnaire that asks about sexual thoughts, fantasies, and behavior. It tests adults for twenty-one paraphilias, cognitive distortions, dangerousness, and recidivism predictability. It is less intrusive (involves no measurement of erection) than the physiological method of phallometry showing excellent (98 percent) specificity and efficiency with prepubescent and pubescent boys. It's not as reliable with prepubescent and pubescent girls, yielding 77 percent specificity and efficiency ratings. This writer has been made privy to a few cases of alleged child sex abuse of twelve-year old girls that rendered false positive results via the ABEL screen. The statistical analyses have shown that guilty offenders are unable to trick the test and falsify results.

The legal system has been kinder to the ABEL screen than the penile plethysmograph. The ABEL screen, unlike the PPG, has been ruled admissible as evidence under the Daubert standard meeting the guidelines outlined in Federal Rule of Evidence 702 (see Appendix F). The recent acceptance of the ABEL screen occurred in Louisiana in federal court in a criminal case whereby a defendant denied sexual interest in underage females. The prosecution filed a motion *in limine* asking the court to exclude information from the ABEL screen because it was not, *inter alia* (among other things) scientifically reliable. However, the court ruled that the ABEL screen did meet Daubert standards and allowed expert testimony from a psychologist corroborating the same. The following countries and states use the ABEL screen within their criminal justice programs for treating sex offenders: The United States of America-Arizona, California, Illinois, Massachusetts, Minnesota, Ohio, Pennsylvania, and Texas; Canada uses the ABEL screen in this capacity. In addition, nearly three hundred therapists who manage sex offender cases use the ABEL screen in thirty-six states and Canada (see www.abelscreen.com on the Internet).

The polygraph is another indispensable tool for both the accused child abuser and attorney. Polygraph testing involves measuring physiological responses from a subject while the subject answers a series of eight to twelve questions. Typically, child abuse polygraphs hold to three or four questions and should be administered shortly after completion of the PPG and ABEL screen testing. Based on the theory of Psychophysiological Detection of Deception (PDD), truth or deception is measured in reactions to blood pressure, peripheral pulse-amplitude, breathing, and an electrodermal response. Most polygraph examiners use a Lafayette Analog instrument or Axciton Computer Polygraph System. The latter is a state-of-the-art digital polygraph system used by many federal and state law enforcement agencies. Zone Comparison Testing (ZCT) is a control question format developed and modified for use by military and federal polygraph examiners. The ZCT is used in the training of all federal examiners at the Department of Defense Polygraph Institute, the foremost polygraph research and training facility in the world. ZCT testing format is recognized as a valid and reliable testing format supported through field studies. Recorded test data should be evaluated via the three point scoring system used by law enforcement polygraph experts and Polyscore, an automated scoring system developed by the Applied Physics Laboratory.

As is necessary in choosing the most competent psychologist to administer sex abuse testing, an accused child abuser must choose the most highly trained polygraph examiner he or she can find. Remember: your lawyer is attempting to admit the polygraph results through the expert's opinion. Thus, it is incumbent upon the attorney to conduct a competent *voir dire* of the polygraph examiner in order to establish him or her as an expert. Your polygraph examiner should be FBI trained and be certified through the American College of Forensic Examiners (ACFE). ACFE polygraphers are *not* considered advocates, but seek only the truth conducting examinations, and report findings in an unbiased and objective manner. Dr. Charles Honts, a recognized expert in the field of polygraph science, recommends all polygraph examiners videotape record PDDs for prospective impeachment purposes in court. I do caution accused abusers against submitting to police issued polygraphs. They are not objective credibility assessments.

On occasion, in criminal cases involving child sex abuse allegations, parents may submit to a Computer Voice Stress Analysis (CVSA) test. The CVSA detects, measures, and graphically displays stress in the human voice from tape-recorded interviews. The police are attracted to the CVSA, but I caution accused abusers who submit to the test because they may become frustrated during police interrogative interviews. Any stress related frustration and resultant anger from an accused abuser can be harnessed by the CVSA.

Polygraph tests are accepted as valid science within the relevant scientific community of psychologists and psychophysiologists. The above statement is supported by several sources of evidence. Susan Amato and Dr. Charles Honts presented a paper: "What do psychophysiologists think about polygraph tests?" The paper was accepted by the Society for

Psychophysiological Research (SPR) for publication in 1994. The SPR is a professional society of scientists (Ph.D. and M.D.) who study how the mind and body interact. In Amato's Masters Thesis at the University of North Dakota a survey was extended to members of the SPR. Roughly two thirds of the SPR professionals felt that polygraph tests were a valuable diagnostic tool when compared with other available information or that they were sufficiently reliable to be the sole determinants. Another more important indicator of the acceptance of polygraph testing in the scientific community is elucidated in the large number of original scientific studies published in peer reviewed scientific journals such as: *The Journal of Applied Psychology, The Journal of General Psychology, The Journal of Police Science and Administration, Psychological Bulletin,* and *Law and Human Behavior,* to name but a few. Hence, polygraphs do meet the criteria under the FRYE test for acceptance in forensic settings.

As I alluded to earlier, an accused abuser litigating a case *Pro Se* (representing himself or herself), or attorney, should not attempt to hasten a polygraph result of *No Deception Indicated,* into evidence. A clean PDD result should be used in concert with clean PPG and ABEL screen results as negotiating tools to stipulate with adverse counsel, CPS, and the GAL, first. If negotiation and stipulation fails, then defense counsel can file a Motion for Daubert or Frye Hearing with the court and litigate the matter, attempting to admit the test results through the experts' opinions.

The Multiphasic Sex Inventory, or the Molinder, is a self-report questionnaire that consists of statements about sexual activities, experiences, and problems. It is a widely used instrument that assesses an accused abuser's sexual proclivities. Another sexual questionnaire graphic in nature is the Derogatis Sexual Functioning Inventory (DSFI). The Derogatis poses questions relative to one's sexual functioning, activities, behaviors, problems, fantasies, self esteem, et al. Lastly, the Sexual Violence Risk-20 (SVR-20) is a twenty-item checklist of risk factors for prospective sexual violence. The actual risk for sexual violence depends on the combination of risk factors present in a given case. The SVR-20 is predicated upon research performed on known sex offenders. It can be a valuable tool to help predict potential sexual violence in both criminal and civil forensic settings.

One measure that requires PPG assessment and predicts sexual abuse recidivism is known as the Sexual Offender Risk Appraisal Guide (SORAG). The SORAG is based on known sex offender populations. SORAG applies to those individuals who have a prior child sex conviction, have been accused again, and are steadfastly holding to their innocence. In this context, the SORAG would be a useful determinant of prospective sex offense recidivism probability. The Violence Risk Appraisal Guide (VRAG) is another actuarial measure that is used to predict male sexual aggression or violence based on one's criminal past. I will delve deeper into the applicability of VRAG in the next chapter.

In today's *parens patriae* society where the government can intervene in the life of your family on the basis of an anonymous phone call, spanking can be easily misconstrued to be physical abuse, requiring testing of an accused abuser. Several written instruments such as the Child Abuse Potential Inventory (CAPI), Adult Adolescent Parenting Inventory (AAPI), and Parenting Stress Index (PSI) are valuable in assessing one's propensity to commit physical child abuse in high stress situations. It is advisable when administering the CAPI Form VI to use the latest version from Psytec which includes a CAPScore computer scoring module.

Fighting back false allegations of child abuse is an expensive, but necessary challenge. Succumbing to an attorney's plea bargain can land you on the local child abuse registry, or worse, in a police database of known sex offenders and on the Internet. I advise all innocent accuseds and their lawyers to consider my two-prong approach: first, prove your innocence by submitting to psychological or psychosexual testing, and second, impeach the credibility of your false accusers. If accused of sexual or physical child abuse and innocent, tests such as the MMPI-2, Penile Plethysmograph, ABEL screen, Polygraph, Derogatis, and Child Abuse Potential Inventory, can bear fruit upon the outcome of your case. Competent defense attorney investigation and interrogation of the background of children's disclosures and *professionals* who reinforce same disclosures are crucial in impugning source misattribution errors. These cases are black or white. Abuse happened or it didn't. If you or your lawyer allows a case to remain in the gray area the court will rule on the side of caution, on the side of the child. If you are fortunate enough to survive a false child abuse accusation, clear your name, and obtain the equitable relief you are seeking, attempt to change public policy. In a 31 January 2001, *National Post* story by Donna Laframboise, Mr. A not only received custody of his 7-year-old daughter after being falsely accused of molesting her, but also the judge ordered an independent review of Winnipeg's Child and Family Services. Now, Manitoba must ensure a team of specially trained social workers investigates child abuse allegations. Moreover, investigators are *required* to interview an accused child abuser.

15.

Fighting Back False Accusations of Domestic Violence

Did you know that a woman is beaten every twelve seconds nationwide (FBI)? Did you know that one out of four women in the United States will be assaulted by a domestic partner in her lifetime? Male children exposed to domestic violence have a 700 percent greater chance of beating their female partners later in life (March of Dimes). It is against the law to hit or abuse another person. Malcontents who perpetrate abuses against children, women, and men should be prosecuted to the fullest extent allowed by law. In 1994, former President Clinton signed Violence Against Women's Act (VAWA) into law as part of the National Crime Act. In doing so, he laid the foundation for the creation of a new industry, the false domestic violence injunction revolution. The new wrinkle in abuse accusations cases, *ex parte* (one party communication) domestic violence protection orders can be obtained upon statements of fear of threatened harm with no proof, without disclosures from the mouths of babes. Public outcry against domestic abuse since the O.J. Simpson saga has fueled scores of reports, many unfounded.

The mixture of VAWA combined with no-fault divorce affords women, and mothers in particular, instant bargaining power, especially in family court. Once accused of spousal assault, unless a respondent or defendant (usually a man or father) proves his innocence and neutralizes the allegation, there's a rebuttable presumption he will not obtain normal child visitation rights or custody. Federal and state laws invite courts to sign domestic violence Orders For Protection-MN & IA (OFP), Protection From Abuse-PA (PFA), 209A's-MA, and other Domestic Violence Injunctions (DVI), based on uncorroborated hearsay contained in a petitioner's or plaintiff's affidavit. An effective weapon for tactical advantage in divorce cases involving marital assets, bitter visitation rights, child custody cases, and move-away cases, the DVI is an equal opportunity accuser. If you think you're immune from accusation because you're a CEO, politician, or sports celebrity, think again!

It is important that one understand the gravity of the VAWA and how it can be used to promote false accusations. Well-meaning, VAWA 2000 provides women shelter, safe homes, payment of expenses for transportation, utilities, child care, job training, and counseling for one year post-victimization, four hundred million dollars in legal assistance, billions of dollars to domestic violence shelters, and a Violence Against Women's Act Office to be located in the Department of Justice in Washington, DC. VAWA was legislated to protect women, not men, who allegedly were physically abused, sexually assaulted, or stalked. The trickle-down effect to the states has been fantastic.

A man in Oregon can be arrested for criminal *menacing* while a father in Maine can be arrested for criminal *threatening*. All states' statutes contain provisions for protecting women from domestic violence. If a man has allegedly touched, hit, punched, bit, slapped, kicked, pushed, choked, shoved, yelled at, stalked, harassed, or *threatened to harm* a woman, he could be arrested. Perhaps it should be called the "In Fear Of Men's Act," instead of the VAWA? If a man violates a civil Temporary Restraining Order (TRO) by directly or indirectly (e.g., E-mail or phone call via a third party) contacting the victim, he will be arrested. Mandatory arrest policies are legion. Police officers spend countless hours enforcing court orders based on statements of fear that women are allegedly in imminent danger, to learn that many of the same are bogus while *real* victims are left unprotected.

The media have exacerbated the prevalence of domestic *violence* through the ideologies of such strident feminists as Steinhem, Walker, Terr, Ireland, and Allred. To battered women's advocates, gripes about the restraining order industry are merely an antifemale backlash. Says Sheara Friend, a Needham, Massachusetts attorney, "lawyers don't want to be pegged as being anti-abused-women." Says former Massachusetts State Representative Barbara Gray in a 1995 interview, "I think judges grant the restraining orders without asking too many questions."

The O.J. Simpson case made it worse for men and fathers in *alleged* domestic violence situations. Coming to fruition in the wake of the 1994 VAWA, the Simpson saga increased public awareness to the issue of spousal abuse. In 2001, temporary no-contact orders can be signed *ex parte*, without the defendant being present or notified, let alone made privy to specific charges, and rely solely on the hearsay of the complainant.

The road to winning the war against domestic violence, like the war against child abuse, is paved with good intentions. Dissemination of public literature tapping men as powerful and controlling beings over women, and billboards doing the same, have fueled a zero-tolerance policy against domestic abuse. That translates into law enforcement departments exercising mandatory arrest policies on the most trivial accu-

sations. The point is, in alleged domestic disputes today, probable cause
to arrest an accused abuser is solely within the subjective discretion of law
enforcement on the scene. Not surprisingly, the feminist paradigm ignores abuse of women against men. Arguably the foremost family violence researcher in the world, Dr. Murray Straus, of the University of
New Hampshire family research laboratory, supports his findings via
empirical data that men are abused by women, equally. Straus' Conflict
Tactics Scales (CTS) research has been developed into a psychometric
instrument for assessing one's propensity toward domestic abuse, the
CTS-2.

The consequences of a restraining order for a man or father on the
receiving end can be quite serious. If he shares a home with the complainant, he will be asked to vacate the premises, and can return to obtain
his personal effects, later, escorted by a police officer, only. *Any* contact
with the *victim,* or the victim's children, is in contravention to the provisions set forth in the boilerplate restraining order. Upon a show cause
hearing, criminal sanctions ensue a defendant being held in contempt for
violation of a civil restraining order. Typically, a defendant must accumu-
late evidence to rebut the complainants version of what allegedly tran-
spired fifteen days after her *ex parte* order is signed. In other words, a
defendant has his day in court, known as the evidentiary or due process
hearing, within two weeks of being alleged to have assaulted a complainant.

Connecticut attorney Arnold Rutkin, editor of the legal journal *Family
Advocate,* says that judges take a "rubberstamping" approach to protection
orders, and the due process hearings that are held later are "usually a
sham." At a 1995 seminar, dispensing advice to other judges, Judge
Richard Russell of the Ocean City, New Jersey, municipal court stated,
"Your job is not to be concerned about the constitutional rights of the
man that you're violating as you grant a restraining order. The woman
needs this protection because the statute granted her that protection . . .
They have declared domestic violence to be an evil in our society. So we
don't have to worry about the rights."

Anecdotally, the abuse excuse is the ultimate weapon available for
parents, usually mothers, to use seven days a week, twenty-four hours a
day, 365 days per year. In today's computer crazed world, women can
utilize the *ex parte* restraining order, *in rem,* on an emergency basis, as
they follow through with Internet lovers and affairs into another state. In
these cases of interstate compact of multi-jurisdiction, a defendant father
must retain not only a local attorney, but also a special appearance attorney in the state she fled to. I recommend in these cases that fathers'
lawyers work in concert to shift jurisdiction back to the home state, the
state she fled from, in accord with the Uniform Child Custody Jurisdiction Act (UCCJA) and Parents Kidnapping and Prevention Act (PKPA).

According to the UCCJA, both judges from each state must converse by telephone to decide which state has jurisdiction. If the fathers' attorney in the state the mother fled to files a general notice of appearance and litigates her domestic assault accusations, he has killed his best defense, the issue of which state has jurisdiction (emphasis added).

Fathers' rights groups argue that orders for protection from abuse, intended as shields for *victims* of domestic violence, are misused by unscrupulous pseudo-victims, strident feminists, and overzealous courts. They claim it is gender profiling. They claim it is stereotyping. They believe men, seen as abusers, are perceived as the more aggressive species, and ultimately, pay the price for it. Many fathers arrested for domestic abuse have told this writer that their significant others perpetrated abuses against them. But, because of state and federal law requirements, he said/she said politics, and subjective mindset, their accounts have been ignored. In fact, men who have been abused were told they were in denial and were narcissistic. Some of their personal stories follow, and should awaken you to the ever-present abuses of protection from abuse orders.

On 29 December 1997, National Public Radio aired as part of their "Morning Edition," the harmful effects on children of restraining orders. James Parakis of Lynn, Massachusetts was meted out a 209A, and prevented from contacting his estranged spouse and then 8-year-old daughter. Subsequently, he attended his daughter's first communion at church, and was arrested. The end result was a *lifetime* restraining order issued against Mr. Parakis by the court. In the interim Parakis' daughter cried, wanting to know when her father would be able to converse with her via phone, or see her again. Of course, the answer was *never*! This writer presented to Fathers and Families of Massachusetts in April of 1999 and was told by same group that Parakis' lifetime restraining order had been vacated. Fortunately, for Jim Parakis and his daughter, the media attention to his plight bore fruit.

Mr. B, the director of a homeless shelter in Miami, Florida, was accused of verbally, physically, and sexually assaulting his wife during the spring and summer of 1999. She forced him to leave their marital home and filed for divorce, shortly thereafter. The wife secured a 741.30 Domestic Violence Injunction against him. Mr. B vehemently denied the accusations of verbal, physical, and sexual assault leveled against him. In fact, he claimed his wife suffered from Dissociative Identity Disorder. Upon psychological testing, Mr. B functioned within the normal limits of psychological adjustment. His Mosher Hyper Masculinity Inventory (HMI) results suggested he did not endorse behaviors or thoughts consistent with a macho personality style. Upon Conflict Tactics Scale-2 (CTS-2) testing, Mr. B communicated positive affect to his partner in negotiating with conflict. His responses to other testing instruments suggested he had not been sexually abusive to his wife. Dr. A concluded his report of Mr. B by stating "This man is not prone to physical violence."

Mr. H and his wife engaged in a heated verbal argument in October of 1999, in Lake Oswego, Oregon. Mrs. H, from a nearby pay phone, called police and informed them Mr. H harassed and menaced her, and she was in imminent fear her husband was going to assault her. She preferred charges against him, not knowing that harassment and menacing were, in fact, violations of Oregon Revised Statutes (ORS). Although she had no pain, bruises, or cuts, law enforcement arrested Mr. H on criminal charges of harassment and menacing. His bail bonds totaled $17,500.00. His legal costs topped ten thousand dollars. Mr. H claimed his wife suffered from borderline personality disorder and delusions (see chapter 16). He steadfastly maintained his innocence. As of this writing it is unclear as to the disposition of the case of Mr. and Mrs. H.

Consider the case of police officer Gregory Schmidt, who in August of 2000, according to published reports in both the *Seattle Times* and *South County Journal* in Renton, Washington, filed a ten million dollar lawsuit against the city of Seattle and King County in connection with his wrongful arrest for domestic violence in 1998. Lieutenant Schmidt, who informed his wife of three months he was divorcing her, called 911 after she allegedly attacked and bit him. Yet officer Schmidt was arrested for fourth degree assault because state statute requires law enforcement to arrest the primary aggressor in domestic violence cases. After an eight-day trial he was acquitted of the misdemeanor offense. Ironically, Lt. Schmidt, a fourteen year Seattle police veteran, said he created the department's domestic violence investigation unit in 1994. Lieutenant Schmidt and his attorney said the officer was the *real* victim of gender profiling, and Schmidt's wife was the actual aggressor in the case.

Mr. K was arrested for Assault D upon his wife in Maine during the latter part of 2000. Like Officer Schmidt in the previous case, Mr. K claims that he was the person abused, not her. Although the police officer's report states that his wife slapped him, it alleges that Mr. K shook her head in an effort to exorcise the demons out of her, attempting to right her wrongs with God. Because he and his wife have a 1-year-old girl at issue, a plea bargain down to criminal *threatening* or conviction would stymie Mr. K's visitation and custody rights with his young daughter. Another case of probable gender profiling, Mr. K went through an extensive battery of anti-domestic violence testing to prove his innocence. Upon testing, Dr. P concluded that Mr. K showed "no attraction to sexually coercive, sadistic, or violent behavior toward either adult or child females. Further, there are no clinical indications that Mr. K is a person prone to resolving conflicts in a violent manner. The results obtained in this assessment are not consistent with profiles of sexual offenders or perpetrators of domestic violence."

According to attorney John Paone from Woodbridge, New Jersey, "the stakes are high and the implications are vast," if a person is falsely accused of domestic violence. Paone, a fellow of the American Academy of Matrimonial Lawyers and AV-rated Martindale-Hubbell attorney, published *Representing Persons Falsely Accused of Domestic Violence* in the 7 July 1997 issue of the *New Jersey Law Journal.* Attorney Paone offers the following sage advise to other lawyers and parents embroiled in an unfounded domestic violence case:

- Obtain a copy of the complainant's affidavit or TRO (Temporary Restraining Order) quickly, due to statutorily imposed time constraints;

- Attack the issue of subject matter jurisdiction, if apropos;

- Move for a continuance, or Enlargement of Time, if the allegations are complex and require further strategizing;

- Weigh the prejudicial impact against your case as it concerns visitation and custody if you are granted a continuance;

- If possible, obtain a transcript of the proceeding at which the TRO was granted for impeachment purposes;

- Examine law enforcement's version of the alleged domestic violence complaint and whether or not same witnessed visible signs of physical injury;

- If possible, obtain a copy of the 911 taped phone call to discern the credibility of the complainant;

- Subpoena all persons who not only witnessed the alleged domestic violence incident, but also knew the complainant prior to the alleged incident;

- Consider the need for expert witnesses;

- Weigh the potential damage to other family members, especially children, before subpoenaing same to court;

- File a Request for Production of Documents, and if necessary, A Motion to Compel Discovery of all tangible evidence, especially medical records;

- File a Motion to Suppress any evidence not produced in response to a request for discovery;

- Move to dismiss a complaint that lacks the requisite intent to commit domestic violence consistent with the rules of criminal procedure;

- Examine the plaintiff's background for a potential history of fostering other frivolous allegations of abuse;

• Request the court take judicial notice of the *timing* of the TRO complaint if a protracted divorce, visitation dispute, or custody battle is pending;

• Have an investigator effect collateral witness interviews to glean if plaintiff has been seen together with defendant since the filing of the TRO complaint. If so, this testimony can be used to show that plaintiff is in *no immediate danger;*

• Become educated on case citations addressing the issue of undue prejudice versus probative value;

• In many states concerning criminal domestic violence actions "self defense" is a defense to domestic violence. Ensure that the alleged perpetrator is not the victim, first. A victim who uses reasonable force against domestic violence by an attacker cannot be criminally charged;

• Be cognizant of the fact that a confession to domestic violence, or plea bargain to the same (as in entering a batterer's intervention program), presumes that custody should be awarded to the non-abusive parent;

• Be cognizant of the fact that a guilty finding of domestic violence imposes upon the defendant supervised visitation restraints with children, at least until a risk assessment is effected;

• Address a TRO with a matter of urgency.

As in alleged child abuse cases, prior to the de facto domestic violence court hearing, I recommend psychological testing for those falsely accused of spousal abuse. In addition to general psychometric instruments such as the MMPI-2 and MCMI-III, which can screen for defensiveness, poor impulse control, anger, or overall personality disorder, parents and attorneys should ensure evaluators administer specific risk assessment testing for prospective violence, and sexual aggression. Let us examine a few of the more common tests utilized by psychologists to rule out one's propensity to be a domestic abuser.

The Psychopathy Check List-Revised (PCL-R) assesses one's antisocial orientation, lifestyle impulsivity, lack of responsibility, and behavioral instability associated with antisocial personality disorders. Bottom third percentile scores indicate an individual would not be likely to participate in criminal behavior or possess antisocial personalities. The PCL-R is also a useful tool in assessing those accused of sexual child abuse.

Parents accused of domestic violence with children are advised to complete the Child Abuse Potential Inventory (CAPI) Form VI, since visitation rights and custody are directly influenced by the disposition of the domestic abuse charge. Since the CAPI is a screening scale for alleged physical child abuse, and studies show that domestic violence and child abuse are directly linked to one another, it behooves a parent to take the CAPI. The test includes an abuse scale, descriptive factor scales, and special scales that measure factors that represent elements of psychiatric and social-interactional models of physical child abuse.

The Conflict Tactics Scale (CTS-2) is one of the most widely used psychometric measures of physical violence among cohabitating and married couples. It is based on research compiled by noted family violence expert Dr. Murray Straus from the Family Research Laboratory in Durham, New Hampshire. The questions posed incorporate every possible definition of violence as outlined in the VAWA. The CTS-2 measures both the extent to which partners in a dating, cohabitating, or marital relationship engage in psychological and physical attacks on each other and also on their use of negotiation or mediation to deal with conflicts. The CTS-2 employs five scale scores: negotiation, psychological aggression, physical assault, sexual coercion, and injury. Typically, a male accused of domestic violence should score within the first standard deviation regarding negotiation and psychological aggression and greater than one standard deviation regarding physical assault, sexual coercion, and injury, to be considered nonviolent and non-sexually coercive.

The HCR-20 is a twenty-item checklist of risk factors for violent behavior. The instrument consists of items organized around historical, present, and future issues. Ten historical items, five clinical items, and five risk management items are addressed. Issues examined are past violent outbursts, substance abuse problems, presence or absence of psychopathy, and stress levels. There is a strong predictive link between a person's past and future violent behavior, and that is the benefit of the HCR-20. The test results are assessed as low, moderate, or high risk to future violent behavior.

Psychophysiological evaluations of accused males of domestic violence using the PPG are very useful. Specifically tailored assessments can be presented including multiple scripts of sexually coercive, physically coercive, and non-consenting female adults, female children, and males. Oftentimes, men will be accused of domestic violence first and then sexual child abuse. Thus, it behooves an accused father and his attorney to *kill all birds with one stone* and partake of the PPG assessment. The desired result post-PPG testing is that Mr. Smith showed no attraction to sexually coercive, sadistic, or violent behavior towards either adult or child females, or males in any age category, nor did he appear to have an interest in any form of sexual behavior with males.

Finally, males who have prior convictions or no contest pleas for domestic violence and are accused again in the future, should be scored for Violence Risk Appraisal Guide (VRAG). A criminally derived actuarial tool like the Sexual Offender Risk Appraisal Guide (SORAG),

VRAG predicts the risk of violent recidivism. As is the SORAG, VRAG is based upon prison inmate populations. To compute the VRAG it is not necessary for the individual to go through PPG testing. PPG testing is necessary to compute the SORAG.

Fighting back false allegations of domestic violence is a tedious and time-constrained challenge. Domestic violence injunctions are easily obtained, based on statements of fear alone. Because society wants to protect and rescue women and children at-risk, in harms way, and in jeopardy, court dockets are flooded with many frivolous cases of alleged domestic abuse. Interestingly enough, University of Massachusetts criminologists Carl and Eve Buzawa, in their 1996 book, *Do Arrests and Restraining Orders Work,* conclude that restraining orders have little if any protective effect. University of Rhode Island sociologist Richard Gelles, a leading authority on domestic violence, also cautions that the more the legal system is bogged down in trivial pursuits, the less likely it is to single out the serious cases that do require immediate intervention. This writer agrees with Professor Gelles and would add that there may be a Sixth Amendment constitutional issue present, also. How can an accused be afforded the right to confront his accuser if the court order is signed *ex parte?*

16.

Borderline Personality Disorder: Survival Strategies for Non-BPs

What kind of twisted and devious mind would use a child as a pawn in a custody battle? What kind of person would falsely accuse another of child abuse or domestic violence, believing in their own mind it really happened? What kind of individual would refuse to mediate a divorce, opting for protracted litigation, in the best interests of the child? This chapter invites you to step into the world of Borderline Personality Disorder (BPD). Its intended audience is non-borderlines, or non-BPs, defense attorneys, judges, and mental health practitioners. A "non" is one who is married to, or cohabitates with a borderline BPD.

It is incumbent upon the reader to understand the machinations of the BPD. Doing so will facilitate realization of the oft-present, never-ending legal battles that ensue. While people with BPD are often bright, creative, and resourceful, they live tumultuous lives and usually wreak havoc in the lives of those close to them. Consequently, we must examine the mental health pathology of the person stricken with BPD before we can address the relevant issue of false abuse accusations. This chapter should send a chilling message to non-BPs, mental health, and legal communities, that BPD is a dangerous, often misunderstood disease. This chapter attempts to help non-BP's and professionals short circuit the pitfalls presented by the BPD.

BPD is defined as a pervasive pattern of instability of borderline, interpersonal relationships, and marked impulsivity beginning by early adulthood as indicated by five or more of the Diagnostic & Statistical Manual (DSM-IV) criteria for BPD. According to psychologists this writer has spoken to, BPD, an Axis II Disorder coded as 301.83 in the DSM-IV, is diagnosed by one meeting five of nine published criteria with corroboration provided by scores on the MCMI-II (Millon) and Gunderson's Diagnostic Interview for Borderlines-Revised (DIB-R). Some of the published criteria are suicidal ideations, impulsivity in at least two areas (e.g., binge spending and promiscuity), efforts to avoid real or imagined abandonment, chronic feelings of emptiness, intense anger, and stress-related paranoid illusions. The latter criterion is key as it affects delusional false accusers. Self-mutilation is common among borderlines. Borderlines are manipulative and attention seekers. They suffer from acute mood swings. While there are millions (about 2 percent of the general population) who suffer from BPD, scores more suffer from BPD traits. The latter represents a large contingent of undiagnosed individuals from all walks of life. BPD is diagnosed predominantly (75 percent) in females.

BPD co-occurs with other Axis I Personality Disorders such as mood disorders, Post Traumatic Stress Disorder (PTSD), and Attention-Deficit Hyperactivity Disorder (ADHD). There are others such as histrionic, antisocial, and dependent personality disorders that can be confused with BPD because of personality features, but can coexist. It is incumbent upon clinicians to exercise proper judgment in diagnosing BPD versus other similar disorders. There are empirical data to support the finding that many adults who suffer from BPD were abused as children (Fonagy, et al., 1996; Paris, et al., 1994; Famularo, et al., 1991 and Herman, et al., 1989). Paris, et al., concluded that trauma and problems with fathers (e.g., children witnessing fathers' domestic violence) are important factors in the development of BPD in males. According to Dr. Peter Fonagy, abused children suffering from disorganized attachments distance their feelings from their abusers and themselves, causing a disruption in their mental functioning. Abused children with low reflective capacities escape mentally and are resistant at looking in mirrors (Schneider-Rosen & Cicchetti, 1991). Later on in life, these same adults are very vulnerable in intimate relationships. This *vulnerability* takes on a life of its own in the form of a multitude of relationships gone bad. While suicide and self-injury are common manifestations of disorganized attachment in borderline women, in borderline men with similar pathology violence against women is more common.

There are several behavioral symptoms and characteristics demonstrated by BPD. Non-BPs must be on the lookout. Each behavior, intentionally, or unintentionally, is aimed at serving the best interest of the borderline, only. It has been said that non-BPs living with borderlines walk on eggshells, functioning like they're on an emotional roller coaster. To say that non-BP's live a *touch-and-go* life with their BPD significant others is an understatement. Here's why: *Splitting* is a common symptom among borderlines. A partial representation of the self, borderlines split mental images of others. Doing so allows them to perceive non-BPs as all good, or all bad. Borderlines resort to black and white thinking. They cannot see gray. Consequently, when a non-BP takes a borderline to court, or vice-versa, e.g., in divorce proceedings, mediation, arbitration, or alternative dispute resolution is impossible. If a borderline sues you for divorce, or accuses you of child abuse or domestic violence, protracted litigation ensues.

Projection is a common psychological occurrence among borderlines. For purposes of discussion here, borderlines as custodial parents project their own pathology onto their children. Perhaps, the borderline was sexually abused as a child, or thinks so. Perhaps, your loving BPD of yesterday, secured an *ex parte* domestic violence injunction against you today. When children become *little BPDs* due to projection, it is a sign that emotional child abuse has begun. It is a sign that Parental Alienation (PA) is in full swing. When same children participate in a denigration, berating, or disparaging campaign against the non-BP, propelled onto them by the borderline, it is called Parental Alienation Syndrome (PAS).

I Hate You-Don't Leave Me, the title of a book by Jerold Kreisman, M.D., is another problem seen with BPDs. They alternate distance and clinging behaviors. They'll get close to you, but then want freedom. You're loving your borderline one day, and the next day your clothes are on the front porch, and the police have been called to enjoin and restrain you from being near her or him.

Hoovering is a mechanism attributed to borderlines when they manipulate non-BPs back into their lives. Conniving, convincing, and clandestine actresses and actors, BPDs are expert at reeling in non-BPs. Many non-BPs are co-dependent, finding it difficult to break off relationships with borderlines, or when they finally do so, succumb to the temptation of reunification. BPDs will shop for experts to corroborate their own delusions. If they've accused you of domestic violence, but lost, they may not stop. The borderline's accusations may escalate to child abuse. This writer cautions all non-BPs to be aware of hoovering. If non-BPs takes the borderline's bait, hook, line, and sinker; it could be a trap.

Non-BPs often fail to address the borderlines behavioral symptoms, or abuse accusations, with a sense of urgency. It's what I refer to as "Nonchalant Syndrome." This is not the time for passivity. This is not the time for the non-BP to be cavalier. Failing to recognize the borderlines guise, their mask, could prove costly in a court of law. Realize that many BPDs are narcissistic and sociopathic, and will blame you for everything while not feeling sorry about it. Borderlines are expert at making you feel guilty for the way they feel. Non-BPs are advised to establish and set boundaries, rules to live by for both themselves and their BPD partners.

Hell hath no fury like a BPD scorned! A non-BP is cautioned against issuing ultimatums to their borderline partners. Borderlines are accusatory. Distortion, exaggeration, and smear campaigns are commonplace. From subtle threats, to launching police and CPS alleged abuse investigations against you, *all* non-BPDs are open season to victimization. Many borderlines do not accuse in bad faith, but are delusional (Wakefield & Underwager, 1990; Hickman & Reynolds, 1994). Many borderlines have wish fulfillments and believe their accusations to be the truth, no matter how farfetched. From stalking, to domestic violence, to physical child abuse, to sexual child abuse accusations, some borderlines are obsessive-compulsive, and will shop for *experts* to corroborate their own delusions. Treating those who want to ruin your life with kid gloves, like fine china, is not doing yourself, or your children any favors. If you're co-dependent, or suffer from "nonchalant syndrome," and don't take even subtle accusations seriously, you're mistaken.

Most of the time borderlines put their words into actions. While you as the non-BP may respect your borderlines abusive and traumatic childhood and while you may want to be nice, consider the jail cell and lack of future with your children that awaits. In my opinion, non-BP's should *not* acquiesce to their borderline partners. In fact, their mindset should be to counter with a howitzer, not a BB gun. Here's why: Without taking gender sides, and adhering to facts, if we do the math, the Mondale Act + Violence Against Women's Act + 75 percent of all borderlines being female = Men and fathers are at-risk to be accused. Anecdotally speaking, borderlines' abuse of allegations and attempts to effect *fathertectomies* in the process are progressive in nature. *Motherectomies* occur, too, but to a much lesser degree. Depending upon whether or not the borderline is high functioning or low functioning, dictates the creativity and speed of the escalating pattern of abuse allegations.

The escalating pattern of abuse allegations and alienation exhibited by BPDs induces legal intervention. Most of the time the borderline strikes first and sues the non-BP for divorce (women initiate divorce proceedings, first, 85 percent of the time) and/or secures an *ex parte* Domestic Violence Injunction (DVI). Should the borderline drop her domestic violence charges, the police can still arrest the accused, and the state can still prefer charges against the same. CPS can be called to investigate domestic violence charges where children are present and/or child abuse accusations and force an accused non-BP into juvenile court. Rarely, does the non-BP initiate courtroom litigation.

What pitfalls face divorcing non-BPs, legally speaking? There are several. A non-BP cannot prevent a borderline from calling 911 and raising stalking or assault allegations. A non-BP cannot prevent a borderline from seeing a therapist, *remembering* being molested years ago, and reporting the same to the appropriate authorities. A non-BP cannot prevent a borderline from calling CPS, promulgating physical, or sexual abuse allegations. A non-BP who voluntarily or involuntarily leaves the marital home during a pending divorce and custody battle, is inviting a borderline to use PAS. Borderlines control what they can. Leaving a child with a borderline in a protracted divorce, visitation dispute, and custody battle is like giving candy to a baby. They wield children as pawns and weapons to gain an unfair advantage in court.

To protect themselves, non-BPs should consider the following courses of action:

- Start a timeline (dated chronology of events);
- Attempt to reconcile the situation with the borderline first, knowing mediation is usually unsuccessful;
- Set out to protect yourself and your children, knowing that you're fighting not only your loved one, but also a severe mental health disorder;
- Contact an attorney (see Appendices C&D);
- Consider hiring a private investigator if you suspect the borderline of having an affair;
- Prepare yourself emotionally, financially, and spiritually for the fight of your life;
- If necessary, have the court appoint a Guardian-*ad-Litem* (GAL), in the children's best interests;
- Consider retaining expert consultants to help effect a legal defense strategy;
- Retain the foremost experts in the field of psychology as it concerns PAS and BPD;
- Consider retaining a Registered Custody Evaluator (RCE) to perform a custody evaluation;
- Do *not* call 911 in the presence of the borderline as it could backfire whereby *you* get arrested;
- If physically abused by a borderline document your injuries photographically, at a local hospital emergency room, and at your local police department;
- Secure all of your bank and credit card accounts.

Distraught borderlines resort to drastic measures. Non-BPs should prepare themselves for acute, knee-jerk, stress-induced reactions by their BPD partners, especially in the midst of protracted litigation. It is not uncommon for a non-BP to come home to an empty house. Since many borderlines are promiscuous (cyber affairs are common), binge spenders, you may find your *loved one* is committing adultery and using your credit cards. Borderlines can stoop to the level of parental kidnapping, moving away without informing you. An even greater problem exists when the borderline accuses the non-BP of alleged abuse in the state she flees to and secures an *ex parte* Order For Protection *in rem* (emergency basis). Now, a case of interstate compact, the non-BP is compelled to retain a lawyer in the foreign state for special appearance purposes only, litigating jurisdiction under the Uniform Child Custody Jurisdiction Act and Parents Kidnapping and Prevention Act. The attorney in the foreign state should address the relevance of the Clean Hands Doctrine, also, to glean if the parent who fled had *unclean* hands. Munchausen Syndrome By

Proxy (MSBP) is a bizarre form of child abuse perpetrated by a parent to make a child ill to gain attention. While there are many false accusations of MSBP, cases involving borderlines usually are not false. There have been extreme cases of MSBP perpetrated by BPD parents that resulted in the tragic deaths of children. This writer advises all non-BPs to quickly secure competent legal counsel (see Appendices C&D) in these cases.

It is important for non-BPs to be aware of their borderline partners psychological makeup and to be cognizant of any behavioral changes that occur. Whether or not the borderline has been diagnosed with the full-blown Axis II BPD, BPD *traits*, or remains undiagnosed, it's crucial the non-BP understand the personality characteristics of false accusers. By doing so, the non-BP is forewarned an abuse accusation may be forthcoming. Being forewarned is being forearmed, and the non-BP can launch a preemptive first strike.

One very important red flag to be aware of is projection. Projection can manifest itself in the form of PAS. In custody cases, mothers who are obsessed with hatred of fathers may bring children to the point of having paranoid delusions about them (Gardner, 1986). As children mirror, parrot, and become mothers' *little borderlines*, and a symbiotic relationship ensues. The children acquire these projected paranoid delusions; e.g., mother truly believes in the absence of evidence that father molested child in the midst of their bitter divorce, and after continually reminding the child that Daddy touched her in bad places, it becomes the child's *reality*.

Falsely accusing parents are sometimes so obsessed with anger toward their estranged spouse it becomes a major focal point in their lives. Evaluators describe such persons as oppositional, hostile, negative, and resistant during the evaluation process. The borderline can become so overwhelmed by anger against the former spouse it supersedes the needs of the child. As pointed out in chapter eight, the SAID syndrome, the female accusing parent often is a hysterical or borderline personality, or is angry, defensive, and justifying. Borderline mothers will shop for expert psychologists and therapists to corroborate their own delusions of abuse. Borderlines function in a highly dysfunctional manner and may lose contact with reality (Blush & Ross, 1990). These same persons often tell of strange events in their past, whether they're true or not. Because the literature indicates most borderlines possess significant psychopathology, accused parents and their attorneys are advised to obtain psychological evaluations of false accusers, if possible. Underwager & Wakefield showed that only one-fourth of all falsely accusing parents did not have a personality disorder. Borderlines can be characterized as having severe mood swings, inappropriate emotional overreactions, a need for approval and attention, difficulties handling anger and conflict, and impulsive tendencies. Several borderlines have been described as being highly unstable, unpredictable, displaying bizarre behaviors, and failing to distinguish between reality and fantasy.

Falsely accusing parents suffer from what I refer to as "Hypersensitivity Syndrome." These parents pleading for one to report abuse at all costs are enamored with public literature. These parents are intrigued by abuse prevention programs and talk show hosts, such as Oprah Winfrey, who lobby Congress for stiffer penalties against real child abusers. This writer does not condone any form of abuse, or maltreatment against children or women, but points out that the incentives to report and disclose abuse are pronounced. Parental victims of "hypersensitivity syndrome," like some social workers and therapists, are true believers. They're child savers, and they will not take "no" for an answer. This class of false accuser falls into what author Mary Pride in her book *The Child Abuse Industry* called, "The Doctrine of Immaculate Confession," meaning that complaining parents and caseworkers believe the child's initial abuse report, only, not the child's recantation that it really did not happen. Since borderlines can be experts at *convincing* family, friends, and even professionals, their abuse accusations are absolutely true, even in the face of overwhelming evidence against them that nothing happened, it's incumbent upon the non-BP and his defense team to select the foremost experts in the field of mental health. Ensure the psychologist has testified in court in both real and fabricated abuse cases and has published in the areas of BPD, PAS, child abuse, and domestic violence.

Now, let us examine some live case studies of BPD parents, false abuse accusations, and PAS. The following case analyses represent actual custody battles in litigation between fathers and BPD mothers. In most of the cases the non-BP fathers were accused of abuse. It is important to remember that because of the borderlines problematic fear of abandonment, child custody is very important, as it reassures her sense of security, need, and control.

Attorney B and Mrs. B, a psychiatric nurse, filed for divorce in North Carolina, and became embroiled in a protracted custody battle over their young daughter. Mrs. B had a long history of depression. She met the diagnostic criteria for major depression at times. Dr. F commented that Mrs. B experienced poor self esteem, and her "expectations are generally that things would not go well." Dr. F further stated that Mrs. B had recurrent suicidal ideations, a strong fear of abandonment, engaged in continual promiscuity, and binge eating. In addition, he reported that she had symptoms which included poor sleep, "felt overwhelmed," hopeless, had a "short fuse," deep mood swings, irrational behavior, and marital problems. She was diagnosed with Axis I major depression and dysthymia (a chronically depressed mood occurring more times than not and lasting at least two years). Mrs. B intimated she would accuse Attorney B of abuse, but to this writer's knowledge never did so. Attorney B was concerned that Mrs. B's dependency upon Prozac, other antidepressants, and her mental illness, rendered her unfit as primary custodian of their young daughter. Moreover, their child was seen playing with knives, scissors, and bottles of various medications while under the supervision of Mrs. B. According to a follow-up review of the records by Dr. C, Mrs. B had *significant* BPD, if not BPD.

The Texas case of *Bell v. Bell* included multiple abuse accusations by Mrs. Bell against Mr. Bell in the context of divorce and custody. Mr. Bell was accused of domestic violence of Mrs. Bell and then fondling and lewd behavior with their young son. Dr. M concluded post-testing that, "Mr. Bell does not pose any threat of physical, emotional, or sexual abuse to the boy. There seems to be increasing evidence that the allegations Mrs. Bell made about Mr. Bell abusing the boy were false. If this turns out to be the case, Mrs. Bell would pose threat of emotional abuse to the boy. The family member who seems best able to provide for the boy's needs is his father, Mr. Bell. It does appear that Mrs. Bell has made numerous false allegations of abuse. I believe Mr. Bell could competently meet the boys current needs as his primary caretaking parent." According to Dr. M's analysis of Mrs. Bell, she presented herself as a "fearful wife and mother who reacted in a hasty and vengeful manner. Mrs. Bell failed to answer eleven items on the MMPI test. Her responses to the MCMI-III indicated histrionic personality traits. These individuals are most often over reactive, volatile, and expressively dramatic. They strongly seek attention and solicit praise."

The cases of Mr. P from Connecticut, Mr. Z from Georgia, Mr. M from New York, and Mr. B from Florida, were similar in many respects. In all cases, the respondents, Mr. P, Mr. Z, Mr. M, and Mr. B, were victimized by *ex parte* orders for protection and wrongly accused of domestic assault by their wives during high conflict divorces. In all cases, the wives possessed the motive, method, and opportunity to falsely accuse the husbands. In all cases, especially Mrs. Z from Georgia, the wives suffered from severe mood swings, narcissism, justification, and delusions of grandeur. In all cases, the husbands claimed they were assaulted by their wives, but the system failed to pursue their complaints. In all cases, except Mr. B's from Florida, children were wielded as pawns by their mothers in vindictive custody battles, and were the products of projection and moderate to severe Parental Alienation Syndrome. None of the falsely accusing women were diagnosed as BPD, possibly because none were seen by mental health experts, but BPD traits were apparent in all. Anecdotally, the cases of Mr. P, Mr. Z, Mr. M, and Mr. B are not uncommon in situations involving mothers with borderline personality pathology. In scattered cases, borderline fathers will falsely accuse mothers of abuse. Men suffering from BPD act more violently than their female counterparts.

Because BPD can be confused with so many other clinical disorders such as Post Traumatic Stress Disorder, Major Depression, Attention Deficit Disorder, Obsessive Compulsive Disorder, Dysthymia, Generalized Anxiety Disorder, Panic Disorder, and Substance Abuse, it is critical psychological testing be administered to the prospective BPD patient.

Do most psychologists and custody evaluators know what psychometric instruments target BPD? The answer is probably most do not know. Most attorneys have *no clue* as to what tests not only help their clients in false abuse accusations cases and custody cases but also extract BPD in pathological parents. The most commonly used tests administered to parents with prospective BPD are the MMPI-2, MCMI-II or MCMI-III, DIB-R, and PDQ-4.

Since borderlines see themselves as all good, their MMPI-2 validity scales depict elevated L (lying), elevated K (defensiveness), and decreased F (psychopathology) scores. In other words, they distort the truth, are very defensive, tend to mask their deficiencies, and employ splitting, projection, and denial. This type of very defensive MMPI-2 profile suggests the person exhibits Parental Alienation, too. Clinicians should be cognizant of the fact that such parental alienators are often more defensive than parents involved in straight custody suits. It's important to note that while same parents appear flawless on paper, they are unaware of the consequences of their own behavior on others, including children.

The MCMI, or Millon, is closely correlated with the DSM-IV, or DSM-IV-TR (Text Revision) classification system of personality disorders. This connection increases the diagnostic utility of Millon's instruments for clinicians. Once a person meets the five of nine diagnostic criteria for prospective BPD, administration of the MCMI-II, or MCMI-III, is necessary to make and corroborate the diagnosis. On the Millon, BPD falls under scale C of the severe personality pathology scales. Since the MCMI-III was updated with response sections for childhood abuse, eating disorders, and adheres more to the DSM-IV system, this writer suggests use of it over the MCMI-II when BPD is at-issue.

Gunderson's Diagnostic Interview for Borderlines-Revised (DIB-R) has gained increasing acceptance and use as a diagnostic clinical research instrument. Revised in 1989, to better differentiate between BPD and other personality disorders, it considers symptoms that fall under four main headings: affect, cognition, impulse action patterns, and interpersonal relationships. The DIB-R has been identified as the best test for diagnosing BPD. Finally, the Personality Diagnostic Questionnaire-Version 4 (PDQ-4) is an interactive program that determines the presence of personality disorders consistent with the DSM-IV, Axis-II. It can be used as a screening or diagnostic tool for prospective BPD.

The final part of this chapter is authored by Psychologist, Dr. L. His firsthand and professional involvement with borderlines and BPD on a daily basis is a vital and compelling addition to BPD: Survival strategies for non-BPs. Readers should be aware that some information may be redundant:

I Do Not Understand

"After a marriage of eighteen years it was impossible to understand what was going on in my life when I could not see my children. Why would my ex-wife deny me the opportunity to be with them? Why would my kids not want to do anything with me, not want to see me, not even want to talk with me on the phone? Up to this point I had been heavily involved with every aspect of my children's lives with their education, religion, medical, and extracurricular activities. For years I had coached many of the sports they participated in, helped with Girl Scouts and Boy Scouts, went to all of the activities, and knew the parents of my children's friends. My life was focused on our family and the responsibilities of being a good parent. Now, I am seen as the bad guy. How could this happen to me? What did I do to deserve this banishment from my kids? This strange course of events is too complex to understand, too unbelievable to comprehend! I don't know what happened, and no one else will ever believe me when I tell my story." This is a story I have heard many times over the last twenty-five years. The story is all too common and tells of the human pain and hurt inflicted upon themselves, their partners, their children, and family members. As a psychologist, I have observed this destructive pattern in therapy with many patients and experienced it up close and personal with my own family. This destructive pattern of behavior, thinking, and relationships is the underlying basis for diagnosing the individual with a BPD.

What Is BPD?

There are no two BPD individuals completely alike in their emotional makeup. The pattern of thinking, feelings, and behaviors may have strikingly similar traits, but it is how the BPD individual responds to perceived stresses in their life that makes them so different from each other. There are very different levels of functioning in the BPD world—high functioning, low functioning, borderlines that internalize and/or implode, and borderlines that externalize and/or explode. Some borderlines fighting to find their own inner peace against the rest of the world live in a world where they're involved in constant drama, excitement, or conflict. Some borderlines withdraw into their own little world and cut off from potential external threats to their existence. There is not one magic pill or one form of therapy that works with all borderlines.

The borderlines' enemy is within themselves, although they perceive the rest of the world as a threat to their own existence. An individual with BPD may experience intense emotional and behavioral conflict when they feel that the world they live in is out of their control. When the borderline feels that the people closest to them have turned against them, the fear of abandonment and perceived loss of control escalates. When this occurs, people with BPD feel a compelling need to be in control of their environment and may take whatever actions they deem necessary to regain control of their life and inner security. This constant struggle to gain control, or regain control is the one way the borderline can fashion a hold on life, to feel safe and secure.

The etiology behind this type of thinking is an intense fear of abandonment going back to an early age where the child did not feel safe and secure. The young infant develops an adaptive response to their environment when they don't feel safe, secure, loved, and wanted. When the young infant is afraid and nobody responds, when they are hungry and not fed, and when they want to be held and nobody is there, the absence of a nurturing response may lay the early foundation for their fear of abandonment. The young infant has no control over their environment and when denied the desired attention will adapt by using whatever primitive means necessary to get any response. This developmental learning theory holds the belief that many of the eating disorders, thought disorders, and personality disorders are set in motion at this early age. This pattern of response is then reinforced and ingrained into the individual's emotional psyche via significant life experiences that can bring BPD full circle. For the adult borderline, the perceived fear of abandonment and the need for control of their lives are the driving forces behind all behaviors, thinking, and feelings.

Living with a BPD partner can be a harrowing experience. The BPD world is very different than that of the non-BP world. One of the traits of a borderline is that quite often they project themselves onto the non-BP. In my experience, the borderline believes that everybody else thinks and feels much like them. If the borderline is angry they project this emotion on their partner and then believe the partner is angry at them. If the borderline fears abandonment, separation anxiety, and that their children may be taken away, this may be projected onto the partner creating a struggle for control of the children. It is this bizarre thinking on part of the borderline that makes a non-BP question their own sanity and wonder if *they* are seeing the world accurately. Until a non-BP can separate their thinking from that of the borderlines, the same may be caught up in a battle to fit their logical and rational world into the illogical and irrational world of the borderlines. This can make anybody feel like they are losing it because nothing makes sense. Over time, nothing seems real, and the non-BP may become dysfunctional without separation from their borderline partner. The good news is that you're questioning your own sanity and wondering if you might be BPD yourself. This indicates that you still possess intact thinking and can separate yourself from the borderlines thought processes.

This concept of transference is very difficult for anybody to understand unless they've been in a BPD relationship. Because of the very nature of BPD and the fear of abandonment, the borderline parent will often see the other parent as a potential threat to their relationship with the children. The reaction of the borderline parent to the fear of losing their children can be catastrophic and will be addressed later in this chapter.

Defining BPD

There are over six million Americans suffering from a BPD, approximately 2 percent of the general population in the U.S. BPD is seen in about 10 percent of the outpatient mental health population and in about 20 percent of all psychiatric patients. Approximately, 75 percent of all diagnosed BPD patients are women. It is estimated that 75 percent of all BPD patients have been physically or sexually abused as children. DSM-IV defines BPD as:

> A pervasive pattern of instability of interpersonal relationships, self-image and effects, and marked impulsivity, beginning by early childhood and present in a variety of contexts, as indicated by at least five (or more) of the following:
>
> 1. Frantic need to avoid real or imagined abandonment.
>
> 2. A pattern of unstable and intense interpersonal relationships characterized by alternating between extremes of idealization and devaluation. (Everything is defined as either good or bad with no shades of gray in between.)
>
> 3. Identity disturbance: markedly and persistently unstable self-image or sense of self.
>
> 4. Impulsivity in at least two areas that are potentially self-damaging (e.g., binge spending, sex or promiscuity, substance abuse, reckless driving, binge eating).
>
> 5. Recurrent suicidal ideations, gestures, or threats or self-mutilating behavior.
>
> 6. Affective instability due to a marked reactivity of mood (e.g., intense episodic dysphoria, irritability, or anxiety usually lasting a few hours and rarely more than a few days).
>
> 7. Chronic feelings of emptiness.

8. Inappropriate, intense anger or difficulty controlling anger (e.g., frequent displays of temper and recurrent physical fights).

9. Stress-related paranoid ideation or severe dissociative symptoms.

To diagnose BPD does not require all nine identifying traits to be present at the same time. If five of the nine identifying traits are present then the proper diagnosis can be made utilizing the DSM-IV criteria for BPD.

Diagnosing BPD

Diagnosing BPD may be difficult because this disorder can involve a wide number of symptoms associated with other disorders. Depression, paranoia, obsessive-compulsive, bipolar, panic/anxiety, addiction, post-traumatic stress, dissociative identity, narcissism, and eating disorders have all been identified as potential symptoms or traits of BPD. In mental health settings quite often these symptoms are used to identify an individual diagnosis for the traits listed previously instead of viewing the full pattern of thinking, feelings, and behaviors for the individual. In other words, individuals with BPD may be easily misdiagnosed as having an eating disorder, being bipolar, having an addiction, a posttraumatic stress disorder, or even severe depression. These individual traits, by themselves, do not identify BPD. However, when these traits are seen in concert, it's more likely that the proper diagnosis of BPD is accurate. *It is estimated that less than 3 percent of the BPD population in the U.S. has been formally diagnosed.* There is also a very large BPD male population unaccounted for as many are incarcerated. Because the vast majority of individuals with BPD do not (will not) seek any form of mental health assistance, the actual number of people suffering from this disorder may be much higher than previously estimated.

Proper diagnosis of BPD is dependent upon establishing an observed pattern of behaviors, thinking, and relationships over an extended period of time. Traditional psychometric testing (as Dean Tong alluded to earlier in this chapter) is a tool that may be employed in an evaluation for BPD. However, most tests do not provide the depth or the pattern for identifying the nine traits listed above. Psychometric tests alone cannot make an accurate diagnosis of BPD. My experience has been that BPD is more accurately and readily diagnosed when the individual is observed over four to six assessment sessions identifying the underlying traits listed previously. Through these assessment sessions a pattern of thinking, feelings, and behaviors can be observed. Psychometric test results can then be useful in helping to confirm a BPD diagnosis with the observed traits listed previously.

Signs to Look For

There are a number of common signs to look for when an individual is suspected of having a BPD. These signs can be observed as functional behaviors, but by themselves cannot diagnose BPD in an individual.

1. Extreme Mood Swings—People with BPD may experience dramatic mood swings from being very happy and in control of their world, to suddenly feeling very depressed, lonely, helpless, and hopeless. In similar fashion, people with BPD can move from a state of total independence to one demanding lots of attention.

2. Mirroring Others—People with BPD are quite intuitive and have the ability to read others very well. In the presence of others, the borderline is able to fit in much like a chameleon by assuming a similar position and mirroring similar feelings and behaviors. Self-image is based on the people around them. This allows the borderline to feel in control and liked by those present. The borderline tends to go in whatever direction the wind is blowing. There appears to be no depth of identity or individuality to their own thinking.

3. Addictive Behaviors—All people with BPD have some form of addictive behavior(s). These addictive behaviors provide an internal sense of security that they view as having control. Eating disorders, excessive spending for unneeded items, sexual compulsions, and drug and/or alcohol abuse are typical addictive behaviors of the borderline.

4. Performance Failures—Many borderline individuals have great difficulty consistently performing in educational and work settings because of the inability to stay focused in completing tasks. Thought disorders along with difficulties in short-term memory and retention and retrieval of information may cause the borderline great difficulty in performing up to their intellectual ability.

5. Self-Destructive Behaviors—People with BPD often have self-destructive behaviors that may threaten their life, or physical well-being. It's estimated that as high as 9 percent of all borderlines commit suicide. Other self-injurious behaviors include self-mutilation (cutting), eating disorders, sexual promiscuity, and potentially life threatening activities such as excessive drug and/or alcohol usage, and reckless driving without regard to their own life or the lives of others.

6. Intense, Unstable Relationships—People with BPD find it difficult to maintain any kind of close interpersonal relationships. Quite often the borderline may quickly develop an intense, exciting relationship with someone. The new partner is perfect, intelligent, gorgeous, fun, caring, loving, etc. Then, when reality sets

in and they feel out of control, the borderline may do a complete reversal. The inability to make decisions or commitments is very frightening to the borderline. Relationships with a borderline often end as abruptly as they start.

7. Black and White Thinking—People with BPD see things as either black or white. There are no shades of gray. The borderline is unable to see another's point of view and understand how they may see it differently. Instead, it is either good or bad, right or wrong, my way or the highway. Compromise or the ability to see other options is not possible for most people with BPD.

If you are in a relationship with an individual who displays a number of the aforementioned signs, you've probably already wondered about your own sanity. The non-BP should regard these signs as wake-up calls, and get help!

High Functioning v. Low Functioning Borderlines

"John is a very successful attorney with a big law firm and well known in the legal community. No one would ever believe me when I told them that he is like Jekyl and Hyde when he's at home with our family. One minute we can be doing something as a family and everything seems to be fine. Then, all of a sudden out of nowhere he can become irate, blame me for everything that is wrong in his life, tell me how worthless I am, and threaten to leave me. I never know when or what is going to cause the next explosion. He makes me feel like I'm a terrible wife and mother."

To much of the outside world, the *high functioning* borderline may be seen as very successful in their work, have a nice home, appear to have a solid family, and be active in the community. Quite often they may have many acquaintances and assume positions of leadership and authority in civic groups. However, the persona beneath this façade may be completely the opposite. High functioning borderlines like to be in positions of authority where they can be in control of their life and all of the people around them. They have the security of knowing that in this position they have the final say.

One of my former high functioning BPD patients was a very high level judge who had the ultimate authority to make life and death decisions in the courtroom. He had a tremendous ability to focus on the details of the cases he presided over. He was extremely intelligent and could organize research in making sound judgments on his cases. However, when he came home the whole family trembled at what kind of judgments he proclaimed to them. There was constant conflict in the family centering around the judge's strange behaviors and bizarre thinking. At times of severe stress I would receive a call from the judge's lifelong assistant, requesting I immediately come to the judge's chambers as he's taken a recess and gone berserk. The judge had many professional acquaintances, but nobody really got close to him, not even family members. Underneath this successful and highly respected judge was a very fearful, insecure individual who saw the world as threatening to his very existence. When the judge felt out of control he internalized much of his crazy thinking and, as a consequence, suffered a number of physical stress disorders, which led to his early demise. As long as he could maintain the façade of being in control of the outside world, the judge had the final say.

The world of the *low functioning* borderline is quite different. There's a constant struggle to maintain an existence with the outside world but without the ability to maintain a focus on thought processes, or the ability to maintain a successful façade to cover-up bizarre thinking and behaviors.

"My BPD ex-wife is very intelligent, has a college degree, and has had some good jobs. The problem is she's never happy with any job and either ends up being fired after a short time or quits because she feels mistreated. Now, she doesn't work because 'it will never work out anyway.' I can't depend on making arrangements with her because she will not make decisions, or else forgets what we agreed upon. Scheduling things with our kids seems impossible. When she forgets to pick up the children, I am blamed for being a bad parent. Although articulate, because of her irrational thought processes, she rarely completes what she starts. She comes across as being stupid and lazy."

In January 1982, I had a young woman in her early thirties come into my office with complaints about her children, ages seven and five. Sally was quite intelligent and had completed two years of college. She was divorced and in the process of raising two small children. My first impression of Sally was a very intelligent woman, quite overweight, and inappropriately dressed with little clothing for winter weather. Sally was animated, lively, and intense in her discussion of her children's problems. She blamed all of her life's problems on the two children and wanted to see how she could get rid of them and still receive state and federal financial assistance. She withdrew into her own little world, and the kids were left to fend for themselves. The 7-year-old daughter fixed food for mom and brother and got herself and brother ready for school. As the children grew older, Sally was faced with both children being in school, feeling abandoned, and with no emotional support at home for her.

The low functioning borderline may be very intelligent but is not organized in his or her thought processes and does not even consider the consequences for the lack of planning. Many low functioning borderlines have been diagnosed with Attention Deficit Disorder because of their inability to focus and maintain thought processes. Retention of information is problematic, and short-term memory lapses are common, making it arduous to perform in a work setting. Their inability to cover up these behaviors or wear an acceptable façade like a high functioning borderline, causes the low functioning borderline to be easily recognized.

BPD, Divorce, and Children

Divorce is a time of crisis for the entire family. However, for the borderline, divorce raises critical abandonment issues that can incite extreme feelings, thoughts, and behaviors. It is during this heightened, emotionally charged time that the borderline may exhibit some of the most dramatic changes in behaviors. When children are involved in the divorce process the borderlines fear of abandonment increases, dramatically. In order to compensate for their fear of abandonment and maintain control, borderlines may resort to some of the following:

1. Discourage or stop visitation entirely with the Non-Custodial Parent (NCP).
2. Allege false claims of physical or sexual child abuse.
3. Involve police with false 911 alleged domestic violence calls.
4. Systematically alienate the children from the NCP.
5. Eliminate the NCP from educational, religious, and medical decisions.
6. Engage in litigation on a regular basis for years post-divorce.
7. Attempt to sabotage the NCP of future relationships with potential partners.
8. Attempt to alienate the children from the NCP's family members or friends.

At the time of divorce, the children of a BPD parent have a significantly higher risk for potential emotional and physical harm as a result of these behaviors. Several research studies estimate that 75 percent of BPD parents employ some form of Parental Alienation Syndrome (PAS). From my professional experience I believe this figure to be much higher. However, this figure compares to an estimated 25 percent for non-BPs who use some form of PAS during divorce. According to these studies a BPD parent is three times more likely to use some form of PAS than a non-BP. Early identification of a BPD partner and the existence of PAS is critical in protecting involved children.

PAS and the BPD Parent

The first time Bob had difficulty seeing his children, ages ten, twelve, and fourteen, was during the process of divorce. For years, Bob had been told by his wife that if they ever got a divorce, the children would never live with him again. That threat had kept Bob in a marriage that had been over for at least five years. Now, after his wife filed for divorce, he was finding out that his greatest fear of losing contact with the children was becoming a reality. When Bob tried to visit his children, they resisted, stating they wished to stay with mom. Then, the children became fearful of dad. Finally, when Bob tried to exercise his visitation rights under the guidelines of the parenting time agreement, he was met by two or three police cars at the children's house. Bob was ordered to assume the position at his car and was frisked. Neighbors watched this real life nightmare with the children watching from inside the house. When Bob showed the officers his divorce judgment awarding him parenting time, they replied, "but they're afraid of you." Bob was told by the police to leave the premises forthwith or face immediate arrest.

To the outside world, a criminal is born. Depicted as an abusive husband and father, Bob faced stereotypical ridicule as a deadbeat dad. How does Parental Alienation (PA), a form of emotional and psychological child abuse, and Parental Alienation Syndrome (PAS), brought about when children participate in a denigration and berating campaign against another, emanate?

The Foundation of PAS

Parental Alienation is the creation of a singular relationship between a parent and child, or children, which excludes the other parent. The alienated child does not wish to have any contact whatsoever with one parent and expresses negative feelings for that parent and positive feelings for the alienator, the *protective* parent. An alienated child loses feelings for both parents that is normal for a child. In order to understand the consequences of PAS and how a BPD parent contributes to the same, first we must look at the natural relationship between the parent and child, for both mother and father. It is natural for a child to love both parents, mother and father. Children yearn affection and approval from both parents. The desire to be with and loved by both parents is apparent when we look at an abused child who still wishes to remain with the abusive parent. It is well known in Attachment Theory that abused children despise separation, anxiety, and loss. What then causes a child to cease to want to be with one of his or her parents? In an excerpt from the book, *People of the Lie*, M. Scott Peck wrote: "The essence of maternal love for the infant is affirmation." The ordinary, healthy mother loves her infant for no other reason other than pure existence. The infant does not have to do anything to earn her love. It's unconditional love with no strings attached. "During the second and third year of its life, the mother begins to increasingly expect certain things, such as toilet training, from her child. And when this happens her love inevitably becomes, to at least some degree, conditional. She now says, "I love you, but . . ." As the child matures and individualism becomes more of a problem for the BPD parent, there's a need for the child to remain dependent and compliant for positive attention. When this takes place, the child learns to either internalize and suppress his or her need for individualism, or act out, rebelling against the controls placed on him or her by the BPD parent. This lays the early foundation for PAS.

Very often the nature of the BPD parent may be controlling, domineering, manipulative, and demanding of complete allegiance to them. When a child is young this does not present as much of a problem for the BPD parent because the child is more compliant than combative. As the child matures and gains independence in their thinking, this becomes more of a threat to the BPD parent. It becomes more of a survival technique for the child to not upset the BPD parent, but express anger upon the *non-BP*, who will continue to love and accept them unconditionally. Children will do whatever is necessary to survive in their crazed world, including accepting the craziness of the BPD parent when they feel there are no other options. The child becomes robbed of developing his or her own personality and instead must mirror the thinking, feelings, and behaviors of the BPD parent. There is no escape for the child without intervention from the non-BP, to protect them and ensure their best interests are truly served.

PAS as Emotional Abuse

A child who has experienced PAS at the hands of a parent has been emotionally abused. They've been robbed not only of their individualism, but also their natural desire to nurture a relationship with the NCP, or non-BP. Early identification of PAS is necessary for the healthy development of the child. If allowed to progress to the *severe* PAS stage, the child could develop their own DSM-IV personality disorder; e.g., Oppositional Defiant Disorder. If a parent is suspected of, or diagnosed as a, BPD, it is critical to identify and document any and all of the following actions by the alienating parent:

1. Discourages or halts visitations entirely with the NCP—via litigation, take immediate steps to re-enforce visitation. File for contempt and sanctions against the alienator.
2. Alleges false claims of physical or sexual child abuse—hire an attorney (see Appendices C&D). Move for the appointment of a GAL, or Court Appointed Special Advocate. Move for a complete family evaluation, psychologically speaking, and home study. Suppress unnecessary therapies of the alleged child victim.
3. Involves police with 911 calls and false domestic violence claims—retain in your possession at all times a copy of the divorce-custody judgment. Follow up by obtaining copies of the police reports.

4. Systematically alienates the children from the NCP—do not talk about the actions or inactions of the alienator with the children. Do not talk about legal problems with the children. Make the most of your visitation time with your kids. Consider a change in custody if the PAS constitutes a material and substantial change in circumstances since the final divorce judgment.

5. Eliminates the NCP from educational, religious, and medical activities—maintain regular contact with the school and exercise your rights under Family Educational Rights and Parents Act. If apropos, during your visitation time, take the child to church and the doctor.

6. Engages in litigation on a regular basis for years post-divorce— create a timeline (log of events of the alienation). Focus on the child, not yourself! Find a good lawyer who understands BPD and PAS (see Appendices C&D).

7. Attempts to sabotage the NCP of future relationships—fit the children into your new familial life slowly. Reinforce in their mindset that they are very special and important.

8. Attempts to alienate the children from developing a bond with the NCP's family members or friends—do not push parenting, but let the children ease into meeting others. Let them become comfortable!

There is a direct relationship between the BPD parent and PAS. The longer PAS goes unchecked the more deeply enmeshed the child becomes in mirroring the alienating parent. Child victims of PAS may suffer pathological symptoms later in life that include, but are not limited to:

- Splitting in their relationships.
- Difficulties in forming future intimate relationships.
- A lack of ability to tolerate anger in relationships.
- Psychosomatic symptoms and sleep or eating disorders.
- Psychological vulnerability and dependency.
- Conflicts with authority figures resulting in brushes with the law.
- An unhealthy sense of entitlement for one's rage leading to social alienation.
- Physical ailments such as irritable bowel syndrome, ulcers, ulcerative colitis, Crohn's disease, and migraines.

The healing process for PAS can be long and difficult. Identifying the pain and attachment issues, removing all of the old hurtful, pain causing negative messages from childhood, and replacing same with healthy, self-caring messages can facilitate the healing process. This process can be expedited with young children when the psychosomatic disorders and/or physical ailments are diagnosed and treated early, and properly. However, it takes a skilled clinician with knowledge and understanding of BPD and PAS to work with the non-BP to help the healing process move at a faster rate.

Richard Gardner, M.D., psychiatrist and founder of the Parental Alienation Syndrome, has suggested performing a *parentectomy* (removing child victims of PAS from parental alienator) via litigation, if the PAS becomes severe enough. Many BPD parents employ PAS to maintain control over their children and keep them dependent. In order to stop the child from internalizing their emotional pain causing psychosomatic disorders and physical ailments, it is necessary to do whatever is required to protect the child. Sometimes a parentectomy may be the only answer when all else fails.

Dr. L possesses a doctorate in counseling psychology and more than twenty-five years experience working with individuals, couples, children, and adolescents in various mental health settings. Dr. L was one of the five original founders of the American Mental Health Counselors Association and was instrumental in establishing the National Academy of Certified Clinical Mental Health Counselors. His personal and professional experiences bring a wealth of knowledge and understanding to his work with individuals who have BPD and exhibit PAS.

17.

A Summary of Problems and Solutions

According to Douglas Besharov, the original director of the National Center for Child Abuse and Neglect and now a legal scholar at the American Enterprise Institute think tank in Washington, DC, 70 percent of child abuse cases are unfounded. A national study done in 1986 by the Child Welfare League showed that 60 percent of child-abuse allegations were proven false. To reach a judgment in cases of child sexual abuse often takes months of juvenile and, perhaps, criminal court time, thousands of dollars in attorney fees, and results in the disruption of the family, the accused's career, and his entire lifestyle. Wouldn't it seem logical that any system producing a 60 to 70 percent error rate should be examined for deficiencies? Wouldn't it seem sensible for any system so rife with errors *on both sides of the child abuse coin* to be tapped for legislative changes?

As we have seen in the case studies presented and others researched, there are a number of problems surrounding the entire question of child sexual abuse allegations, beginning with the credibility of the alleged child victim and running through the social services agencies, the mental health profession, the court system, and the issue of individual rights. I make no pretension of having the answers to all these problems, nor do I propose to offer a quick solution. This is not a problem that began yesterday and can be solved tomorrow, but an intricate network of issues and attitudes that must be approached in a careful, consistent, conscientious, and compassionate manner. Indeed, the pervasive problem of false allegations of child abuse has resulted from actions that were initially presented as a solution to the concerns engendered by abuse of children. The solution has become a problem itself, a not uncommon occurrence when the long-range ramifications of decisions are not considered.

In this chapter, I will attempt to first define and summarize the problems surrounding false allegations of child abuse and domestic violence that I have discovered. It is hoped that this summary will provide a map of potential obstacles for anyone who is falsely accused. It is further hoped that this presentation will encourage agencies, legislators, lawyers, judges, and individuals in the mental health care professions to carefully analyze the manner in which our current system operates, with an eye toward developing a system that better serves the best interests of the child. I will then examine some potential solutions to these problems, in the hopes that involved agencies, legislators, and individuals may begin to fashion a system whereby true perpetrators are properly identified and prosecuted, while innocent victims of false allegations are exonerated and allowed their full rights to their children, their good reputation, and a full life. These solutions have been proposed by various experts in the field of child development and, in some cases, include legislation that has been passed or is pending in various states. Unfortunately, the list of solutions is much shorter than the list of problems.

Problems:

Definitions of child sexual abuse, like most other definitions of abuse and neglect, are ambiguous at best and most often nonexistent in the statutes that address the issue. During Dr. Spiegel's trial, a physician was asked if it was sexual abuse for a father to kiss his 2-year-old daughter on the posterior. The physician responded "yes" but qualified the response by adding, "Yes, if the mother is out of the room." During a supervised visit, I kissed my daughter on the cheek and was told by a horrified social worker, "Mr. Tong, that is inappropriate behavior!" Under the VAWA a father can be prevented from visiting his children based on a statement of fear of threatened harm with no proof of abuse. While I respect victims' rights it appears we've turned our backs on the Constitution and the Bill of Rights, and, in specific, the Fourteenth Amendment and one's right to due process.

Not only are definitions of abuse ambiguous, but the definition of "evidence" is equally flexible. In cases of child sexual abuse allegations, which generally involve young children, there is rarely any medical evidence. A physician's statement that behavior is "consistent with abuse" is an opinion, not evidence. A mother's contention that the child said it happened, particularly when the child will not repeat the accusation or, in fact, denies the abuse, is not evidence; it is a statement made by the mother. A social worker's, or GAL's statement that he or she believes the child's behavior is indicative of abuse is, again, an individual's opinion, not evidence. In these situations, juvenile court judges have too much latitude to find for the government and adjudicate children dependent.

The submission and acceptance of hearsay evidence in the family courts, with judges accepting the statements and opinions of social workers and child protection team members as expert opinions, is a distortion of the laws and the constitutional rights of the victim and "the accused."

The current trend in using hearsay testimony makes it too simple for a prosecutor to resort to hearsay in lieu of live testimony, in order to gain a tactical advantage. In doing so, it deprives the accused his right to confrontation under the Sixth Amendment.

The automatic acceptance of self-proclaimed "experts" by the courts needs to be closely examined. Many social workers, child protection team members, agency therapists, and law officers have little, if any, education or training in the areas of child development, play therapy, or play projection. Few of these individuals have qualifying clinical experience. The individual investigating allegations of child sexual abuse or domestic violence may be untrained, incompetent, or personally biased.

Hechler's book included a case study in which the state called an "expert witness." This expert witness was a police officer who had taken a forty-hour course in child maltreatment. This witness had no other credentials, no associated degrees, and no advanced psychological courses. The witness introduced information on pedophiles and homosexuals and stated that, although the accused had done nothing but hug the child, there was always an escalation of activities in the seduction of children. He further advised the jury that if the accused hadn't been arrested, he might have gone on to perpetrate all manner of heinous crimes on the children he supervised. (The accused individual was convicted.)

There is a noticeable difference in the treatment of the accused and the accuser. State statutes and procedures almost always act to the detriment of the falsely accused. An allegation of child sexual abuse brings immediate concern and support to the accusing parent, who is afforded belief, therapy, sympathy, and legal counsel by the state. The accused is rarely made aware of what's occurring until the case is built and then has no where to turn for support, objective and helpful counseling, or funding for the legal counsel necessary to prove his innocence. Rarely are the accused and accuser afforded the same opportunities to present their sides of the issue, the accused often is not even afforded the courtesy of an interview by child protective services. The alleged perpetrator must pay for his own attorney, evaluations, and any court costs, while providing child support and sometimes alimony, even though he may be denied any contact with the children he is supporting.

There is a startling lack of effort or interest in interviewing/investigating the accused. Often, the accused is unaware of the allegations until the state agency and prosecutors office have had time to build their case. Particularly in cases where there is the potential of a SAID syndrome situation, the omission of interviews with the accused parent shows a glaring lack of objectivity in gathering pertinent information. The accused is denied access to his own records, in regard to allegations made by the social services agency or child protection team. In most states, these records are considered strictly confidential, and it requires a court order for the accused to learn the exact nature of the allegations and its source, the results of interviews, evaluations, and allegations, and exactly what he is defending himself against.

Given the way the system currently operates, it is all too easy for an individual to manipulate it to their benefit, particularly in cases of custody or visitation. The accusing parent may exaggerate a nonexistent or inconsequential sexual contact. The child, in order to ingratiate himself with the accusing parent, or feeling the necessity of approval from the custodial parent bringing the accusation, goes along, not necessarily even understanding, if they are young. It is a widely known fact that, in the instance of a sexual abuse accusation, custody is almost instantly awarded the complaining parent and, in most cases, visitation of any sort is denied the accused parent.

There remains, throughout much of our judicial and social services systems, the automatic assumption that the mother is the best parent, regardless of her ability to function adequately in that role. This gender bias provides parenting classes and DCF supervision and instruction to a mother, but rarely is this considered for the father. This bias resulted in Mark Doe's children living with a convicted abuser, the man to whom their mother is married. This bias resulted in my children living with my ex-wife, even after she was proven to be an unfit mother.

Many of the so-called "standard tests" are in violation of the tenets of the American Psychological Association. Judges and lawyers need to be aware of this.

There is some question as to the value of psychological evaluations done on parents where allegations of child sexual abuse have occurred as an add-on to a divorce and custody battle. There are many "experts" whose qualifications are miles apart and whose methods of testing and manner of interviewing are diverse enough to result in different results from the same type of test. These experts are seeing the individuals at a time when they are hurt, angry, confused, frustrated, and frightened, yet attempt to draw a profile of how these individuals think and act under "normal" circumstances. Moreover, many of the tests like the Rorschach and TAT are not generally accepted into the scientific community and shouldn't be administered.

Often, the individuals involved in substantiating and treating the abuse are not acting in the best interest of the children. It appears we have a bureaucracy that perpetuates the problem, combined with the subtle establishment of a system of experts who can be relied upon to substantiate allegations of abuse. The child abuse industry is an extremely lucrative one, pumping vast dollar amounts into various agencies in the mental health field, whether state or federally funded or private. There are too many payoffs involved in the levying of false allegations. Attorneys receive large fees, the ex-wife obtains custody of the children, state agencies receive grant funds and larger budgets, and evaluators, therapists, and mental health professionals and institutions receive large fees for unnecessary treatments. One individual has pointed out that if we were to take the profit out of child protective investigations, where child abuse allegations are concerned, the problem would go a long way toward correcting itself.

The effect of the accusation on the falsely accused is not often realized. An allegation of child sexual abuse automatically paints you guilty until proven innocent in the eyes of the public, society, and social workers. There is frustration, anger, and anxiety. Through the court battles and investigations, there is tremendous financial expense. All of these build to a level of depression that makes the falsely accused begin to question the sense of continuing the fight. It would be much easier to give up. Support groups for the falsely accused are appearing across the nation, but all too often there is nowhere for the individual to turn.

The proposed conditions for allowing the accused to see his children again too often include a requirement that he attend child sexual abuse counseling or therapy. This condition is frequently imposed before there is any valid evidence of abuse and is often stipulated even after criminal charges have been dropped, or the individual has been acquitted and creates a no-win situation. If you want to see your children, you must enter the required therapy. To be accepted into therapy, many therapists require that you admit to child sexual abuse. If you do not, there will be no therapy and therefore no contact with your children. If you do admit to the abuse, you're admitted to therapy, but the family court has reason to deny you any contact with your children. And, if you're lucky enough to see your children you will do so at *family visitation centers*, designed to be family friendly, but at best are very tense, non-parenting centered settings. While visiting his daughter under the supervised confines of a family visitation center in Tampa, one father told me he could cut the air with a knife.

The use of anatomically complete dolls encourages a child to fantasize, which is then treated as fact. Investigators resort to other methods of interviewing alleged child victims such as scripting, stereotype induction, and guided imagery, which can lead to source misattributions errors.

In too many states and counties, social workers are dealing with two to three times the recommended number of cases. With the tremendous increase in allegations, false and valid, this overload prevents a thorough investigation and evaluation. In addition, burnout resulting from this situation leads to high turnover among social workers. As a result, many social workers, agency mental health workers, and child protection team members are undereducated, untrained, and inexperienced, resulting in a high degree of incompetency, particularly in areas of comprehensive and objective investigative techniques and skills. In a number of agencies, the social worker's job performance is measured by the body count of cases discovered or convictions gained.

Caseworkers may see a great deal of real suffering on a daily basis. As a result, objective analysis and reaction are replaced by emotional decisions. When the same caseworker who is responsible for emotional therapy is also responsible for investigative work on the case, there is inevitably a crossover of efforts and information that should have been uncovered during an investigation but is smothered in the immediate desire to "help" the *victim*. A lone social worker, whose interest is primarily therapy, cannot conduct a qualified, objective investigation, looking for answers to the question, "What is the basis of this allegation?"

In regard to investigators serving as therapists, Hechler's book includes this insight. "To avoid this very conflict, the Federal Standards for Child Abuse and Neglect Prevention and Treatment Programs and Projects suggests that social services departments assign specific staff for the purpose of intake (receipt and evaluation of child abuse and neglect reports) when the local unit has two or more child protective service workers, and assign specific staff for the purposes of treatment (provision and/or obtainment of services and resources to meet the needs of the child, individual members and the family as a unit)."

The manner in which the system currently treats allegations of child sexual abuse provides that only the accused has accountability responsibilities. The individual making the accusation has historically suffered no legal or financial ramifications if the allegations were false. This is slowly changing in some states. "Expert" witnesses, who use unproven testing or interviewing techniques and who provide biased opinions of test results, suffer no legal or financial ramifications. Social workers and child protection team members operate under the protection of "sovereign immunity." The lack of checks and balances, the absence of accountability to legislators, heads of state, or the court system, guarantees that DCF agency workers can dictate the lives of the falsely accused and his family. The establishment of anonymous hot line reporting of child abuse, which in my opinion is an open invitation to malicious slander, allows an individual to make the allegation without identifying himself/herself, therefore making it impossible to hold that individual accountable for the devastation that may ensue.

The theory held by most social workers is that "children don't lie and must be believed and protected *at all costs*." Even though the statement is made by the mother, it is held that the child must have said it, and so it is truth. When the child denies the allegations during an interview, the theory shifts to the fact that he or she is now ashamed or frightened of repeating the accusation, that he or she has been threatened not to tell. Called the "Doctrine of Immaculate Confession" by author Mary Pride in her 1986 book *The Child Abuse Industry,* child protective investigators often ignore children's recantations of abuse and rely on their initial disclosures, only.

The practice of placing the young child into therapy as soon as an allegation is filed is not in the best interest of anyone involved except, perhaps, the therapist and governmental agency. This therapy often teaches the child more about the accusation and the role of victim they are to play. In many cases, we are treating young children for a condition that doesn't exist.

Solutions:

A review of the type of evidence and testimony that is allowed and accepted by the court is a necessary initial step. Today's technology provides various means by which hearsay testimony can be avoided and the child witness can provide actual testimony without undue stress or trauma. The use of closed circuit television, either one-way or two-way systems, provides the defendant the right to face and cross-examine the alleged victim without subjecting the child to an adult courtroom filled with strangers. Another option is the possibility of using videotaped testimony, taken in the defendant's presence. All initial and subsequent interviews of the alleged victim should be video, or audio recorded.

Laws need to be passed that protect the right of the accused and include consequences for a false allegation. The 1990 Ohio legislature passed House bill 44, assessing liability against anyone making false and malicious allegations of child abuse. Florida statute chapter 98-111 makes bad faith false accusations a third degree felony providing for prison time for accusers of the same. Currently, a bill introduced in Ohio would forbid agencies to override a judge's decision or the decision of one's peers. It will also address appropriate access to one's own records and will contain a penalty clause making agencies and caseworkers accountable for their actions. The 1989 Arizona legislature passed a bill amending their Section 6, Title 13, Chapter 36 to provide that a person acting with malice, who knowingly and intentionally makes a false report of child abuse or neglect, or a person acting with malice who coerces another person to make a false report of child abuse or neglect, is guilty of a class three misdemeanor.

Social workers, child protection team members, attorneys, and judges need to become familiar with the signs and potential of the SAID syndrome when handling allegations made during the course of custody/ visitation battles. Social workers and mental health care professionals should also be cognizant of factors that may be indicative of the Parental Alienation Syndrome. In the context of divorce and custody battles, when allegations of child sexual abuse are made, particular attention must be focused on the accuser's psychological makeup, psychological needs, hidden agendas, and his/her influence on the child's allegations.

"Experts," such as social workers, child protection team interviewers, and policemen, need to be closely examined as to their actual "expertise" and qualifications before their diagnoses, opinions, and recommendations are considered or accepted. Many juvenile courts run forty cases through each hour, relying solely on the social services recommendations and rubberstamping those recommendations.

Regarding social workers as expert witnesses, we should ask the following questions about the individuals and their interviewing techniques: What are the social worker's qualifications? How are those qualifications defined? Do they qualify as experts under Federal Rule of Evidence 702? What are the interviewing techniques? When are there enough questions, too many questions? How many times must the child go through the same questions in order to satisfy everyone's requirements for expert testimony? What are the results of this repetition?

Childcare workers need to be trained to have equal suspicion of untruth and of truth in allegations of child molestation. They need training in child development and child pathology to learn that children can be tricked or trained to lie by adults/parents, professionals whom they wish to please or whom they fear.

Before a case moves into the courts or criminal charges are filed, each situation should be reviewed for outside factors that may be indicative of a motive for false allegations. Is there a divorce or custody battle in process? Does this case have any of the red flags of the SAID syndrome? Is the family intact? Which patent filed the complaint? Did the child actually indicate there had been abuse or did the complaint come from a parent or other adult? How was the investigation handled and what professionals were involved? Were all individuals directly interviewed, as well as friends, neighbors, relatives, and so forth?

Anonymous reporting of alleged child abuse should be abrogated and changed to *confidential*. This would ensure accountability for a person who was vindictive and attempting to wield the system as a weapon. In juvenile-dependency court, the burden of proof upon the government should be *clear and convincing* evidence, not a preponderance of evidence, to prove a child has been abused, neglected, or abandoned and is in need of assistance.

Initial interviews must be videotaped, to identify the credibility of the information acquired, the circumstances in which statements were made, the manner in which the interrogation was conducted, and the competency, if any, of the professionals conducting the interviews. Child competency and hearsay relevancy hearings should be used to determine the effect of the child's age, the ability to communicate, and to discern truth from falsehood at the time the out-of-court statements were made. This may shed light on the child's competency and the trustworthiness of his/her hearsay statements. Guidelines must be established, determining when a child witness crosses the line from merely being uncommunicative to unavailable.

Any investigation of child sexual abuse should be done by a team of qualified individuals, preferably a designated task force. A responsible team should include individuals trained in objective investigation, psychiatric/psychological intervention, medical evaluation, social work, and logical legal work.

The court monitor system, discussed under "The Courts" in chapter twelve, could serve as an excellent informal research system to identify areas of concern regarding types of evidence and investigative techniques that do not serve in the best interest of either the alleged perpetrator or the alleged victim. It is essential that the validity of using anatomically detailed dolls be closely examined. With no standards for either the production of the dolls as a testing mechanism or for the manner in which they are used, this protocol is not accepted by the scientific community and considered highly suspect by the majority of expert professionals involved in the areas of child development and play therapy. If the dolls were used to gain "evidence" from the child, both sides should be allowed to speak of the validity of the use of such methodology.

Judges and attorneys need a better understanding of various tests, such as the Minnesota Multiphasic Personality Inventory, the Child Abuse Potential Inventory, ABEL screen, TAT, and Rorschach, to be able to identify biased reporting, unreliable tests, or too much reliance on any one given test. The various psychological tests available measure different facets of the individual's personality and psychological makeup and need to be used as a set of tools to reach valid conclusions.

Consistent and objective actions by support groups, such as VO-CAL, National Father's Resource Center, Children's Rights Council, CASA, and other similar organizations can identify the problems within the system and work toward forming and proposing solutions that will protect the innocent, as well as, the children.

In cases of alleged domestic violence, the ten or fifteen day TRO hearing should be pushed back to thirty days, affording the accused more legal discovery time to prove his innocence. Moreover, the accused should be awarded supervised child visitation upon the signing of an ex parte TRO. Until such time that the complainant proves by clear and convincing evidence the accused is guilty and should not receive visitation rights at all. As stated in a report filed by an investigative committee reviewing the actions of a child protective services agency in Texas, "Regrettably, an infusion of resources alone will not be sufficient to address these problems . . . Judgment, ethics, and attitude cannot be purchased or legislated. Money cannot buy common sense . . ."

18.

A Self-Help Guide

This chapter contains the "dos" and "don'ts" for anyone who may be in a position to face false allegations of child abuse or domestic violence and for anyone who is already embroiled in the battle against such false allegations. It incorporates all the suggestions and recommendations that have been discussed throughout the book, as well as additional recommendations from psychologists, attorneys, support groups, and other individuals who have been victims of false allegations. I have grouped the information by category, i.e., relationship with the children, emotions, attorneys, expert witnesses, and court appearances.

If You Suspect the Potential of False Allegations:

If you are in a high risk situation, i.e., in the process of filing for separation or divorce, involved in or anticipating a custody battle, or considering an attempt to get a change in custody or visitation schedules.

If the marriage or separation has been stormy, watch out for over cooperativeness or friendliness as a behavioral change. This may be a prelude to false allegations.

Document everything throughout the divorce/custody suit. Create a timeline or dated chronology of events. Note what the children say during your visits (particularly anything out of the ordinary), anything your spouse/friend says that is rash or unusual, and whether or not there's a male or female friend in the picture. Take copious notes. If your state is a one-party state, tape record the conversations.

If something seems wrong have an eyewitness present at all visits with your child to corroborate your testimony, if needed. Don't be alone with your child if you have any suspicions about your spouse's actions or potential actions.

If the child appears to be psychologically, emotionally, or physically abused, take the child to an independent expert Ph.D.-M.D., before you bring the child back from a visit with you. This may alert you to factors or events in the child's home environment of which you are unaware.

If you foresee a bitter divorce/custody battle ensuing, hire an expert attorney who is familiar with SAID-Parental Alienation Syndrome cases and who will litigate in your best interests. This may help you avoid making mistakes in dealing with your spouse's demands or proposed conditions of divorce and/or custody.

If you suspect your wife is going to file for divorce and you live in a no-fault state, file first, seeking an *ex parte* order granting you temporary custody, effective immediately.

Close joint accounts and cancel credit cards. It's going to take every cent you have to fight the allegations.

Remain in the house, unless ordered to move out by the court or advised to do so by a professional you trust. Once you leave the house, your wife or ex-wife has full control of the children. Once you've lost temporary guardianship of the children, the other parent can begin the projection and PAS process, programming the children to not want to see you.

If You Are the Victim of False Allegations, DO the Following:

Treat the accusation very seriously. This accusation will affect every area of your life.

Hire a competent and qualified lawyer immediately, one familiar with false allegations of child sexual abuse and domestic violence and with the SAID and Parental Alienation Syndromes (see Appendices C&D). Recommendations may be made by VOCAL or other support groups or the State Bar Association. Query consultants and psycho-legal strategists who are experienced with the kind of case you are litigating.

Find the necessary resources to defend yourself properly. An inadequate defense team, due to financial constraints, may result in you losing your children, or in a longer than necessary court battle.

Immediately retain a civil rights attorney to sue for damages against false allegations once you've been vindicated. The accuser and participating individuals of the state agencies may be liable for damages you suffer as a result of the false allegations.

Do everything possible to halt any further interviewing or treatment of the alleged child victims. Continuous interviews using scripting, guided imagery, and/or play therapies may be used to train children to give desired responses or tell pre-programmed stories.

Attempt to require that all further interviews will be videotaped. This assures the ability to check for objectivity and validity of questions asked and methods used.

Have an independent psychologist suggested by your attorney appointed to evaluate the entire family.

Pay for all evaluations yourself or split the cost with your ex-wife. This assures you have access to the results.

Prohibit interrogation of the child until the independent evaluation is complete. Again, this is to avoid training the child to give desired responses during interrogation.

Attempt to regain custody or visitation immediately, with the understanding such custody or visitation will include constant adult supervision by a third party. This reduces the potential for parental alienation syndrome.

Shift the court's focus from the alleged conduct of the accused (you) to the psychological functioning of the accuser. This may show the accuser fits the typical profile of a SAID syndrome case or specific type of accuser.

Go immediately on the defensive and demand accountability.

Persuade the court that any delay in addressing the issues raised is detrimental in the extreme to the child.

Maintain contact with the alleged victim. This will make it more difficult for the child to believe what others are saying because it will conflict with their firsthand experience.

Steadfastly maintain your innocence.

Learn about the judges who might sit on your case. Request a different judge if you are assigned one with a history of being prejudiced.

Keep detailed records of everything. Document the children's visits or reasons visits were canceled, conversations, comments, and actions.

Maintain files of all documents and review them often for inconsistencies. You may be better able to spot inconsistencies than an attorney unfamiliar with your family.

Keep a daily journal of events. This shows where you were and what you were doing and may pinpoint inaccuracies of statements made by the accuser.

Keep records. If it is legal in your state (i.e., if your state is a one-party state), buy a mini tape player to record any conversations with your wife, your ex-wife, social worker(s), or anyone remotely connected with the case. A calendar, diary, expenses, photographs, and videotapes may show inconsistencies.

If you are denied a normal visitation, note when and why, where you were, and what you were doing. This may contribute to raising questions as the good faith efforts of your wife on the part of the children and their best interests.

Track past, present, and future events on the calendar and in the diary, noting where you were, whom you were with and what you did, whether you had your children or not. This may prove that you were at a ball game with a friend when the alleged abuse or any future allegation was supposed to have occurred.

Obtain evidence that is admissible in court . . . affidavits from friends, children, and character references. This can be used to indicate that there has been no previous indication of problems and again point interest to the accuser's personality profile.

Have a reliable witness at all meetings, interviews, and phone conversations. This assures accuracy and credibility in a their word/your word situation.

After all meetings, interviews, and phone calls, write to the person with whom you spoke, listing the main points discussed and asking that if you have misinterpreted anything they respond by return mail to your letter. Mail the original certified, return receipt requested, and keep a copy. This forces accountability from the other party involved.

Obtain and keep transcripts of all proceedings. These should be reviewed for inconsistency or inaccuracy.

Be careful what you say, it will be used against you. Your ex-wife and those working with her are looking for anything that can be used to cast suspicion on your denial.

Scrutinize all prior statements on the subject by the complainant. You may be able to identify discrepancies regarding the allegation.

Attempt to ensure that child is not being coached. This frequently occurs in the home or during successive interviews.

Educate and be helpful to Child Protective Investigators. Be firm, but cordial with social workers and CPT members. This attitude projects a positive, cooperative image of you as an individual. They will be expecting anger that they can use to place you in a negative light. Remember, if you're *angry*, that is consistent with being a probable abuser!

When and if a DCF home study is ordered, be sure studies are the same in all respects. If they view two different sets of circumstances, they cannot make a valid comparison.

Get depositions of anyone and everyone involved in working with the child and the prosecution. If nothing else, this establishes the qualifications, protocol, and techniques used, the basis upon which the professional came to the conclusion of abuse.

Recognize the social worker is trying to build a case against you, no matter how they try to impress you as being helpful.

Get involved-help yourself and your attorney.

Where flight to another state takes place, make use of the Uniform Child Custody Jurisdiction Act and Parents Kidnapping and Prevention Act.

Try to win the case "before going to court" by pointing out weaknesses to the investigator's attorney.

When you've won the case, follow up immediately, e.g., get court orders, certify them, serve them.

File appeals immediately when your constitutional rights are violated.

Motion to recuse, or disqualify the judge, or file a Writ of Prohibition if you've been prejudiced by the court.

Ensure your attorney is kind and gentle with the child witness. Badgering a child has negative impact on judges and juries.

Take a lie detector test, paid for in cash. Effect anti-domestic assault testing or psychosexual testing, if accused of domestic assault or sexual child abuse.

Learn as many facts as possible and keep them in manageable form. The more you know, the better able you'll be to fight statements and hearsay allegations.

Be prepared and willing to go to court.

Learn as much as you can about the laws in your state and the requirements child protection agencies must fulfill to receive their funding. This may indicate funding is based on a number of cases filed or successfully convicted.

Assist in researching cases that may be of help to you and your attorney. There may be precedents you can apply or motions that you could use in your own case.

Require child competency and hearsay relevancy hearings. This may prevent invalid or suspect evidence from being presented.

Check to see if the accuser has levied allegations against any other individual or organization. If so, the accuser's credibility may be in question. This is particularly helpful in countering false Protection From Abuse orders.

Have a family doctor with whom you can substantiate any injuries. If alleged child sex abuse, ensure an independent pediatrician critiques the colposcopic photographs, or drawings of the abnormal genital findings at-issue. If unexplained fractures or broken bones, ensure there are no genetic abnormalities such as Osteogenesis Imperfecta. Have your pediatric orthopedist critique the child's X-Rays, MRI scans, etc.

If possible, have the child independently examined. Do not consent to the child being examined by a doctor associated with social services.

Request through the courts an independent psychiatric and/or psychological evaluation of the alleged victim be done immediately. This will counterbalance any subjective evaluations the agencies may attempt to use against you.

Get professional medical and psychological help. Don't try to battle the stress and depression by yourself. You must be strong for yourself and your children.

Subpoena the Standard Operating Procedure Manual (SOPM), or Policy and Training Manual of CPS, ESPECIALLY IN CASES OF ALLEGED PHYSICAL CHILD ABUSE.

The CPS book should outline the color scheme of bruises and what constitutes physical abuse from corporal punishment.

Obtain expert psychological /psychiatric review. If you are forced to accept a court appointed psychologist, establish what protocol will be used, if you will be examined in the presence of your child, if the mother is to be interviewed, where the interview is to take place, and when the report can be expected. This establishes your expectation for accountability from all involved.

Question the use of anatomical dolls and improper interview techniques. Hire an expert psychologist or psycho-legal strategist to assist you in rebutting the validity of the dolls and results of any interviews involving their use.

Have videotaped interviews analyzed by nationally recognized experts in the field of child developmental psychology, interrogation, and sexual abuse. This analysis may point out the leading questions and modeling behavior that would call the results of the interview into question.

Reach out for support from family, friends, doctors, psychologists, and VOCAL. This allegation will cause frustration, anger, and depression that is almost impossible for one to bear alone.

Become an activist in family rights and for the rights of the falsely accused. Be objective and be an advocate for the children and the entire family.

Expect the unexpected.

Channel your anger into constructive methods of fighting back.

Allow yourself to grieve, for the loss of time with your children, for your loneliness, and for your child's current circumstances.

Accept as normal your feelings of anxiety and depression, and find an individual or support group with whom you can talk through your emotions and concerns.

Forgive yourself for mistakes you have made or may make, and apply what you have learned to all future situations.

If supervised visitation is required, attempt to have supervision by a third party who is not from social services.

Upon consent from your attorney, use the media to your advantage. But, try to win your case in a court of law, not the court of public opinion.

If You Are a Victim of False Allegations. DO NOT DO the Following:

DO NOT accept a public defender to represent you. Few, if any, are qualified or experienced in this area. If indigent, file an Affidavit for Indigency, Insolvency, or *In Forma Pauperis* and request the state pay for your expert's fees.

DO NOT accept an attorney who is inexperienced in such allegations and who knows nothing of the SAID syndrome. He or she will be unaware of the machinations of a typical accuser.

DO NOT be afraid to change lawyers if you feel your current one is unable to defend you adequately against the charges that have been brought. This charge could cost you your freedom and your children, quickly!

DO NOT expect common sense in the activities of child protection workers, prosecutors, or the courts. Their motivations and objectives are often misguided.

DO NOT admit to anything you have not done. You have too much to lose by plea-bargaining!

DO NOT be over trusting and open yourself up to vulnerable weak spots.

DO NOT offend the child protection workers. They will be looking for anything that can be used to cast you in a negative light.

DO NOT sign anything without legal counsel being present or notified.

DO NOT agree to a plea bargain at *mediation* by consenting to a finding of dependency at a CHild In need of Protective Services (CHIPS) or CHild In Need of Assistance (CHINA) Petition Hearing, or enter a plea of *Nolo Contendere* (No Contest). Either of these qualifies you as guilty, and you're perceived by the system as a child abuser.

Never take your spouse/friend for granted and succumb to naivete. Do not underestimate them, particularly if jealousy, insecurity, adulterous threats/actions, and arguments persist.

DO NOT interrogate your child at all about the mother's intentions/actions or the child's acute transformation of behavior if any. You must prevent the child from becoming a pawn or tool for your own wishes.

DO NOT be nonchalant. You must be aggressive and nip any potential problems in the bud ahead of time.

DO NOT act guilty.

DO NOT make any concessions. Doing so will be looked upon as evidence of guilt.

DO NOT waive any rights, especially to a hearing.

DO NOT underestimate the effect of the initial pleading against you.

DO NOT underestimate the effect your responsive pleading may have.

DO NOT hesitate to advise your attorney to advise the court of attitudes, practices, and behaviors that would help prove your wife unfit. Perhaps, she suffers from Borderline Personality Disorder and/or fits the justified vindicator, hysterical, or psychopath accuser profile as outlined in the SAID syndrome chapter.

DO NOT play the gentleman. Pretending the accuser is still the woman you loved and married can get you a jail sentence and cost you the children. At best, it will lengthen the process of disproving the allegations and being reunited with your children. If co-dependent, this could induce you back into a relationship with same accuser, which could seal your doom if accused again. Remember, where there's smoke, there's fire! Read the book *Co-Dependent No More!*

DO NOT submit to a psychiatric/psychological evaluation for yourself before discussing this with your legal counsel.

DO NOT succumb to the Parental Alienation Syndrome. Utilize this syndrome to your advantage to aid you in your custody endeavors. Do not contribute to it!

DO NOT allow the situation to drive you into self-imposed isolation. You need support, assistance, and understanding at this time.

DO NOT attempt to influence the children by telling them horror stories about their mother. The children will resent this and may well become confused.

DO NOT agree to have the matter continued, under any circumstances, unless some sort of visitation can be arranged. It is important that your children see you regularly to counteract the negative information they may be receiving from others.

DO NOT be afraid of the media. Work with your attorney to work with the press.

DO NOT give up. Your life and the lives of your children depend on you.

19.

An Attorney's View

Charles Jamieson, Esq.

Introduction

When Dean Tong requested I write a chapter in his book, *Elusive Innocence*, regarding "Defending Against False Child Abuse Allegations," I was at first somewhat dismayed. This is a subject matter that one could write several books about and still not fully and comprehensively cover all the aspects of litigating a false child abuse allegation case. Consequently, in this short chapter, I have not tried to provide a comprehensive overview, but rather I have attempted to discuss some important aspects that must be confronted by an individual litigating a false child abuse allegation, regardless of what forum it may occur in: divorce court, criminal court, juvenile court, or civil court.

Many of the comments contained in this chapter may seem, at first, to be based on nothing more than a common sense, assertive approach in defending a client. However, it is amazing how many times a lay person or an attorney will apparently become confused and discouraged and not act in an assertive fashion in the defense against a false child abuse allegation. Because of this dynamic, one should never overestimate an attorney's ability to devise even what appears to be the most common sense and simplest response to a child abuse allegation. As an educated consumer of legal representation, a layperson should always assume that his attorney is open to suggestions and should always proceed, during any interview with your attorney, with the attitude you have certain things you wish to discuss or suggest to your attorney. Inevitably, you will find that the attorney is willing to sit back and speak to any individual about any alleged grievances, which they may have.

Most cases are won or lost prior to the commencement of trial. Consequently, I have focused my presentation on important pretrial issues that the falsely accused must confront in the context of preparing for trial. Like any attorney, I begin this chapter with a disclaimer. This should not be viewed by any individual as a "paint by the numbers" method of defending against a false child abuse allegation. Every case must be tailored to its own facts to fit its own facts and dynamics. Consequently, the suggestions made in this chapter, should not be followed blindly by any individual in forming or instituting a strategy of defense against a false child abuse allegation.

Negative Impact of the Allegation

No issue stirs such emotions in our society today as the issue of child abuse. It is an issue that is in the forefront of media, including newspapers, television, or radio. It is easy to comprehend why child abuse evokes such an overwhelming negative reaction. We are socialized from the time we are quite young to be protective of children. It is a message that is communicated to us in many forms on a daily basis throughout our entire lives. Consequently, it is not unreasonable to expect that an allegation of child abuse will evoke a uniformly negative response. The negative reaction associated with child abuse allegations cause many individuals to forget rational thought, and results in an atmosphere of hostility and prejudice toward an individual falsely accused, which must be overcome in order to preserve the principles of justice and due process. As attorneys and lay people involved in these types of cases, we cannot forget that this is a powerful dynamic which causes an individual falsely accused of child abuse to have to overcome the major unspoken, underlying premise in such cases, "An accused is presumed guilty until proven innocent." The most effective way to counter this dynamic is the planning and implementation of a comprehensive and assertive legal strategy. The watchwords for the strategy to counter the opposition's case should be, "object, object, object" and "limit, limit, limit." The watchwords for the implementation of a defense should be, "educate, educate, educate" and "explain, explain, explain."

Choosing Sides

Despite their protestations to the contrary, Americans, by their nature, choose sides in any controversy. It is part of our national ethos. Almost every person, in traveling, has turned on a television set and found themselves gazing idly at a sports event about which they know nothing, which involves players of whom they know nothing. Inevitably, within the first few moments of watching this sport, the viewer will start consciously or unconsciously rooting for one side or the other. This "rooting" may not be of the obvious, boisterous kind, but it will always inevitably occur.

In the same fashion, do not believe the statement that people will not choose sides in a child sex abuse allegation. Every significant person in the accused's life either consciously or subconsciously will determine which party to side with: the accuser or the accused. Even if they do not verbally state a preference, many people will state, "I don't wish to become involved." Even by this apparently neutral statement, the individuals are in fact stating a preference because they are not going to support the accused.

Because of this dynamic, it is absolutely important to immediately reach out and obtain a written statement from those individuals who may be potential witnesses on your behalf. As soon as possible, it is important to try and have these individuals commit their support to you in the form of a written statement. This statement can be obtained by an attorney, or preferably by an investigator. Any investigator who attempts to obtain these statements should be educated as to the themes of your case so that the appropriate questions can be asked.

An investigator is also useful in attempting to obtain statements from potentially hostile witnesses. Unless there is a specific court order entered that prevents your side from having contact from the opposition's witnesses, then it is appropriate and essential that your investigator attempt to contact these individuals to learn what they have to say about the issues in this case. If an individual refuses to talk to your investigator, then the tactic of sending them a certified, return receipt requested letter requesting that they permit your side to ask them questions about what they may know about the case is needed. Inevitably, those individuals, who have been instructed by the opposition's attorney that they don't have to talk with your side, will ignore the letter. If that occurs, then a second, similar letter should be sent. Such letters create the opportunity whereby you can have potent cross-examination of this witness before a judge or jury by creating an innuendo that these individuals had something to hide. At the very least, it permits the opportunity to have your attorney pose the closing argument, "What do these individuals have to hide, and why did they refuse to cooperate on a very simple request regarding the knowledge they have of the case?"

Chronology

Among other things that the O.J. Simpson trial brought to the national spotlight was the importance of time lines or chronologies. A chronology is one of the most important devices that a falsely accused individual, or his or her attorney, can create in the preparation and presentation of a defense. Chronology is a documentary procedure of organizing the information available in a child abuse case in a chronological or time oriented fashion. A chronology can be used to organize consistent and/or conflicting information concerning how an incident or accusation occurred, the events that preceded and occurred after the allegation occurred, how the investigation was conducted after the allegation occurred, what potential effects or influences various events may have had on the child or other major characters involved in the allegation, and it also produces an insight as to how an allegation occurred and/ or escalated. A chronology is a standard method of organization which can help your attorney establish his or her themes of the case and bring out causal links between seemingly related and sometimes seemingly unrelated events.

There is no easy way to prepare a chronology other than rolling up your sleeves and writing down all the important facts and incidences that have occurred in the case in a painstaking fashion. This requires that the creator of the chronology obtain information from every source available, including, but not limited to the accuser's recollections, friends of accuser's recollections of events, all possible records of the alleged child victim (including medical, school, and mental health), the section notes and evaluation reports of any mental health professionals involved in the case, civil case records from dependency or divorce court, criminal records if appropriate, and the views of all witnesses. Chronology is not a onetime task. It should be consistently and thoroughly updated with the production of each new piece of information and/or report. It should be reviewed from beginning to end on several occasions by both the accused and the attorney, and their impressions should be carefully compared and discussed. A chronology should be kept for each child in a multiple child case and for each defendant in a multiple defendant case. As the chronology is being generated, it has several uses. It can help the attorney to create a trial strategy and theories of defense. In addition, it can be used to help generate emotions, discovery requests, develop material for the jury, and help develop the opening and closing arguments of the attorney.

Learning about the Child Victim

It is important to discover everything one can about the child victim or victims involved in the case. What are their favorite movies and books? Once identified, it is absolutely essential that these books and movies be carefully reviewed. Sometimes the children's allegations will mirror particular themes contained in children's G-rated movies. In addition, particularly with young children, the fantasy elements contained in movies sometimes generates their own fantasy and may cause them to make allegations about things that have never occurred.

It is also important to find out what sources of potential sex education and/or stimuli to which the child has been exposed. Has the child victim ever had any playmates who were sexually abused? What kind of sexualized stimuli has the child been exposed to in the form of X-rated films, cable television shows, daytime soap operas; in what child abuse awareness or educational programs has the child participated? (Be sure to obtain a copy of the curriculum of each presentation, adult magazines-such as *Playboy* or *Penthouse,* and R-rated movies). These may all provide explanations as to why a child may be acting or stating things in a sexualized fashion, but yet has not been sexually abused.

In preparing for litigation, one must also obtain all records concerning the minor child. This includes all medical records, educational records, and mental health records. These records should be obtained through a direct request by the alleged perpetrator (if the alleged perpetrator is a parent of the alleged child victim) and through discovery requests and motions. The medical records are critical in attempting to ascertain if there are other medical conditions or incidents in the child's life that may have created a physical condition which may offer a benign or non-abusive explanation for the physical findings at issue in the case.

School records are often vital in exploring whether the child has disciplinary problems or behavioral problems that may lead to development of a possible theory for the defense. Mental health records are critical in reviewing whether appropriate procedures have been followed in the evaluation of the alleged child victim and the subsequent therapy sessions. In addition, a review of the mental health records are useful in determining whether evaluation and/or therapeutic techniques of mental health professionals have led to memory contamination, particularly in the case of younger children.

An extensive knowledge of the child's background, as well as his or her likes and dislikes, is essential for an attorney to be able to create an appropriate form of cross-examination of the alleged child victim needs. Children have different levels of maturity, sophistication, and articulation. Those developmental levels differ between children of the same chronological age, as well as children of different chronological ages. Consequently, in order to formulate a successful cross-examination, extensive knowledge of the alleged child victim is important.

Contextual Defense

In formulating a defense during any child abuse case, it is absolutely critical to determine if the alleged child victim is really indicating that something inappropriate happened to him or her. The proverbial sixty-four million dollar question is, "Did something really happen and if so, what was it?" The seemingly simple question is critically important. Today males are encouraged, more than at any other time in our recent past, to become actively involved in all aspects of child rearing. Those aspects include bathing, diapering, and administering medication to anal/genital areas of babies who have rashes, urinary tract problems, and other medical problems. Despite this change in child rearing practices, it is surprising the number of times a child will say that his or her father has touched their genital or anal areas, and the investigating agency automatically assumes that the child is talking about being sexually abused. Consequently, it is critical in the review of the history and materials in an investigation of child abuse to ascertain if there was an exploration into the context in which the alleged abuse occurred. If the touching occurred in a situation where the alleged accused has participated actively in childcare, then a potential defense may be created on the basis of the agency's misconstruing a benign or appropriate action.

In contextual exploration of an allegation, it is also important to ascertain whether the allegation is a by-product of other parties. This may be a stereotypical coaching of an estranged parent or mistakenly aggrieved relation or acquaintance of the accused. Although not frequently, children are sometimes brainwashed into making allegations.

Expert Witnesses

It is a sad fact that without the assistance of expert witnesses, the falsely accused stands a good chance of being found to have committed child abuse. Attorneys are trained in law school in legal logic, in the formulation of legal questions, and how to research and find the applicable statues and case law regarding legal questions. Attorneys are not trained in the areas of psychology, sociology, and medicine, which factor prominently in most false charges of child abuse. There is a common expression among individuals who are experienced in child abuse litigation, "A mediocre attorney can win a child abuse case with a good expert; however, a good attorney will have a hard time winning a child abuse case without the assistance of an expert witness."

An explosion of research has occurred in the past few years in the fields of medicine and psychology concerning the issues of child abuse. An expert is useful in helping educate the falsely accused and their legal counsel as to current accepted principles within the fields of medicine and mental health, regarding child abuse. Such current knowledge is critical in attempting to expose some of the commonly held myths which were created approximately ten years ago and which have entrenched themselves in some areas of the medical and mental health field. An example of such an outdated myth would be: children do not lie about sex abuse, or a relaxed anal tone is a diagnostic sign of child sexual abuse.

Expert witnesses are also essential in helping to formulate areas of cross-examination of the opposition's experts at the trial. Experts will also indicate information as necessary to be acquired in order to adequately review your case and help formulate themes for the defense. Finally, experts are critical in helping to explain some of the critical questions that occur in any child abuse trial (whether by judge or jury). Some of those questions include:

1. Did the child suffer from any medical conditions or incur any kind of injury that would result in the physical condition that is similar to a condition resulting from child physical or sexual abuse?

2. If the accused did not sexually abuse the child, then why is the child claiming that the accused abused him or her?
3. Has there been an overreaction or misinterpretation of a benign incident or statement?

Experts are also useful in educating the attorney and the trier of fact as to what research has been done to establish what behavior or findings are normal. For example, there is surprisingly little data as to what is the normal base rate for children touching their genital or anal areas. Although most parents are aware that all children touch themselves in this area, there is little knowledge as to what should be considered normal touching and at what age. Any experts you can retain will help neutralize the opposition's experts and will provide valuable assistance in the preparation and presentation of your defense.

Another useful purpose for an expert is to educate the trier of fact. Most people do not know the true facts about child abuse. Their beliefs and ideas concerning child abuse have been molded by the media and by myths that may have been accepted as being fact by mere repetition. This shortcoming affects both judges and many potential jury members. By the use of your expert, you can obtain research and data by which you can construct an aggressive, defensive strategy that can help counteract the prejudice that is inherent in a child abuse charge and the "myth and folklore" espoused by the opposition.

Collateral Proceedings

The importance of the institution and active participation in collateral proceedings cannot be underestimated. In the event you are falsely charged in a criminal action of child abuse, then a collateral action might be some kind of civil action whereby you could participate and involve the same allegations. The advantages of doing are many. In the majority of the states, discovery that is permitted in criminal proceedings is quite limited. However, the discovery that is permitted in a civil action, such as a divorce case, is far more liberal. Consequently, in the event the former spouse brings a false accusation of child abuse, a collateral post-final judgment motion for modification action could be utilized to engage in discovery and find out information which would not ordinarily be available to you and your attorney in a criminal case. For instance, most states do not allow depositions in criminal proceedings. To circumvent this "road block" and be able to use this powerful engine of discovery, institute a collateral or corresponding civil case, and take the depositions in the civil proceeding.

In those jurisdictions where the family court may try to limit your criminal attorney's involvement in a proceeding, it may be appropriate to hire a separate attorney to pursue the modification proceeding in divorce court. However, your criminal attorney would continue actively working in the background to help direct the discovery strategy in the civil case and to make available to you any information which could be gained in this matter.

Pretrial Practice

One of my first legal mentors taught me that any case, no matter how strong it may appear, has weaknesses. It is the job of any good defense attorney to probe constantly in every case to discover those weaknesses in an attempt to wedge them open to the advantage of his or her client. This is the basic attitude of an attorney defending against false allegations of child abuse. Essentially, the attorney should raise every objection that he thinks appropriate and must move to limit the majority, if not all, the evidence offered by the opposition in their case.

Both the medical and mental health fields have undergone a revolution in recent years. Research has indicated that many of the "sacred truths" held by these professions, regarding issues in child sex abuse cases, have either been modified or been found to be erroneous. However, there has been an uneven distribution of these developments throughout the medical and mental health fields. There is no child abuse case in which it is not appropriate to file motions to suppress, motions in *limine*, or motions to limit the introduction of evidence. For instance, such motions can be filed regarding the suppression of evidence concerning anatomical dolls, child sexual abuse accommodations syndrome, and sex offender profiles, just to name a few. However, the need to file such motions only highlights the critical need for attorneys to be educated in the medical and mental health aspects of defending false child abuse allegations.

A more practical aspect regarding the effect of an active pretrial practice, exists in terms of obtaining discovery and filing motions. The underlying approach should be to paperwork the opposition to the maximum. This is not a vehicle of harassment. Instead, it is also a method to defend effectively against a false allegation and a means to obtain necessary information for your defense that the opposition may possess. The prosecutors, for the most part, are understaffed and overworked. They possess heavy caseloads, which usually prevent them from spending a great deal of time on any one case. In similar fashion, the majority of attorneys in private practice carry a rather heavy caseload in order to maintain a volume to meet the ever- increasing demands of overhead expenses and their own individual salaries. Consequently, opposing attorneys may not respond promptly to informal, or formal requests for production of discovery.

An aggressive approach to making discovery demands is oftentimes an effective method for obtaining needed information. It sends a message that your case is not *business as usual*. In some cases, prosecutors or

Assistant District Attorneys (ADA) may provide a better plea bargain offer if they see they have a major fight on their hands. In family court matters, you may get a better settlement if the opposition believes they have an unduly expensive and litigious fight on their hands. Aggressive pretrial motion practice and discovery practice is the most effective tactic to be utilized by those individuals who cannot afford to hire a battery of experts and may not have the financial wherewithal to withstand a protracted and lengthy trial. It is also the most effective fashion in which to start preparing your case for court. The focus of your pretrial practice is to limit the evidence of the opposition, to ask for every piece of information pursuant to discovery requests, including the *kitchen sink*, and to educate the court regarding the themes of your case. An attorney representing an alleged perpetrator of abuse should understand from the beginning that many, if not the majority, of his or her motions will be denied. However, unless vigorous motion practice and discovery practice are pursued, those few breaks the falsely accused may obtain from the legal system, will not occur.

Conclusion

Child abuse allegations immediately stir negative emotions in nearly everyone, including attorneys and judges. The only way to counteract the assumption that an accused is guilty, until proven innocent, is to carefully plan and institute a comprehensive, defensive strategy. Such a strategy must include obtaining all the information you can about the players in the development of the child abuse allegation, obtaining experts to assist you, instituting an aggressive strategy to obtain all the possible information you can, and to object and limit in any way possible the opposition's case. If one follows this basic strategy, then you will maximize their chances for a successful outcome if they find themselves falsely accused of child abuse.

Note: Charles D. Jamieson is an attorney in the law firm of Glickman, Witters, Marell, and Jamieson, P.A., 1601 Forum Place, Suite 1101, West Palm Beach, Florida 33401, telephone number (561) 478-1111. His practice is focused in the area of child abuse issues.

Epilogue

False abuse accusations are equal opportunity exterminators. They can affect parents, old and young, teachers, a host of other professionals, and even children. Everyone is vulnerable. Nobody is exempt. These accusations can hit, anonymously, or via *ex parte* avenues, at any time, on any day. They work all day, every day . . . holidays included. And, when they hit, they do so like a hurricane, leaving a path of destruction that seems infinite. The negative effects of false abuse accusations felt by non-abused children are severe. Judges and prosecutors must acknowledge these consequences before "erring on the side of caution, on the side of children" in gray area cases.

Children and families have been and will continue to be victimized by a behemoth known as Child Protective Services. Charged by our legislatures to protect children at-risk, in harm's way, and in jeopardy, CPS intake caseworkers have the burdensome duties of detecting which children have been abused and which have not been so. On the defense of CPS, many departments are strapped for personnel and resources, while at the same time overwhelmed with cases. Many workers are forced to make snap judgment calls and do leave children at-risk, subject to further abuse. Similarly, CPS workers investigate frivolous complaints because the law states they have to. Most unfounded, but vigorously investigated complaints of sexual or physical child abuse are the result of undereducated and under-trained CPS workers. Social workers who combine the problems of confirmatory bias and poor child interview techniques will create source misattribution errors. Their often-heralded dogma that children must be believed at all costs is troubling. Scientific studies conducted by Ceci, Lamb, Poole, Lindsay, Esplin, et al., have proved that many children's stories are credible, but inaccurate.

But, this book was not written to be an indictment of CPS. It was written to describe the terrible injustices that occur within our system designed to protect children and women. From its accusation-driven laws, to its confounding policies and procedures, and finally to its wide latitude of adjudicatory powers held by omnipotent judges, fathers and families are the usual recipients of *Elusive Innocence*. Recent studies by the American Association for the Protection of Children indicate a 1700 percent increase in the number of child abuse reports since 1975. Nationally, over 65 percent of the more than three million alleged child abuse and neglect reports in 1998, were unfounded. In Massachusetts, over one-half of the sixty thousand restraining orders in alleged domestic abuse cases issued every year, according to a 1995 state report, did not involve so much as an accusation of physical abuse. The number of false positives in alleged child abuse and domestic violence cases is chilling and troublesome.

This book was my attempt to educate system professionals, help falsely accused parents and naïve attorneys in real time, and capture the minds of our public policy makers with thought-provoking suggestions and recommendations to effect change. The rest is up to you!

Appendix A

A Questionaire

The following questionnaire was developed by J. Petty as a suggested guide in identifying true versus false allegations of child sexual abuse.

Identification of False Allegations

1. Relationship of reporter to perpetrator:

2. Was there any evidence that the abuse/neglect reporter:

A. Was generally hostile or resentful toward the perpetrator for reasons not directly related to the abuse?

B. Had something of personal value to gain if the abuse was substantiated (such as gaining child custody, eliminating visitation, or parental rights, financial gain, etc.)?

C. Suffers from posttraumatic stress disorder?

1. History of being abused themselves?

2. Stressors that would evoke significant symptoms of distress in anyone?

3. Response numbness to external world?

4. Recurrence of recollection of trauma via dreams or intrusive remembrances?

[NOTE: Mothers who have been abused tend to over-identify with their child and believe abuse has occurred.]

D. Had a serious psychiatric disorder and had a pathological symbiotic relationship with the child?

1. Histrionic Personality

2. Borderline Personality

3. Schizophrenia

4. Paranoid Disorder

5. Munchausen-by-Proxy

6. Other

E. Appears to be an over-concerned professional who has prematurely committed themselves to believing the allegations and has influenced others to believe the same?

F. Tended to offer progressively more elaborate versions of the original story?

3. Did the child repeat the story consistently to more than one person?

4. How many?

5. Did the child repeat the same story to the same person over time?

6. Was the story consistent with information gathered from other mediums, such as drawings or dolls?

7. Did other involved children repeat the same story? If so, how many?

8. Does the child tend to make up stories, exaggerate, or fantasize excessively?

9. Has the child progressively offered more elaborate versions of the story with unexpected adult words and phrases?

10. Does the child have any reasons, other than having been abused by the perpetrator, to be resentful, hostile, or revengeful toward the perpetrator?

11. Is there any evidence that the child has been influenced by others through leading questions or threats?

12. Were stories told by the child challenged to determine whether the child is consistent or suggestible to adult influence?

13. Did the child maintain consistency following challenge or leads?

14. How influenced by suggestibility does the child appear to be (highly, moderate, not influenced)?

15. By whom? Relationship?

16. Did the child go beyond expected details by telling sensible, credible stories?

17. Is there evidence of the accommodation syndrome?

A. Has the child substantially diminished or withdrawn the allegations?

B. Has the child stated that he/she has been told what to say?

C. Has the child been threatened with harm or loss if they don't withdraw the allegations?

D. Have you directly observed anyone attempting to get the child to change their story?

E. In the presence of particular reporters the child appeared:

Guarded?

Intimidated?

Ambivalent?

Frightened?

In whose presence?

18. Did the mood or affect of the child match what would be expected during disclosure?

Appendix B

Fake or Factual?

Speedy Identification of Child Sexual Abuse Allegations

The Joint Custody Association, Los Angeles, California

Bona fide sexual abuse:

  Mothers will generally be upset, secretive, and embarrassed

  Child will be fearful and timid in presence of abusing parent

  Description of abuse will be consistent, real, and serious

Fabricated sexual abuse:

  Mother has a need to tell the whole world, expresses no shame

  Child also wants to tell the whole world

  Child is comfortable in presence of the accused, and may even
    scream the accusations in the face of the accused parent

  Descriptions often have preposterous scenarios

Children from four to seven:

  Tend to over generalize

  Fabricate in an effort to fill in the blanks

  Will begin to believe what they have said

Common problems among individuals involved in parent-child abuse:

  Impulse control problems

  Difficulty monitoring or directing emotional reactions

  Excessive self-centeredness

Strong dependency needs

Poor judgment

Divorced women who accuse spouses of incest:

Usually overzealous and dishonest

Histrionic or combative

Aggressively demand the decision-makers act quickly

When questioned for specific details, they can provide little information and are reluctant to have their children interviewed alone

Mothers who are child focused and not fabricating, or exaggerating:

Express remorse for not protecting child sufficiently

Willing to consider other explanations for poor behavior

Willing to have child interviewed without their presence

Concerned about impact on child if child testifies

If allegations can't be verified, willing to let go of the investigative process as long as child's well-being can be monitored

Mothers interested primarily in attacking fathers:

Insist on being present when child is interviewed and prompt the child

Are unwilling to consider other possible explanations for child's statements

Are eager for child to testify at all costs

Shop for other professionals who will verify her suspicions

Involve the child in multiple examinations

Demand the investigation continue, irrespective of the impact on the child

Three types of data, in assessing the child, to be considered are:

Child's verbalizations

Child's test responses and play interviews

Reports of parents, teachers, and others knowing child

Appendix C

How to Choose Your Attorney

They are called esquires, officers of the court, barristers, solicitors, counselors-at-law, juris doctors, attorneys-at-law, or simply, lawyers. But, when accused of child abuse, especially child sexual abuse, or domestic violence, one should be on the lookout for a *litigator*. There's a difference. A litigator is a lawyer who not only is good on paper, drafting pleadings (motions), but also is aggressive in the courtroom. A litigator is fearless and willing to come on the verge of contempt in court. A litigator is a pit bull, not a poodle.

As I've pointed out throughout this book, the falsely accused must prove their innocence. Even if CPS doesn't meet their burden of proof in juvenile court to sustain their CHINA Petition, or even if the DA can't gain a conviction beyond a reasonable doubt against you for alleged sexual battery, in the eyes of the family court you're *still* guilty. You *still* must prove your innocence. This necessitates retaining an educated, trained, and highly skilled trial attorney who has had experience litigating and/or trying like cases. Realize the most important decision you'll be making in any alleged child abuse or domestic violence case is the selection of counsel. Realize in most cases, your attorney represents you the accused, and your children, too. If you lose, your children lose, too. Thus, your attorney must try to kill two birds with one stone. Your attorney is the navigator of your ship. He or she will be responsible for navigating a course to keep you out of jail and/or reunify you with your family. Likewise, he or she could be responsible for navigating your case like the Titanic, hitting an iceberg and ruining you and your family.

I don't recommend finding your lawyer in the yellow pages, or via a friend or family members advice. There are very few lawyers who will advertise as having experience in handling fathers' rights, CPS, false accusations, or domestic violence cases. Chances are those are not the only types of cases they handle. When falsely accused of child abuse or domestic violence you need a specialist, a litigator who handles these types of cases, perhaps an experienced matrimonial or criminal lawyer. That said, I'm against the falsely accused being represented by public defenders or court appointed counsel in criminal and juvenile cases, respectively. And, I'm very much against the falsely accused litigating *pro se*, or *in proper persona* (*in pro per*), representing themselves. In my opinion, that is legal suicide! Remember, the person who acts as his or her own attorney has a fool for a client.

Where to shop for and find a litigator?

- Call expert consultants who are familiar with attorneys who handle false abuse cases.
- Call father's rights groups, such as the Father's Resource Center at 1-800-515-DADS, family rights groups such as VOCAL at 1-800-745-8778, or children's rights groups such as the Children's Rights Council at 1-800-787-KIDS.
- Call your local County or State Bar Association for attorney referrals.
- Search the Internet at lawyers.com or other apropos websites (see Appendix G).
- Search Law Journal Review articles authored by expert attorneys.
- Query local University Law School Professors.

It is incumbent upon the consumer shopping for an attorney to question the expert's credentials and qualifications. When doing so, be diplomatic, but be forthright. Since you're employing the attorney, and his or her retainer fee may be ten thousand dollars billed out at 250 dollars an hour, it is your obligation to determine that your hard earned dollars will be well spent.

Conduct an attorney interview, perhaps several attorney interviews, before you commit in writing to signing a retainer agreement, or contract. Since the falsely accused can be forced into litigation in several different courts at the same time, it is recommended the attorney be competent to handle criminal, family, juvenile-dependency, administrative review, and even appellate cases. As part of the attorney interview, I suggest you ask the following questions:

- Do you have a current CV or resume I can peruse?
- Are you affiliated with American Academy of Matrimonial Lawyers?
- Are you affiliated with Association of Trial Lawyers of America?
- Are you affiliated with National Association of Criminal Defense Lawyers?
- Are you AV Rated in Martindale-Hubbell?
- Are you Board Certified in your particular area of legal specialization?

- How many cases of false abuse accusations have you litigated successfully?
- Can you show me any published appellate decisions you've won?
- Have you authored any legal journal articles?
- Do you litigate cases *Pro Hac Vice* as foreign counsel in other states?
- What are the titles of the Continuing Legal Education courses you've taken during the past biennium?
- What do you do to keep abreast on domestic violence issues, child sex abuse issues, and child physical abuse issues?
- Do you belong to any niche professional organizations targeting your legal areas of specialization; e.g., American Professional Society on the Abuse of Children?
- Does the attorney have a comprehensive library of professional journal articles and/or books relative to child abuse and domestic violence issues?
- What is your experience with the judges of the court the case-at-bar is being tried in?

There are several reasons why the falsely accused should retain *pro hac vice* attorneys. The most obvious reason is the fact that there may not be an outstanding litigator such as Barry Scheck, or Charles Jamieson in your entire state. Therefore, it may be appealing to bring in a specialist from out of state. Another advantage in using foreign counsel is the fact that politics will not be an issue. In other words, who do you think will fight harder for you: the local attorney who must appear next week before the same judge, or the foreign attorney, who most likely will never see that judge again? (I'd surmise the latter.)

Most, if not all, states, in accord with their Rules of Judicial Administration, allow foreign attorneys to appear in their courtrooms. There are certain conditions that must be met: e.g., in the Central District of California in United States District Court, according to Rule 2. (83-2), and in specific Rule 83—2.2.3.1, for an attorney to be afforded permission *pro hac vice,* he or she must be a member in good standing with the local Bar Association, must be eligible to practice before the Bar of any United States (Federal) Court, must be of good moral character, must be retained to appear before this court, and must make written application to the court to appear, *before* the court considers and permits same attorney to appear in a particular case. The same applies to foreign lawyers entering the Florida courts *pro hac vice.* According to Rule 2.060 (b), pro hac vice attorneys entering Florida cases must also provide evidence of motions for permission to appear in Florida for the preceding three years.

Throughout this book I've tried to impress upon readers the need for science, psychology, and experts in court, when one is falsely accused of abuse. As attorney Jamieson pointed out in chapter nineteen, lawyers are not trained in psychology. In fact, lawyers are not trained to litigate false accusations cases, period! There are no legal courses that I'm aware of offering Trying False Accusations in Court 101. They learn to do so by getting on the job training and attending legal, mental health, and medical conferences on abuse issues for Continuing Legal Education credits.

Because most attorneys have little or no experience in tendering expert witnesses, conducting experts' *voir dire,* cross examining adverse *experts,* or admitting scientific test results into evidence, it's necessary the falsely accused legal consumer be privy to this potential obstacle. Most lawyers representing falsely accused clients suffer from what I call "Legal Naivete Syndrome," meaning they're naïve concerning the urgency of warlike litigation and the necessity of retaining experts for the defense. Clients must ensure their attorneys retain the most highly credentialed and objective experts that money can buy. Because the falsely accused are allotted as much justice as they can afford, and it's not just what you know but who you know that is vital to your case, it's imperative to query consultants to offer assistance on experts. Be leery of the attorney who claims that "experts are unnecessary."

Be leery of the attorney who says, "I'm the best lawyer in town on these cases, and I've been doing them for twenty-five years." Perhaps the attorney has handled one or two child sex cases over the past ten years, but none in the past five years. The science and laws surrounding child abuse and domestic violence are dynamic, changing constantly. Lawyers must stay current with the scientific literature regarding children's suggestibilities and memories, as well as normal versus abnormal anogenital findings. Likewise, your attorney should be familiar with current federal laws such as Child Abuse Prevention and Treatment Act, Adoption and SAFE Families Act, and VAWA, previously discussed in chapters fourteen and fifteen of this book.

It is difficult, if not impossible, to find a competent lawyer who can handle three-ring circus (juvenile, criminal, and family law) cases. Some states, like Florida, possess a multitude of procedural rules for each court one enters; e.g., Rules of Juvenile Procedure, Rules of Criminal Procedure, Rules of Civil Procedure, Family Law Rules of Procedure, Rules of Appellate Procedure, Rules of Administrative Procedure, et al. Thus, attorneys must hone their skills when it comes to litigating child abuse and domestic violence cases. Legal consumers should conduct laborious searches before selecting counsel. While the falsely accused may be in a state of shock filled with emotions, thinking that time is of the essence in choosing an attorney, haste can make waste in doing so. Be diligent, but yet deliberate in picking your lawyer. Don't be hoodwinked because the lawyer charges a mere five hundred dollar retainer. Likewise, don't be feigned because the attorney's lowest retainer is twenty thousand dollars. Read over the retainer agreement very carefully before signing the same, realizing that you'll probably have to replenish the retainer somewhere along the line. And, don't be intimidated into thinking that the bigger the law firm, the better the legal representation. There is no directly proportional pattern regarding law firm quantity and quality. The falsely accused client may be better served by a solo practitioner versus a large law firm that houses fifty lawyers.

How will I know if I chose the right attorney? Unfortunately, in law, there are no guarantees. In reality, you won't know if you picked the right lawyer until litigation ensues. I do recommend you ask yourself the following questions *before* signing a retainer agreement:

- Is the attorney fully qualified and credentialed?
- Can the attorney litigate all of my legal problems?
- Am I on the same page as the lawyer regarding retainer and other fees?
- During the initial consultation, do I feel like the lawyer and I have formed some type of chemistry?
- Does the lawyer appear to be not only a litigator, but also an advocate and confidant?
- Will the lawyer return phone calls and afford you individualized attention, or are you *just another client*?
- Does the attorney seem passionate about your case and representing your best interests?
- Does the attorney have on-board ancillary help such as paralegals, trial consultants, and investigators?
- Is the attorney familiar with the work of the foremost scientists in the fields of children's suggestibilities and domestic violence, e.g., Ceci, Bruck, Esplin, Yuille, Clarke-Stewart, Lamb, Poole, Bull, Straus, Gelles, and Steinmetz?
- Does the attorney have his or her own crop of experts?

Effecting the selection of counsel is an arduous and lengthy process. Although I've just scratched the surface here, it's clear to see that achieving an attorney-client *match made in heaven* is not easy to do. There are several hoops a prospective client should jump through before inking a contract and check. Is the lawyer highly qualified, possessing board certifications and AV ratings in Martindale-Hubbell? Is the attorney experienced in the types of litigation I'm involved in? Does the lawyer return phone calls in timely fashion? Does the attorney believe in using experts to prove my innocence? As you would choose the best construction company to build your new house brick by brick, so goes it with selecting attorneys. There are a plethora of attorneys waiting to take your hard earned dollars. Don't be hoovered by lawyers who *appear* to have all of the answers before they've read over your case file. As an employer of legal services, choose cautiously and choose wisely.

Appendix D

Attorney Referral List

According to my information, the following North American defense lawyers have concentrated their practices in the areas of child abuse, domestic violence, and child custody. Some litigate in criminal court, only. Some litigate in family court, only. Others specialize in handling juvenile court cases, or appeals, only. In my opinion, these are some of the finest defense lawyers for those that have been *wrongly* accused of child abuse, repressed memories, or spousal abuse. I suggest you retain any attorney *only after* you have perused the lawyers' CV. Be certain the lawyer has defended similar cases to your own successfully.

Disclaimer: This writer does not receive any remuneration for referring potential clients to any of the following lawyers. To do so would be considered fee splitting, and that is in contravention to the canons of ethics of each state bar association. Moreover, this writer is *not* responsible for any negative ramifications that may ensue out of litigation via representation from the following lawyers.

Jes Beard, Esq.
737 Market Street
Suite 601
Chattanooga, TN 37402-4820
423-267-4391

Roy Black, Esq.
201 S. Biscayne Blvd.
Suite 1300
Miami, FL 33131
305-371-6421

Lawrence Braunstein, Esq.
11 Martine Avenue
White Plains, NY 10606
914-997-6220

John Henry Brown, Esq.
821 2nd Avenue
Suite 2200
Seattle, WA 98104
206-624-7364

Patrick Clancy, Esq.
1600 S. Main St.
Suite 185
Walnut Creek, CA 94596-5431
510-256-6884

Eliot Clauss, Esq.
291 Broadway, 13th Floor
New York, NY 10038
212-349-6775

Danny Davis, Esq.
P.O. Box 3516
Beverly Hills, CA 90212
213-659-5800

Douglas Dougherty, Esq.
2955 Donnylane Boulevard
Columbus, OH 43235
614-798-1933

Robert Estrada, Esq.
1007 11th Street
P.O. Box 2006
Wichita Falls, TX 76307
940-723-9749

John Finn, Esq.
49 Main Street
Yarmouth, ME 04096
207-846-1429

Walter Fox, Esq., Barrister & Solicitor
The Sheraton Centre-Richmond Tower
100 Richmond Street
Suite 312
West Toronto, Ontario, Canada M5H 3K6
416-363-9238

Friedman & Manning, P.C.
2 Norman Skill Boulevard
Delmar, NY 12054-0069
518-439-0375

Clifton Fuller III, Esq.
7 Market Street
Belfast, ME 04915
207-338-1311

Robert Gidding, Esq.
29 Bala Avenue
Suite 204
Bala Cynwyd, PA 19004-3206
610-664-4530

Charles Jamieson, Esq.
The Centurion
1601 Forum Place
Suite 1101
West Palm Beach, FL 33401
561-478-1111

Barbara Johnson, Esq.
6 Appletree Lane
N. Andover, MA 01810-4102
978-474-0833

Louis Kiefer, Esq.
21 Oak Street
Suite 310
Hartford, CT 06106
860-249-3600

Dennis Levin, Esq.
Park Center II
3681 Green Road
Suite 410
Cleveland, OH 44122
216-839-3939

Jeffery Leving, LTD.
19 S. LaSalle
Suite 450
Chicago, IL 60603
312-807-3990

Bruce Martin, Esq.
Wichita Tower
705 Eighth Street
Suite 600
Wichita Falls, TX 76301
940-322-7517

Jerry McDougal, Esq.
P.O. Box 50898
Amarillo, TX 79159
806-355-1202

Mark Mestel, Esq.
3221 Oaks Ave.
Everett, WA 98201
206-339-2383

Jay Milano, Esq.
600 Standard Building
Cleveland, OH 44113
216-241-5050

James Murdoch, Esq.
131 Main St.
P.O. Box 363
Burlington, VT 05402-0363
802-864-9811

Michael Oddenino, Esq.
444 E. Huntington Drive
Suite 325
Arcadia, CA 91006
818-447-8084

John Paone, Esq.
146 Green Street
Woodbridge, NJ 07095
732-750-9797

Barton Resnicoff, Esq.
287 North Boulevard
Great Neck, NY 11021
516-829-2940

Tom Ryan, Esq.
1600 W. Chandler Boulevard
Suite 220
Chandler, AZ 85224
602-963-3333

Skip Simpson, Esq.
2828 Woodside Street
Dallas, TX 75204
214-922-7078

Michael Snedecker, Esq.
1752 S. E. Hawthorne
Portland, OR 97214
503-234-3584

Sverre Staurset, Esq.
725 Yakima
2nd Floor
Tacoma, WA 98402
206-572-8880

Rowe Stayton, Esq.
13140 E. Mississippi Avenue
Aurora, CO 80012
303-745-5578

Robert Storrs, Esq.
45 W. Jefferson
Suite 803
Phoenix, AZ 85003
602-258-4545

Joel Thompson, Esq.
4500 N. 32nd Street
Suite 100
Phoenix, AZ 85018
602-957-2010

Robert Van Siclen, Esq.
4508 Auburn Way N.
Suite A-100
Auburn, WA 98002-1381
206-859-8899

Steven Varney, Esq.
100 Pearl Street
Hartford, CT 06103
860-659-0700

Paul Wallin, Esq.
2020 E. 1st Street
Suite 300
Santa Ana, CA 92705
714-571-0227

Appendix E

Case Law and False Accusations

The following list of case law citations is brief but identifies major decisions related to evidence issues: the interpretation of the confrontation clause, hearsay and child competency, the admissibility of expert testimony, scientific evidence in court, the questionable acceptance of anatomically exaggerated dolls, play therapies, and repressed memories in the scientific community in sex abuse cases. Also, there are cases addressing parent's accused of *prospective child abuse or neglect*, abolition of a child abuse registry, the right to redress, duty owed to a third party, immunity issues, and the government.

Disclaimer: This writer takes no responsibility for the use or misuse of the following citations by in *pro per* litigants, public defenders, or retained counsel. If you question the proper usage of a given citation, albeit, contained within an appellants brief or motion accompanied by a memorandum of law in e.g., Federal Court, consult a qualified attorney.

Santosky v. Kramer, U.S. Sup. Ct. 88-5889 (1982). Held that there must be conclusive evidence beyond a reasonable doubt (not merely a preponderance of evidence) to terminate a parent's right of access to his or her child.

Felix v. State of Nevada, 109 Nev. 151, 849 P.2d 220 (Nev. Sup. Ct. March 18, 1993). The High Court reversed the convictions, finding the trial court erred in not properly establishing child competency, in disregarding the lack of medical evidence, and in allowing a lack of spontaneity in reporting by the children and leading questions to be admissible.

Hellstrom v. Commonwealth of Kentucky, No. 90-SC-262-Mr (Kentucky Supreme Ct., 1992). The High Court reversed and remanded, holding that "neither child sexual abuse syndrome nor the symptoms that comprise the syndrome have recognized reliability in diagnosing child sexual abuse as scientific entity and thus testimony on the syndrome and the symptoms is not admissible.

People of New York v. Knupp, 579 N.Y.S. 2d 801 (N.Y. Sup. Ct., App. Div. 1992). Held that accused was denied right to a fair trial by the improper admission of mental health testimony. Admission of expert testimony of a "validator," who had previously testified in several other cases that children suffered from "intra-familial child sexual abuse syndrome," was held improper. Undue prejudice outweighs probative value. Upon retrial, Knupp, who had served two years in prison, was acquitted of sexual assault charges.

State of Idaho v. Wright, 497 U.S. 805, 110 S. Ct. 3139, 111 L. Ed. 2d 638 (1990). A child sex abuse conviction was reversed because hearsay statements made by the child and reported by the physician did not bear adequate indicia of reliability. The doctor failed to videotape the interview, asked leading questions, and had a preconceived notion the abuse took place.

State of New Jersey v. Michaels, 136 N.J. 299, 642 A.2d 1372, 1994 N.J. LEXIS 504, (N.J. Sup. Ct., 1994); previous history—264 N.J. Super. 579, 625 A. 2d 489, 1993 N.J. Super. LEXIS 174 (N.J. Superior Ct., 1993). Kelly Michaels, a nursery school teacher at the Wee Care Day Nursery, was convicted by a jury of 115 counts of sexual assault of children in 1988. After spending five years in prison, her convictions were reversed by two higher courts, which held that to re-prosecute the defendant the state must prove by clear and convincing evidence that the statements and testimony extracted from the children were done so by proper interviewing techniques and reliable at pretrial. In December 1994, the state decided not to retry the case.

United States v. Tome, No. 93-6892 (U.S. Sup. Ct., argued Oct. 5 1994); decided January 10, 1995. Reversed a conviction of a New Mexico man for allegedly raping his 4-year-old daughter. The High Court of the land considered the admissibility of hearsay statements made by a child complainant "of recent fabrication or improper influence or motive," In a 5-4 decision, the court held that Federal Rule of Evidence 801(d)(1)(B) rendered inadmissable hearsay statements of accusations made to others after the alleged motive or influence first arose.

Ward v. State of Florida, 519 So. 2d (Fla. App. Ct. 1988). The court held that "child sexual abuse syndrome is an area sufficiently developed to permit an expert to testify that the symptoms observed in the evaluated child are consistent with those displayed by victims of child sexual abuse." However, the court noted that the testimony of the syndrome is circumstantial evidence and may not be received as corroborating evidence that the defendant committed the criminal act charged on the specific occasion.

Hadden v. Florida, 690 So. 2d 573, 574, 575 (1997). The court held that the Child Sexual Abuse Accommodation Syndrome is not generally accepted in the scientific community, does not pass the FRYE test, and is therefore inadmissible in court as evidence of abuse.

State v. F.Q., 617 A.2d 1196 (N.J. 1993). The court held that although the "Child Sexual Abuse Syndrome" was sufficiently reliable as generally accepted within the relevant scientific community to explain *traits* often found in abuse victims, it may not be used to establish substantive fact of abuse.

White v. Illinois, 112 S. Ct. 736 (1992). The U.S. Supreme Court considered requirements for assessing the reliability of a child's accusatory hearsay statements made against a defendant before their admission into evidence. The unavailability analysis is a necessary part of a Confrontation Clause inquiry only if challenged out-of-court statements are made in course of prior judicial proceedings.

Coy v. Iowa, 487 U.S. 1012 (1988). The U.S. Supreme Court reversed a sexual child abuse conviction because the trial court permitted the prosecution to use screens to block the children's view of the defendants. The court held that, without a finding of necessity, such a procedure violated the Confrontation Clause.

Maryland v. Craig, 497 U.S. 836 (1990). The court held that shielding child witnesses from sexual abuse defendants is constitutional, but only if the lower court finds: 1. One-way closed circuit television is necessary to protect the child's welfare. 2. The child would be traumatized in the presence of the defendant. 3. The emotional distress suffered by the child witness in the presence of the defendant is more than *de minimis*. The defendant's right to cross examination is upheld. And the court, jury, and defendant have the right to observe the child's demeanor.

Ohio v. Roberts, 448 U.S. 56 (1980). The High Court of the land ordered a two-part test for determining when the right to confrontation must yield to the admissibility of hearsay: The proponent 1. Must show the necessity for using the hearsay declaration (witness unavailability) and 2. Must show the inherent trustworthiness of the declaration.

State of Florida v. Townsend, 635 So. 2d 949 (Fla. 1994). The Supreme Court held that the competency of a child is a factor that should be considered in determining the trustworthiness and reliability and thus the admissibility of hearsay statements.

Frye v. United States, 54 U.S. App. D.C. 293 F. 1013 (1923). *People v. Kelley*, 17 Cal 3d 24 (1976). "The Kelley-Frye Rule of Reliability" stipulated that novel scientific testimony is admissible if generally accepted by the relevant scientific community.

Daubert v. Merrell Dow Pharmaceuticals, 113. S.Ct. 2786, 125 L.Ed 2d 469 (1993). Here, the High Court of the land expounded upon Frye and applied the Federal Rules of Evidence. The Daubert opinion, written by Justice Blackmun, specifies that under Rule 702 an expert's testimony pertaining to "scientific knowledge" must be grounded in the methods and procedures of science and derived from the scientific method. In order to be admissible, the trial judge must examine the scientific validity of the underlying methodology. In addition, under Daubert, the criteria for admissibility (see Appendix F) is:

1. Whether the theory has been tested and is scientifically reliable;

2. Whether the theory has been subjected to peer review and publication;

3. Whether the theory or technique has a known rate of error;

4. Whether the theory has attained general acceptance within the relevant scientific community.

Several judicial decisions reflect the view that evidence generated by the use of anatomically exaggerated dolls do not pass the FRYE Rule and meet general scientific acceptance criteria:

In re Amber B, 236 Cal. Rpt. 623, (Cal. App. 1 Dist. 1987), 191 Cal. 3d 682 (1987).

In re Christine C, 191 Cal. 3d 676 (1987).

U.S. v. Gillespie, 852 F2d 475 (9th Cir. 1988).

State of New Hampshire v. Hungerford, Superior Court of Hillsborough County, N.H., Case No. 94-S-045 thru. 94-S-047, May 23, 1995. After a Frye/Daubert hearing and factual review, the court held that repressed memory testimony was not sufficiently reliable under Frye or Rule 702 to be admitted as evidence.

Hunter v. Brown, Tenn App. LEXIS 95, 1996 WL 57944, Feb. 13, 1996. In this case of first impression, the Tennessee Appellate Court declined to apply the discovery rule to toll the statute of limitations in repressed memory cases. "We find that there is too much indecision in the scientific community as to the credibility of repressed memory."

S.V. v. R.V., Supreme Court of Texas, 1996 Tex. LEXIS 30, March 14, 1996. The court held that because Plaintiff relied on the discovery rule, the evidence must have met a higher level of proof. This case did not survive as the court ruled against the discovery rule.

Engstrom v. Engstrom, Superior Court, Los Angeles County, CA, Case No. VC016157, Oct. 11, 1995. The court granted a motion to exclude the testimony regarding repressed memories, repression, or dissociation, finding that the phenomenon of memory repressions is not generally accepted as valid and reliable by a majority of the scientific community and that the procedures used in the 'retrieval' process have not gained general acceptance in the fields of psychology or psychiatry.

Hafer v. Melo et al, 912 F. 2d 628, 636-37 (3rd Cir. 1990), U.S. Sup. Ct. 90-681 (Nov. 5, 1991). The High Court of the land held that a plaintiff can sue a governmental official in his/her personal or individual capacity for monetary damages.

Wilkinson v. Balsam, DC VT 4/95 - No.2 94-CV-375, 4/17/95. The Federal Court rejected the claims of a psychiatrist and two state social workers that they were cloaked under a shield of absolute immunity. The court based its findings upon shoddy investigative work of the social workers and deceitful behavior by the doctor, in that the reporting physician overstepped his bounds in going beyond simply reporting a case of child abuse.

Montoya v. Bebensee, 761 P. 2d 285 (Colo. App. Ct. 1988). A Colorado Appeals Court reinstated a father's negligence and outrageous conduct claims against his daughter's therapist for her behavior in a SAID case. The court held that a therapist who counseled a child owed a duty of care to the father because the harm he suffered from unfounded child abuse charges was foreseeable.

State of Minnesota v. Huss, 506 N.W. 2d 290 (1993). High court of Minnesota overturned a father's conviction for criminal sexual assault, concluding the child's accusations were "improperly influenced" by a highly suggestive book on sex abuse, which was shown to her repeatedly by a therapist.

Caryl S. v. Child Adolescent Treatment Services, Inc., 614 N.Y.S. 2d 661 (N.Y Superior Ct., 1994). The court found factual basis for the grandparents' claim of negligent misdiagnosis and denied defendants' motion to dismiss. The court further found that a duty of care was owed to not only the child, but also the alleged abusers, the grandparents.

James W., et al., v. The Superior Court of San Diego County, Kaddeen Goddfriend, et al, 17 Cal. App. 4th 246 (Calif. App. Ct. 4th Dist. July 1993, modified August 16, 1993). Therapists' activities went far beyond the intent and spirit of the statute. The court recognized when counselors "abuse" a therapeutic relationship with family members they are liable to both the child and the parents. The case was settled out of court for 2.5 million dollars in May 1994.

Commonwealth v. Stewart, 422 Mass. 385, 389, 663 N.E. 2d 255 (1996). The court allows inquiries to be made of polygraph examiners at Daubert hearings based on the case of *Commonwealth v. Lanigan*, 419 Mass. 15, 641 N.E. 2d 1342 (1994). The examiner's qualifications, experience, and test methodology can be argued on a case-by-case basis.

Commonwealth v. Rosenberg, 410 Mass. 347 (1991). The prosecution's expert testifies to the relevancy of the penile plethysmograph and results from the same are admitted into evidence.

Spencer v. Commonwealth, 240 Va. 78 (1990). A trial court must make a "threshold finding of fact with respect to the reliability of the scientific method offered."

General Electric v. Joiner, 522 U.S. 136 (1997). The court amplified its Daubert holding by adding that appellate courts must find lower courts have abused their discretion in order to reverse and remand cases. The basis for the same includes the lower courts admission or denial of expert testimony, its decision on the reliability or lack thereof of the test or method, and the ultimate conclusions rendered by the expert.

Kumho Tire, Inc. v. Carmichael, 119 S.Ct. 1167 (1999). "Daubert-like" standards, tests, methods, or other measures of validity and reliability also apply to *technical* or *other specialized knowledge*. The same Daubert factors may apply to the opinion testimony of nonscientist expert witnesses. This case paved the way for trial courts to exercise more judicial discretion regarding expert testimony claiming that the Daubert factors do not constitute a definitive litmus test.

State v. Jackson, No. S97A1791 (March 20, 1998) and *Fulton Co. Dept. of Family and Children's Services v. R.S.G.*, Nos. S97A1904, S97X1905 (March 20, 1998). In appeals from Decatur and Fulton counties, the Georgia Supreme Court declares the Child Protective Services Information Act (Child Abuse Registry) unconstitutional.

In re M.F., 742 So. 2d 490 (Fla. 2nd DCA 1999). Addressing past abuse or neglect adjudications of dependency in juvenile court relative to prospective abuse or neglect against other children, the Florida Supreme Court held in the case of *In the Interest of M.F. and M.F., etc. R.F., Petitioner, v. Florida Department of Children and Families, Respondent.* No. SC96883, October 12, 2000, that there "must be a totality of circumstances surrounding the petition which is legally sufficient to support an order for dependency." The court wrote that "A simple showing by DCF that a parent committed a sex act on one child does not by itself constitute proof that the parent poses a substantial risk of *imminent* abuse or neglect to the child's sibling, as required by statute. While the commission of such an act may be highly relevant, it is not automatically dispositive of the issue of dependency. A court instead should focus on *all* the circumstances surrounding the petition in each case."

Ex parte Peterson, 253 U.S. 300, 312 (1920); *Reilly v. United States*, 863 F.2d 149 (First Cir. 1988). Whereby Federal Rule of Evidence 706 should encourage more courts to appoint independent experts in custody and other family law cases.

Beekman v. Beekman, 645 N.E.2d 1332 (Ohio Ct. App. 1994). False allegations are sufficient to alter custody.

L.R.M. v. P.R.M., 780 S.W.2d 111 (Mo.Ct.App. 1989). A father was awarded custody in a case of false allegations of abuse and deliberate parental interference.

Blazel v. Bradley, 698 F. Supp. 756 (W.D. Wis. 1988). Ex parte Protection From Abuse orders can deprive a person of their right to liberty or property interests, and as such there must be a pre-deprivation hearing, unless there is a showing of "immediate harm."

Pennsylvania v. Ritchie, 107 S. Ct. 989, 480 U.S. 39 (1987). The court will entertain an *in camera* review of sought after documents, should requests for production and motions to compel fail.

United States v. Addison, 498 F.2d 741, 744 (D.C. Cir. 1974). Those experts most qualified to assess the general validity of a scientific method will have the most determinative voice.

Appendix F

Frye v. Daubert: A Look at Science in the Courtroom

In today's unpredictable and unsafe world where no-fault divorce, SAID syndrome accusations, protracted custody battles, borderline personality disorder, parental alienation syndrome, and ABEL screening are *norms*, it's crucial to understand why and how law and psychology *must* form a marriage in court. Courts frequently struggle over the use, or misuse of scientific evidence at trial. Most judges, lawyers, and jurors lack scientific training when the adjudication of a case *requires* an understanding of scientific concepts, procedures, and test results, and experts must explain them. Examples of clear forensic inadmissibility would be psychic predictions and horoscope readings. Examples of clear forensic admissibility would be blood and breathalyzer tests for alcohol consumption. The use of a novel scientific theory, especially one developed by a small group of scientists, will unfairly burden one's opponent because few qualified experts will be able to evaluate the evidence. However, novelty does not imply invalidity, because every scientific theory must at some point be *new*. Perhaps, the theory of PAS and penile plethysmography apply, although neither is "new." Nobody knows for certain whether novel scientific evidence is reliable, especially our courts; because courts cannot define the line between good science and junk science, evidence admissibility criteria had to be adopted.

There are two camps fighting on different sides of the child abuse and domestic violence coins, litigating hotly debated and contentious *scientific* arguments surrounding the Child Sexual Abuse Accommodation Syndrome, Battered Women's Syndrome, Parental Alienation Syndrome, SAID syndrome, and penile plethysmograph, to name but a few. Hence, it is necessary for judges to have legal foundations in place to determine and decide if the theory, method, test, science, or syndrome is valid, reliable, or generally accepted, and should be admitted as evidence into court. The foundations or bedrock are grounded in two United

States Supreme Court decisions known as Frye and Daubert, respectively.

Frye v. United States, U.S. App. D.C. 293 F. 1013 (1923), was an early attempt to create a standard of admissibility of scientific evidence, holding that "general acceptance" in the field for which it belonged had to be met. Frye defers to the judgment of the scientific community. The Frye court stated its *test* as follows, "While courts will go a long way in admitting expert testimony deduced from a well-recognized scientific principle or discovery, the thing from which the deduction is made must be sufficiently established to have gained general acceptance in the particular field in which it belongs."

The problem with the Frye test is that "thing." Frye does not describe that "thing." That "thing" can point to a technical procedure or its underlying scientific principle. As a result, a court intent on disallowing certain evidence can require both the technical procedure and the underlying scientific principle to be generally accepted, while a court intent on admitting the evidence may require only one, but not both; e.g., under Frye, the polygraph must be generally accepted in the fields of both psychology and physiology, since it is a measure of Psychophysiological Detection of Deception. Hence, if judges in a Frye state incorporate their own "confirmatory biases" against a given scientific theory, e.g., PAS, their subjectivity can wreak havoc for a defense lawyer trying to admit the same into evidence. Yet, the trial court's gatekeeping role in Frye is one of conservatism, helping to keep "pseudoscience" out of the courtroom. In addition, the definition of "general acceptance" became a problem with the Frye test. General acceptance could mean anything from 51 percent to unanimity. One court stated that "the standard is acceptance by a substantial section of the scientific community concerned." One could presume such a standard to be less than that of a majority. Thus, establishing general acceptance became and still becomes a "battle of the experts" in itself, allowing a judge to choose who to believe and thereby whether or not to admit the evidence.

The rigid and non-flexible Frye test was replaced by the Federal Rules of Evidence (FRE) in 1975, although twelve states still adhere to Frye, and others adhere to a modified Frye test. In Frye, courts could abdicate their judicial responsibility and defer to the widespread scientific community. Courts cannot do so when the Federal Rules are used. "General acceptance" is not a necessary precondition to the admissibility of scientific evidence under the FRE, but the FRE, especially FRE 702, do require a trial judge to ensure that an expert's testimony rests on a reliable foundation and is relevant to the case-at-bar.

The adoption of the FRE provided courts and scholars with a reason to depart from Frye. The general framework for scientific evidence is contained in FRE 402, 702, and 403. FRE 402 states that "all relevant evidence is admissible, except as otherwise provided by . . . the FRE." Writing for all nine judges of the United States Supreme Court, Justice Blackmun said "the court read FRE 402 literally as admitting all relevant evidence and setting a standard of relevance that the Court called *a liberal one*." This is tantamount to Ga. Code Ann. 24-9-67. FRE 702 states that "if scientific knowledge will assist the trier of fact to understand the evidence or to determine a fact in issue, a witness qualified as an expert by knowledge, skill, experience, training, or education, may testify thereto in the form of an opinion or otherwise." The precedent setting Daubert test and factors that superceded Frye and will be discussed at length later in this appendix, comports with FRE 702. Faced with a proffer of expert scientific testimony under FRE 702, a trial court must act as the gatekeeper and make a preliminary assessment of whether the testimony's underlying reasoning or methodology is scientifically valid and can be applied to the facts at issue. The criteria to determine scientific validity are: has the theory or technique been subjected to testing providing replicable data? Has it been subjected to peer review and publication? Does it have a known error rate and standards controlling its operation? Has it attracted widespread acceptance within a relevant scientific community? The assessment is a flexible one and focuses on methodologies, not on conclusions. FRE 702 applies to technical, or specialized knowledge, also, which will be discussed *in Kumho Tire v. Carmic*hael later in this appendix. On the opposite pole, FRE 403 allows for the exclusion of relevant evidence "if its probative value is substantially outweighed by the danger of unfair prejudice, confusion of the issues, misleading the jury, or by consideration of undue delay, waste of time, or needless presentation of cumulative evidence."

Attorneys representing the falsely accused faced with unproven, or questionable scientific syndromes, such as the Child Sex Abuse Accommodation Syndrome or Battered Women's Syndrome, might consider using FRE 403 as an affirmative defense at a Frye or Daubert hearing. Motions *in limine* are effective in limiting or excluding questionable scientific expert opinions. Other means of challenging questionably valid scientific opinions are to use cross-examination, the presentation of rebuttal evidence through your own experts, and careful instruction on the burden of proof. Defense attorneys should consider aggressive cross-examination of social workers and therapists whom tender as expert witnesses under FRE 701 or 702. While the prosecutions or plaintiffs' *experts* may *qualify* as experts, savvy attorneys can still impeach their professional expert *scientific* opinions.

FRE 701 allows for testimony by lay witnesses. In these instances, testimony by witnesses in the form of opinions or inferences is limited to those that are rationally based on the perception of the witnesses and helps determines facts in issues. As alluded to above, FRE 702, which ties in the landmark Daubert decision, compels a trial judge to ensure that an expert's opinion is both relevant and scientifically reliable. General acceptance akin to Frye is not required, but pertinent evidence based on scientifically valid principles is so.

FRE 703 allows experts to rely on data that might not be independently admissible. The source of controversiality hugging FRE 703 is that it invites expert opinions on facts or data falling under the category "of a type reasonably relied upon by experts in the particular field." In abuse cases, it's common for experts championing either the prosecution or defense, to cite, *inter alia* (among other things), literature and statistics in social sciences as a basis for opinions. Because anecdotal data can come in as well-grounded science if not objected to, it's advisable to require tying in FRE 703 with FRE 104(a) and FRE 403, so as to require the proponent to establish some modicum of trustworthiness or reliability for the underlying data.

FRE 704, as it applies to both expert and lay witnesses, is an application of the basic "helpfulness" approach of Rules 701 and 702. Thus, if testimony is helpful to the finder of fact, beyond the knowledge of the average person, and satisfies the admissibility requirements under Rules 702 and 703, it should not be excluded simply because the expert testimony embraces the ultimate issue in a case. Defense lawyers must be cognizant of *expert* therapists for the prosecution who testify to conclusions based on play therapies; e.g., a silent or fearful child may be said to be in denial, or a child who recants may be suffering from a sexual abuse syndrome. According to author Mary Pride in her 1986 book, *The Child Abuse Industry,* many social workers cling to the "Doctrine of Immaculate Confession," believing a child's initial disclosure of abuse but not believing a recantation.

FRE 705 allows experts to testify in terms of opinions or inferences and gives reasons for the same without testifying to the underlying facts or data, unless the court requires them to do so. Defense lawyers can extract these underlying facts or data upon cross-examination.

FRE 706 allows the court at its discretion, *sua sponte* (upon its own motion), to obtain an expert of its own choosing. *Daubert v. Merrell Dow Pharmaceuticals,* 509 U.S. 579, 587, 113 S.Ct 2786, 2794, 125 L.Ed.2d 469 (1993), abandoned the Frye test, adopted FRE 702, and is consistent with the movement in alleged child abuse and domestic violence cases as the basis of expert opinion in courts. In its opinion, the United States Supreme Court recognized that general acceptance by the scientific community was a relevant factor in determining the admissibility of expert testimony. But, such acceptance, the paramount criterion in the Frye test, is not the sole test in Daubert. The court, in its role as gatekeeper, accepts relevant and reliable scientific evidence to assist the same in determining admissibility. The subject of an expert's testimony must be "scientific knowledge." That implies grounding in the methods and procedures of science. It compels more than subjective belief or unsupported speculation. It is here that defense lawyers can decertify *experts'* opinions based on e.g., the Child Sexual Abuse Accommodation Syndrome or Battered Woman's Syndrome. The proffered science must be tested, subjected to peer review and publication, possess a known or potential rate of error, also. Because "general acceptance" is not a precondition for admissibility, defense lawyers can attack the naivete of *experts* who purportedly claim that sexual abuse syndromes saying "children don't lie," and relaxed anal tones are evidence of sexual abuse are erroneous at 702 or Daubert hearings. Likewise, defense lawyers can move into evidence testimony surrounding PAS, Penile Plethysmography, ABEL screening, and the Psychophysiological Detection of Deception, with the correct experts and supporting peer reviewed professional journal information. The fact of publication (or lack thereof) in a peer-reviewed journal will be a relevant, though not dispositive, consideration in assessing the scientific validity of a particular technique or methodology on which an opinion is premised. Since Daubert states require as an admissibility factor, the existence and maintenance of standards controlling a technique's operation, see *U.S. v. Williams*, 583 F.2d 1194 (CA2 '78), defense lawyers can file motions in limine, and, *arguendo*, prevent any testimony surrounding anatomically exaggerated dolls from entering into evidence. The APA has not established standardized usage of the dolls, or normal controls governing their falsifiability, refutability, and testability. Currently, there are twenty-four states that adhere to Daubert, fourteen states that still adhere to Frye (including the District of Columbia), and thirteen states in a state of flux between Daubert and Frye with their own test. The following chart shows the states supporting Daubert, Frye, or their own test, as it concerns the admissibility of science and expert testimony in forensic settings:

Daubert	**Frye**	**Standard in State of Flux**
Alabama	Arizona	Alaska
Arkansas	California	Colorado
Connecticut	District of Columbia	Georgia
Delaware	Florida	Hawaii
Indiana	Illinois	Idaho
Iowa	Kansas	Minnesota
Kentucky	Maryland	Missouri
Louisiana	Michigan	Nevada
Maine	Mississippi	North Dakota
Massachusetts	Nebraska	Oklahoma
Montana	New Jersey	South Carolina
New Hampshire	New York	Tennessee
New Mexico	Pennsylvania	Wisconsin
North Carolina	Washington	
Ohio		
Oregon		
Rhode Island		
South Dakota		
Texas		
Utah		
Vermont		
Virginia		
West Virginia		
Wyoming		

There is a growing trend for states and judges to move toward acceptance of the Daubert factors in court, regarding the admissibility or inadmissibility of scientific and expert testimony: e.g., in the case of *Commonwealth v. Lanigan*, 419 Mass. 15 (1994), Dr. Bruck's opinion was determined to be admissible, not intruding upon the province of the jury to assess the credibility of witnesses; in the case of *United States v. Rouse*, 111 F.3d 561, 567-573 (Eighth Cir.), cert. Denied, 522 U.S. 905 (1997), the court held that expert opinions regarding suggestive interviewing techniques and their effects upon children are admissible under Daubert. In criminal action No. 99-20063-01, in the U.S. District Court, Western District of Louisiana, on 17 April 2000, Judge Tucker Melancon ruled that the ABEL Assessment for sexual interest (ABEL Screen) met all of the Daubert factors, and the testimony of the psychologist was admissible as evidence.

This writer supports defense lawyers' filings of motions in limine and litigation of Frye, Daubert, or taint hearings to rule out junk, or bad science. Because Ms. Jones, the Sexual Abuse Nurse Examiner *expert* who this court recognized as such for the past ten years, examined four year old Sally and testified that her finding of "vulva erythema" was *consistent with sexual abuse*, does not mean it is! Defense lawyers, as Jamieson alluded to earlier, should challenge, object to, limit, and move to exclude any *science* or *scientific findings* that could be based on ideology or in error.

The Daubert standard fits well with the ethical standards for psychologists. In accord with the APA's 1992 ethical principles of psychologists and code of conduct, relevance to Daubert can be seen under Ethical Standard 2.02 (a), which states that "Psychologists who develop, administer, score, interpret, or use psychological assessment techniques, interviews, tests, or instruments, do so in a manner and for purposes that are appropriate in light of the research on or evidence of the usefulness and proper application of the techniques." Ethical Standard 2.04 (a) states that "Psychologists who perform interventions, or administer, score, interpret, or use assessment techniques are familiar with the reliability, validation, and related standardization or outcome studies of, proper application and uses of, the techniques they use." Clearly, in alleged abuse cases, social sciences opinion testimony proffered by *experts* must now under Daubert be supported by well-grounded scientific principles and studies that are relevant and reliable.

In *General Electric v. Joiner*, 522 U.S. 136 (1997), the court held that the court of appeals must use an abuse-of-discretion standard when it reviews a trial court's decision to admit, or exclude expert testimony. In *Kumho Tire, Inc., v. Carmichael*, 119 S.Ct. 1167 (1999), the court held that the Daubert factors may apply to the opinion testimony of nonscientist expert witnesses, also. Without equivocation, the United States Supreme Court held that the obligation imposed on trial judges by Daubert to act as gatekeepers applies not only to scientific testimony but also to *all* expert opinion testimony. The Daubert factors may be used by courts to determine reliability of either the underlying technique or expert's conclusions. But in Kumho, the Daubert factors are no litmus test, just a guiding light. Because of the indoctrination of flexibility via the Daubert and Kumho decisions, courts can utilize their wide judicial latitude in cases. The point is, the Kumho Court allows "technical and other specialized knowledge" into evidence; e.g., assessing the evidentiary reliability of the instruments used for sexual predator evaluations necessitates consideration of both Frye and Daubert, as further defined by Kumho.

There are *experts*, and then there are experts. There is *science*, and then there is science. As the falsely accused proceed down the meandering path of litigation, they will undoubtedly be confronted by experts against them. Likewise, they will require experts to rebut the testimony of the states' experts. The battle-of-the-experts wars have fueled controversies in our courtrooms. Fortunately, for Americans, because of Frye, Daubert, Kumho, and Joiner, our courts possess well-defined guidelines in deciding evidentiary admissibility requirements of experts' testimonies.

Appendix G

Internet Resources

The following list of World Wide Web addresses will help you locate a plethora of information on false accusations of child abuse and domestic violence that is available over the information super highway. Of course, you must own or have access to a computer system and be on-line to do so.

Disclaimer: This writer is not responsible for the dissemination of inaccurate information that is transmitted over the Internet. Because information can be intercepted and altered due to lack of safeguards, I urge you to proceed with caution when on-line. And, since website contents and E-mail substance can be used against you in court, I suggest you refrain from typing-in information about your own case.

World Wide Web Addresses

http://bsd.mojones.com/mother_jones/JA96/levine_jump.html
    A Question of Abuse

http://www.ags.uci.edu/~dehill/witchhunt/cases.htm
    Alleged Witch Hunt Cases

http://www.vix.com./men/index.html
    Men's Issues Page

http://www.bpdcentral.com
    Borderline Personality Disorder

http://www.onedaly.com
    Lawrence Daly, Expert Private Investigator

http://www.ncfm.org
    National Coalition of Free Men

http://fact.on.ca
    Father's Are Capable, Too, of Canada

http://www.gocrc.com
    The Children's Rights Council

http://www.fathersresourcecenter.org
    Fathers' Resource Center

http://www.mensdefense.org
    Men's Defense Association

http://www.vix.com/pub/men/falsereport/resources/
    False Accusations of Sexual or Physical Abuse in Custody Cases

http://www.pacegroup.org
    Parents' and Children's Equality of Ohio

http://www.vix-com/pub/men/falsereport/wsj-witchhunt.html
    Modern Witch Hunt

http://childsbestinterest.org
    Children's Best Interest of Tennessee

http://www.usc.edu/dept/law-lib/legal/topiclst.html
    Legal Resources on the Internet

http://www.safe4all.org
    Stop Abuse For Everyone

http://www.abusedmen.com
    Abused Men

http://www.rutherford.org/
    The Rutherford Institute

http://www.parentsdb.com
    Parenting Resources

http://www.divorcesource.com/wi/articles/harris7.html
    Divorce and Custody for the USA and Canada

http://www.ojp.usdoj.gov/bjs/
    Bureau of Justice Statistics

http://www.accused.com
    False accusations of child abuse and repressed memories

http://www.lawlib.uh.edu/handi/
    HANDI Home Page

http://www.ipt-forensics.com
    Institute for Psychological Therapies

http://www.apsac.org
    American Professional Society on the Abuse of Children

http://oif.org/tier2/childabuse.htm
    Osteogenesis Imperfecta

http://www.vocal.org
    Victims Of Child Abuse Laws

http://www.os.dhhs.gov
    U.S. Department of Health & Human Services

http://www.allencowling.com
    Allen Cowling, Private Investigator

http://www.atlanet.org
    Association of Trial Lawyers of America

http://www.kruglaw.com
    Forensic Research & Criminal Law

http://www.criminaljustice.org
    National Association of Criminal Defense Lawyers

http://www.fmsfonline.org
    False Memory Syndrome Foundation

http://www.family.org
    Focus on the Family

http://www.injusticebusters.com
    Home of the $10 Million Lawsuit

http://www.parentalienation.org
    Douglas Darnall, Ph.D.

http://www.parental-alienation.cc
    J. Michael Bone, Ph.D.

http://www.geocities.com/heartland/pointe/3171
    Recovered Memory Accusations of Sexual Abuse

http://breakingthesilence.com
    Sexual Abuse Consultant Linda Halliday-Sumner of Canada

http://www.reenasommerassociates.mb.ca
    Reena Sommer, Ph.D., of Canada

http://www.onedaly.com
    Lawrence Daly, Private Investigator

http://www.mother.com/~randy/law.html
    Substantive Law on the Worldwide Web

http://www.falseallegations.com
    Barbara Johnson, Esq., and Massachusetts Law

http://www.dadsrights.com
   Jeffery Leving, Esq., and Father's Rights Attorney

http://www.ellenross.com
   Ellen Ross, Esq., and Law Guardian of New York

http://www.dvmen.org
   Abused Men and Dr. Charles Corry of Colorado

http://www.apa.org/practice/childprotection.html
   Guidelines for Psychological Evaluations in Child Protection
   Matters

http://www.deltabravo.net/custody/rorschach.htm
   The Rorschach Test

http://www.deltabravo.net/custody/psychtests.htm
   Common Psychological Tests

http://www.expage.com/page/childcustody
   Ken Lewis, Ph.D., Registered Custody Evaluator

http://hometown.aol.com/jayceco
   Joel Charles, Video and Audio Expert Witness

http://www.people.cornell.edu/pages/sjc9
   Stephen Ceci, Ph.D., Cornell University Professor of Child
   Development

http://www.rachelfoundation.org
   Pamela Stuart-Mills Hoch: Helping Alienated and Abducted
   Children

http://www.abuse-excuse.com
   Dean Tong, Trial Forensic Consultant and Author

Appendix H

"Consistent With . . . What, Exactly?"

Pediatric medical examinations of alleged child victims of sexual abuse performed by Child Protection Team (CPT) doctors, physician assistants, advanced registered nurse practitioners, Sexual Abuse Nurse Examiners, and Sexual Abuse Response Teams more times than not conclude that abuse occurred. A defendant in an alleged criminal sexual battery case of a minor child may encounter some of the following catch-all phraseology: "consistent with sexual abuse," "cannot rule out the possibility of sexual abuse," "can neither confirm nor deny sexual abuse," "suspicious for sexual abuse," "inconclusive for sexual abuse," "suggestive of sexual abuse," or "nonspecific findings." Any of these aforesaid *findings* can induce a judge or jury to err on the side of caution, on the side of the alleged child victim, to find the accused guilty.

In the Archives of Pediatric and Adolescent Medicine in November of 1999; 153: 1121-1122, 1160-1164, in an article entitled "Clinical Training in Assessment of Childhood Sexual Abuse Found Lacking," it was found that pediatricians and family physicians are poorly trained to detect or rule out child sexual abuse on the basis of physical examination. Dr. Kathryn Bowen and Dr. Michael Aldous from the University of Arizona College of Medicine in Tucson stated, "Many children referred to specialists for abnormal findings have, in fact, normal anatomy. There is a need for better education on normal genital anatomy. Regardless of history, examination of findings were normal or nonspecific in 83.5 percent to 94.4 percent of cases," Drs. Bowen and Aldous report. "Only two children (3 percent) with no reported history of abuse had suggestive physical findings, and none had definite findings." Dr. Joyce Adams of the University of California, San Diego, agrees that many physicians are unfamiliar with both the normal and abnormal appearances of genital and anal tissues in children. "If they are not familiar with children's genital anatomy, they should not look at all unless there is bleeding, discharge, or pain," she wrote.

Noted forensic pediatrician Robert Fay, M.D., F.A.A.P., contributed the following digest concerning his views of medical assessments of child sexual abuse cases:

> In the entire spectrum of American jurisprudence, very few criminal allegations evoke a greater emotional response than those involving abuse of a child. A child's innocence and presumed "clean hands," evoke a plethora of understandable, but professionally undesirable reactions, among them: anger, outrage (with concomitant high blood pressure and pulse rate), facial flushing, and almost a literal desire to attack and pummel the perceived perpetrator(s).
>
> The reader might legitimately inquire as to why such emotions (initially perceived as 'normal' and 'healthy') are undesirable? Regardless, only a modicum of reflection should be necessary. In the competent and fair practice of criminal law, emotion or emotional reactions should be granted *no* merit or credibility when one seeks to objectively evaluate the veracity of a set of accusations, which if indeed they are true, are despicable, and would have very severe life ruining results for the person found culpable.

Where protection of the *victim* is always purported to be the sole purpose of any child sex abuse investigation, and prosecution of the accused *the* priority, the mere recitation of such accusations invariably elicits a presumption that the accused is guilty. Such accusations elicit a concomitant desire by the participating authorities to *prove they happened*, regardless of the nature and strength of the accusations, or other *evidence*. Long term incarceration of the accused (often a parent), and/or permanent removal of the accused from the child's life, are often the end results. This loss of a parent would hardly be "protection," or in the "best interest of a child," should such allegations be erroneous.

The very use of the term *victim* is impermissibly gratuitous, and will surely plant in a judge or jury's mind that:

- The child is indeed a victim of a crime.
- The accused has indeed committed the crime.

This gratuitous, and legally sloppy term, *victim*, is invariably used by everyone on the sexual abuse evaluation *team*, and, on occasion, even by naïve defense attorneys. Sadly, misuse of the term victim is often not the only *verbal gymnastics* defense lawyers will encounter.

In the approximate 350 child abuse allegation cases in which I have been consulted over the past fourteen years, forensically speaking, I have inevitably encountered in *each* case words or clauses, which though frequently true, are *seductive* and assertively unfair to the accused and tailored to draw empathy from a judge or jury, thereby tilting the judgment or verdict on the side of the prosecution.

One of the most common, and foulest of such phrases is *consistent with abuse, or not inconsistent with abuse.* What, exactly, do these words mean? To attentive and concerned, but legally naïve jurors, the assertion by a doctor for the state, prosecution, or child, that claims findings "consistent with the child's story," or "consistent with the history given," or "consistent with sexual abuse," means *he did it!* And, the prosecution team knows that! What prosecutors also know, or should know, is that medical examination findings that are interpreted as "consistent with a child's history," *do not confirm, nor should they be interpreted as confirming* that the accusatory child, the "victim," has indeed been molested, or is indeed a victim at all.

The status of being "consistent with" a statement or accusation merely infers that the particular alleged acts *could have happened!* The status of an accusation being "not inconsistent with" particular examination findings means nothing more than the examination findings *did not rule out* the substance of the accusatory statements. The cornerstone of American jurisprudence, however, in criminal cases, mandates that accused defendants need not have to prove their innocence but requires assistant district attorneys prove (rule in) beyond a reasonable doubt, guilt. Physicians are trained similarly.

I will never forget the response of a wise and experienced physician who heard an intern assess the sad history and physical findings of a 50-year-old man who smoked heavily, coughed severely for several weeks, lost thirty pounds, and had a large mass visible upon x-ray of his right lung. My assessment stated: "This man has lung cancer, *until proven otherwise.*" My mentor responded: "Doctor, I agree with your initial assessment, and commend you for the very thorough history and physical examination you've performed. It does seem likely that this man has lung cancer to the exclusion of any other pathology. However, your last clause concerns me deeply. It shows a pattern of thinking, which, if retained after you assume medical practice, can lead to serious and even medically dangerous presumptions and diagnoses, which will affect patient care, negatively. I notice in this case that you have not ordered diagnostic tests for any other diseases, e.g., tuberculosis or fungal or parasitic conditions. I suspect the fact that because this man is a heavy smoker with a strong family history of cancer, *led you to this supremely confidant—dare I say presumptuous—conclusion*? Your attitude, 'until proven otherwise,' is, I suspect, the real problem. How can we, indeed, prove any 'otherwise' diagnosis, if we don't order smears and cultures? We cannot! And, by the way, we won't make interesting, rewarding, and rare diagnoses, unless we *consider and look for them!*"

We, as physicians, have no right whatsoever to pontificate about anyone proving anything, or any disease. *You* have an obligation to prove any diagnosis in which you are confident, but have no right to impose on others an *obligation* to prove you're wrong! This attitude is arrogant, and sullies your good efforts to diagnose this patient's (or any patient's) illness. It is also a very showy cloak to hide woolly thinking. Your patient, who has come to you in good faith for help, deserves better than a doctor who challenges someone to *prove* anything, "otherwise." Confidence in your knowledge, or skill will not be inspired by imposing condescending obligations on your colleagues; rather, it will be inspired by intelligent and industrious practices which establish your reputation as a good diagnostician.

Ambitious prosecutors and aggressive "it couldn't have happened any other way" social workers would be well advised to listen. "Guilty until proven innocent" is a repugnant and all too common attitude adopted when abuse allegations surface. Wisdom and prudence therefore dictate that in abuse allegation cases involving young children, raising our voices (and, our blood pressure) is far less persuasive than strengthening our investigative skills, and therefore our arguments. By the way, the patient discussed above had *pulmonary tuberculosis*!

I have seen many cases in which an accusation is made that a child has been genitally molested (touched or fondled), or digitally penetrated. In all such cases, *either* act may cause physical changes that are visible, or may leave the genitals undamaged, i.e. normal. In the former instance, accusations of rubbing or fondling (sometimes referred to as lewd and lascivious behavior), *any* findings, however mild (e.g., irritation or redness), will be reported as *consistent with the child's story*, or *consistent with sexual molest*, even if the history is that the event occurred weeks or months prior to the accusation. The statement that molestation *might* have occurred (i.e., "is consistent with the child's history) is true; yet, it is also assertively true (and almost never mentioned) that absent of any findings is also *consistent with the total innocence of the denying defendant!* The presence of irritation or redness of the genital area is also fully *consistent with* tight panties worn on a hot day, or poor hygiene/lack of cleaning after urinary accidents, or sensitive skin/diaper area irritation.

When fondling is alleged, and there are absolutely no abnormalities found on genital examination (not a rare event), it will almost invariably be asserted that the findings are still *consistent with the history given by the child*, or it is *not inconsistent with the child's story*. Often, at the end of the report, the doctor will assert that the "absence of abnormal findings does not preclude the possibility of sexual abuse having occurred." While these statements, in light of the alleged history are technically true, a better and fairer statement would be: This examination neither proves nor disproves that sexual abuse occurred. Where digital penetration has been alleged, it's still quite possible to find no abnormalities upon genital examination. But, the same prosecutorial *doublespeak* can be expected; i.e., consistent with, or not inconsistent with, sexual abuse.

When minor labial or mucous membrane scratches are encountered in cases involving alleged digital penetration, the report will very likely assert that the findings are "very consistent with" the allegations, when in fact, they're also consistent with a child who has scratched an itchy labial area, or who engaged in (or whose parent might have engaged in) over-vigorous post-urination wiping. Inflammation and scratches can most definitely occur as a result of over-vigorous wiping. Often, in a rush-to-convict mode, prosecutors will ignore, or not consider critical *time* information; e.g., the child was examined fifteen to twenty days after the alleged incident occurred, when minor findings like redness or small scratches would be ascribable to some *non-abuse related event* that occurred subsequent to the date of accusation. Prosecutors might contend that the above possibility is remote. I would inform him, or her, that I have encountered five cases that have unfolded precisely in this manner in fourteen years of pediatric forensic consultative work. In fact, in one sad case, redness of the labia, irritation, and a vaginal discharge were seen (in a multiple fondling over time case), and even though the last *abusive* event was alleged to have occurred thirty-three days prior to the medical examination, the report depicted "the findings were consistent with the child's history of abuse." This happened despite the examiner's diagnosis of a vaginal yeast infection, monilial vaginitis, which was the obvious probable and proximate cause of *all of the examination findings*!

A fair and objective report emanating from such a case as illustrated above would be: "While these findings certainly can occur and be present subsequent to genital fondling or other abusive activity, they are also found when vaginal yeast infection is present, which it is in this case. Therefore, on the basis of the findings in this examination, it is *impossible to prove or disprove* whether sexual abuse trauma was perpetrated upon this child." It is indeed rare that such a fair and accurate statement is found in a sexual abuse evaluation report. I have two such known statements in my voluminous stack of reports compiled over fourteen years of practice.

Many reported findings in these cases are quite nonspecific, i.e., they could be due to non-abuse causes such as redness, or swelling of genital areas. Alternative reasons for such findings (see Chapter 14 and "source misattributions") are almost never mentioned. Many findings are puzzling, or very slight, and therefore quite difficult to point to child abuse, specifically. However, child abuse evaluators show very little hesitation or temerity in reporting these findings as "consistent with the history," or "supportive of the child's history," as was seen in the above case.

Therefore, defense attorneys must be ready for such truthful, but highly deceptive reports and extremely wary and cynical of verbal reports stating "she was all torn up," or "her hymen was ruptured," or it was "consistent with her story." I am humbled, as a nonlawyer, to have been asked to try and demonstrate to lawyers how the truth (or particular facts) can be manipulated with statistics. I'm also uncomfortable.

My ethics and tradition dictate that all facts should be honestly and objectively sought, and then, similarly reported. I am shocked and appalled that many of my colleagues, apparently influenced by the "history" that a particular little girl was molested, will examine her knowing that a finding of "no findings," and/or a dispositive conclusion stating "findings neither prove nor disprove abuse" will almost *certainly* result in a discontinuation of their employment as child sex abuse evaluators and child *advocates*. In the field of forensic child abuse examinations, in an area of pediatric medicine whose time has come, objectivity and fairness are necessary. An accusing child is *not* hurt or endangered by being fairly and objectively examined and evaluated, and juries (or judges as finders of fact) will not be hindered or obstructed when afforded *straight* stories in these difficult cases. We should ask for no more and insist on no less!

Robert Fay, M.D., F.A.A.P., is a board certified pediatrician and forensic consultant in child abuse allegation cases. After twenty years of clinical pediatric practice in upstate New York and Massachusetts, Dr. Fay noted with heightening concern, a marked increase in child sexual abuse allegations which were oft associated with flawed physical "findings." He proceeded, in 1987, to obtain specialized training in pediatric sexual abuse anatomy, i.e., differentiating between normal, doubtful, suspicious, very likely, and certain findings, in non-abused and truly abused children. Since then, he has forensically evaluated hundreds of cases of alleged sexual molestation of children, testified in seventy-five cases in many jurisdictions, and submitted forensic case evaluation reports in many more. In a substantial number of evaluations, he reported findings in agreement with the original case evaluators, who believed that abusive acts *had occurred*. In addition, he's attended multiple conferences sponsored by the American Professional Society on the Abuse of Children. Now, he is consulted almost exclusively by defense attorneys (not by choice) in these complex and heart rending cases.

Appendix I

Defense Interrogatories for False Accusers

Used with Permission from High-Risk Action Council, Inc., and Heyward Bruce Ewart, III, Ph.D.

The following questions must be adapted to each individual situation. They are based on an actual case of false accusation, whereby a father was accused of molesting his daughter from ages five through thirteen. Certain models of interviewing and testing are included.

- Name all persons helping you answer these questions.
- A "forensic evaluation model" has been used since 1995 by hundreds of communities to interview children claiming sexual abuse. The "model" was developed by the National Children's Advocacy Group. This standard of interviewing is very well known by the types of workers who interviewed you, including people from Children and Families, and the Sheriff's Office. Testing of the model involved more than forty children's advocacy centers across the United States. Did anyone mention the name of the type of interviewing model that was used in your case when you accused your father of molesting you?
- Before you ran away the last time, did you have any intention of "getting even" with your father if he reported your absence to the police?
- Did you disclose your plans to make up a story about your father to any friends?
- How many interviewing sessions took place that dealt with accusations against your father?
- Who conducted these interviews?
- Were you asked to take any tests?
- How long did each interview last?
- Did you take a test called the "Briere Trauma Symptom Checklist?"
- Were you administered an oath when you were interviewed?

- Who was the witness to this oath?
- Was a family history obtained from your mother?
- Did your mother complete a "Child Behavioral Checklist?"
- Did your mother complete a "Child Sexual Behavior Inventory?"
- The model mentioned above recommends eight sessions to examine your accusations and whether or not they are true. The first session is conducted with the parent you are not accusing, and the other seven are with you. How many sessions were spent on you, only?
- Was the first session with you devoted to establishing a good relationship with the interviewer before any questions were asked about your accusations?
- Was the second session devoted to your self-esteem, your understanding of yourself, and your ideas about your support system?
- Did the third session involve education about good, bad, and secret touching?
- Did the fourth, fifth, and sixth sessions cover information such as family violence, substance abuse, care routines, bathing, eating, environment, people, and discipline?
- Did the final session regarding your accusations cover safety and prevention education?
- If you have ever been sexually active with boys, at what age was your first experience?
- Were you at any time reluctant to make an accusation against your father?
- Did you foresee any benefit for you personally by making these accusations?
- When you made these accusations against your father, were you angry toward him?
- What are all the reasons you were angry toward your father?
- Were you also angry toward your mother?
- What are all the reasons you were angry toward your mother?
- When your mother brought you to live with your father, did you feel that this was a form of punishment?
- Why did you wait until your last runaway to make the accusations rather than after the first or second runaway?
- Why did you not tell your school counselor or private therapist that your father molested you?
- Why did you not tell your pastor or your sister that your father molested you?
- Why did you not tell any close adult that your father molested you?
- Why did you not tell your brother your father molested you?

- If your dad really molested you, wouldn't you have warned your little sister, so that you could protect her, too?
- What reasons can you give as to why your father would get you a counselor, take you to a priest, encourage you to stay overnight with your sisters and their families, as well as friends, if he knew that you could tell any one of these people that he molested you?
- Did the fact that your father has devoted his professional practice and life to child abuse and domestic violence figure in to what kind of accusations you would level against him?
- Describe in detail your first remembrance of your dad molesting you. Include the place and room, what you were wearing, what you were doing right before, what time of day it was, what your father was wearing, whether he wore glasses, whether he had a moustache, what he said, what you said, where you were touched and for how long, whether you experienced pain, how you felt, whether there was blood, whether there was discharge, whether you cried, whether you begged him to stop, and any other pertinent details you can convey.
- Please describe your most vivid and horrific memory of being abused.
- Do you suffer from flashbacks, night sweats, or nightmares due to the abuse?
- Can you describe in detail the feelings and premise images you envision due to flashbacks and nightmares from the abuse?
- If you told your counselor other things, why did you not tell her about your dad molesting you?
- If you made any complaints to your school counselor about your upbringing, discipline, and interactions with either parent, what did you say?
- Have you ever made any complaints to anyone about these matters, and if so, to whom?
- What was the substance of your complaints to these other persons?
- Do you have any friends who have made similar accusations against a parent, and if so, please identify these friends and a secure method to contact them?
- Please give the names and a method of contact for each person you have ever had sex with, albeit, minor, or adult.
- Do you understand that any adult who had sex with you, or sheltered you while considered a runaway, will be prosecuted criminally?
- If any of the persons who sheltered you during your runaway episodes were drug dealers, please identify same and give a sure method of contact.

- Do you know that purposefully withholding information in an interrogatory under oath is in itself a crime?
- Has an authority informed you of your right to know the penalty for perjury when a false accusation of a criminal act is made?
- Of the adults who sheltered you during your runaway episodes, to whom did you claim that you were being molested by your father?
- Please afford us any contact information about people who befriended you during your runaway episodes.
- If you know, please identify which classification your accusation was placed:
    - Credible disclosure-suspicion of abuse supported.
    - Credible non-disclosure-no or low index of suspicion remains.
    - Non-credible disclosure-evidence of coaching or other factors decreases, or removes suspicion of abuse.
    - Unclear-high index of suspicion remains, but no disclosure or problematic disclosure exists.
- Do you feel that your mother has added credibility to your accusations against your dad, and if so, how?
- What kinds of accusations have your mother made about your father's behavior to other members of the family, and identify which members?
- To whom has your mother made detrimental comments about your father's alleged sexual exploitation of you?
- What is the substance of these comments?

Note: Dr. Heyward Bruce Ewart, III, Ph.D. is a professor of psychology. He specializes in victimology and traumatology. The founder of the High Risk Action Council in Sumter, South Carolina, Dr. Ewart has tendered as a forensic expert on abuse related subjects in Florida and South Carolina. He can be reached at 803-773-3536.

Appendix J

Investigative Intake Process—Flow Chart
Used with permission from Systematic Investigations,
Lawrence Daly, President
10751 S.E. 272ⁿᵈ St., Suite 43-# 231, Covington, WA 98042

I. Multiple Sources of Referrals
- Case Referral

II. Case Received
- Assign Account Number - Enter In MC Database
  - Accountability Process
  - Copying - Long Distance - Backgrounds

III. Create Computer Client Files
- Create Client Folder   - Create Client's Notes & File

IV. Case Organized

A. Police Reports	J. Timeline of Events
B. C.P.S. Records	K. Case Breakdown Statements
C. Police/Other Agencies Statements	L. Background Investigations
D. Legal Documents	M. Notes to File
E. Medical Records	N. ODC Statements
F. Correspondence	O. Case Assessment Form
G. Case Analysis	P. Miscellaneous
H. Case Action Plan	Q. Case Status Report
I. Witness Contact Database	R. Witness Statement Interview Notes

V. Reviewing Case File

- Identifying Issues   -Preparing Witness Contact Database
- Preparing Allegation   -Identifying Missing Discovery
  Breakdown

VI. Client Interview - Witness Interview

- Meeting with Client
  - Reasonable and Logical Explanation to Allegations
  - Determine Validity of Response
  - Counseling - Referral to Sexual Treatment
  - Evaluation
  - Treatment

VII. Case Analysis

-Identifying

- Alleged Victim(s)   - Teachers
- Relatives/Children   - Medical Personnel
- Other Witnesses   - Daycare Provider
- Child Protective Services - Records
- Police Personnel   - Suggestions (Case Action Plan)
- Councilors   - Notes/Comments
- Foster Homes   - Motions

VIII. Case Action Plan

- Initial Plan - Summary - Milestones

IX. Timeline Of Events

- Preparing Timeline from Discovery
- Identifying Missing Time/Dates of Relevance
- Create Initial Hypothesis

X. Backgrounds

- All Parties, Including Client
  - Complete Criminal, Civil, Domestic Checks
  - JIS - Public Access
  - Other Agencies - User Services
- Searches Should Be Done By Computer First
  - Conduct Follow-up with in Person Check

- Federal Criminal and Bankruptcy Checks
  - Analyzing Background Findings
  - Searching for Criminal History
  - Searching for Personal History Information
  - Searching for Additional Witnesses

XI. Preparing For Interviews

- Prepare Questions For Interviews
  - Who, What, When, Why   - Court Transcriptionist
  - Where, Which, How   - Shorthand
  - Tape   - Summary

XII. Conducting Interviews

- Decision Making - Value of
  - In Person
  - Summary Prepared by Investigator
  - Transcription Prepared by Typist
  - Telephone
  - Summary Prepared by Investigator
  - Transcription Prepared by Typist
  - Deposition
  - Transcription Prepared by Transcriptionist

XIII. Analyzing Findings to Date

  - Reviewing Documentation to Date
  - New Case Action Plan
  - Prepare Case Status Report to Attorney
  - Revise Initial Hypothesis

XIV. Receive and Review Discovery Requests

  - Organize and File into Case File (On Going Process)
  - Identify Any New Information
  - Witnesses - Allegations - Issues

XV. Meeting with Client

  - Present Investigation Fact Findings
  - Identify if Hypothesis is reasonable and logical
  - Review Investigation to Date

- Identify Priorities
- Identify To Do List

XVI. Court Preparation

- Identify Your Role
- Identify Witnesses
- Identify Evidence
- Identify Demonstrative Evidence
- Identify Your Testimony

XVII. Conclusion of Case

- Pull Case and Store
- Provide Summary Conclusion of Case

References

Abel, G., et al. 1994, Screening Tests for Pedophilia, *Criminal Justice and Behavior*. Thousand Oaks, CA: Sage Publications, 21: 115-131.

Besharov, Douglas J.D. 1990. *Gaining Control over Child Abuse Reports*. Washington DC: Public Welfare.

Blush, Gordon & Ross, Karol, 1986, *The SAID Syndrome*. Sterling Heights, MI: Family and Conciliation Courts Review.

Ceci, S., & Bruck, M. 1995-99. *Jeopardy in the Courtroom*. Washington, DC: American Psychological Association.

Ceci, S., et al. 1999. *Psychology in Litigation and Legislation*. Washington, DC: American Psychological Association.

Ceci., S. & Bruck, M. 1993. *The Suggestibility of the Child Witness: A Historical Review and Synthesis*. Psychological Bulletin, vol. 113, no. 4: 403-439.

Child Maltreatment 1998. *Reports From the States to the National Child Abuse and Neglect Data System*. Washington, DC: U. S. Government Printing Office.

Clauss, Eliot. 1989. *Counterattack and Control: Keys to Successful Defense of False Child Abuse Accusations*. Northfield, MN: Institute for Psychological Therapies.

Davies, G., et al. 2000. The Impact of Questioning Style on the Content of Investigative Interviews with Suspected Child Sexual Abuse Victims. *Psychology, Crime & Law*, vol. 6: 81-97.

DSM-IV Sourcebook, 1994. *Diagnostic and Statistical Manual of Mental Disorders*. Washington, DC: American Psychiatric Association, vol. 1.

Endres, J., 1997. The Suggestibility of the Child Witness: The Role of Individual Differences and Their Assessment. *The Journal of Credibility Assessment and Witness Psychology*, vol. 1, no. 2: 44-67.

Eberle, Paul & Shirley. 1986. *The Politics of Child Abuse.* Secaucus, NJ: Lyle Stuart, Inc.

Fonagy, P. 13 May 1999. *Pathological Attachments and Therapeutic Action—A Transgenerational Model of Personality Disorder.* Paper presented to the American Psychoanalytic Association Meeting, Washington, DC: psychematters.com/papers/fonagy3.htm.

Gardner, Richard. 1992. *The Parental Alienation Syndrome.* Cresskill, NJ: Creative Therapeutics Publishing.

Gillespie, Sean. 2000. Officer Sues for $10 Million—Acquitted cop says he was victim of 'gender profiling' in his arrest for domestic violence. *The Journal Reporter.* Renton, WA: 15 August.

Giovannoni & Becerra. 1979. *Defining Child Abuse.* New York: The Free Press (Division of Macmillan).

Goldman, S.J., Dangelo, E.J., & DeMaso, D.R. 1993. Psychopathology in the Families of Children and Adolescents with Borderline Personality Disorder. *American Journal of Psychiatry,* 150, 12: 1832-1835.

Hechler, David. 1988. *The Battle and the Backlash.* Lexington, MA: Lexington Books.

Hickman, J., & Reynolds, C. 1994. *Effects of False Allegations of Sexual Abuse on Children and Families.* Texas Legal Resource Center for Children and Travis County Bar Association.

Kiefer, Louis. 1989. *The Child as Witness in Allegations of Sexual Abuse Part III:. Defense Strategies for the Falsely Accused Individual.* Northfield, MN: Institute for Psychological Therapies.

Liberator. 1990. Fighting False Abuse Charges taken from *The Liberator,* Forest Lake, MN: June, quoting Thomas W. Pearlman, Esq., in *FACE,* April 1990.

Malcolm, P.B., et al. 1993. Discriminant and Predictive Validity of Phallometrically Measured Sexual Age and Gender Preference. *Journal of Interpersonal Violence,* 8: 486-501.

Mason, P., & Kreger, R. 1998. *Stop Walking On Eggshells.* Oakland, CA: New Harbinger.

McBrien, C.M., & Dagenbach, D. (1998). *The Contributions of Source Misattributions, Response Bias, and Acquiescence to Children's False Memories.* American Journal of Psychology, 111, No. 4, 509-528.

McIver, William II, Hollida Wakefield, Ralph Underwager. 1989. *Behavior of Abused and Non-Abused Children in Interviews with Anatomically Correct Dolls.* Northfield, MN: Institute for Psychological Therapies.

Paone, John., Esq. 1997. Representing Persons Falsely Accused of Domestic Violence. *New Jersey Law Journal,* vol. CXLIV, no. 1: 1-4.

Parry John, et al. 1998. *National Benchbook on Psychiatric and Psychological Evidence and Testimony.* Washington, DC: American Bar Association: Commission on Mental and Physical Disability Law.

Petty, J. 1998. *Comprehensive Child Abuse & Neglect Evaluation Program.* Wilmington, NC: Human Growth and Training Associates.

Prescott, D. 1997. *The Hydra Hypothesis.* Portsmouth, NH: Peter Randall, Publisher.

Pride, Mary. 1986. *The Child Abuse Industry.* Westchester, IL: Crossway Books.

Schultz, Leroy. 1989. *One Hundred Cases of Unfounded Child Sexual Abuse: A Survey and Recommendations.* Northfield, MN: Institute for Psychological Therapies.

Schultz, Leroy. 1989. *The Child Protection Teams: Defenses for the Falsely Accused.* Northfield, MN: Institute for Psychological Therapies.

Siegel, J., & Langford, J. 1998. MMPI-2 Validity Scales and Suspected Parental Alienation Syndrome. *American Journal of Forensic Psychology,* vol. 16, no. 4: 5-14.

Spiegel, Lawrence. *A Question of Innocence.* Parsippany, N.J. Unicorn Publishing House, 1986.

Tong, Dean. 1997. *ASHES to ASHES . . . Families to Dust.* Tampa, FL: FamRights Press.

Tong, Dean. 1992. *Don't Blame ME, Daddy.* Charlottesville, VA: Hampton Roads.

Underwager, R., & Wakefield, H. 1990. Effective Use of a Mental Health Expert in Child Sexual Abuse Cases. *The Champion:* 20-22.

Underwager, R. & Wakefield, H. 1990. *Personality Characteristics of Falsely Accusing Parents in Custody Disputes.* Northfield, MN: Institute for Psychological Therapies. Paper presented to the Sixth Annual Symposium in Forensic Psychology.

Underwager, Ralph and Wakefield, Hollida. 1990. *The Real World of Child Interrogations.* Springfield, IL: Charles C. Thomas.

Weiss, M., M.D., et al. 1996. Psychopathology in Offspring of Mothers with Borderline Personality Disorder: A Pilot Study. *Canadian Journal of Psychiatry,* vol. 41, 5: 285-290.

Wood, J., & Garven, S. 2000. How Sexual Abuse Interviews Go Astray: Implications for Prosecutors, Police, and Child Protection Services. *Child Maltreatment*, vol. 5, no. 2: 109-118.

Wright, L., & Adams, H.E. 1994. Assessment and Sexual Preference Using a Choice Reaction Time Task. *Journal of Psychopathology and Behavior Assessment*, 16: 221-231.

Notes